My Father's House

My Father's House

a midcentury memoir

Janet Dillon

My Father's House

Names and specific addresses have been changed to protect the privacy of persons involved.

Imprint: Independently published

Cover photography by Tom Namey, Namey Design Studios, Knoxville, TN

Author contact: janetdillon351@gmail.com

for the five grandchildren

of my mother and father

Do not let your hearts be troubled. You believe in God; believe also in me. My Father's house has many rooms...I am going there to prepare a place for you. ...I will come back and take you to be with me.

Jesus

John 14:1-3

Chapter 1

I first met Jesus under the family Christmas tree, which was strategically placed in the center of the picture windows facing the street. My father was very deliberate in this. The trend-setting architects of those days sought to bring the outside in; Daddy took it one step further by bringing the inside out. The tree thus provided both indoor and outdoor Christmas decoration. Voila! Simple, dignified, dramatic. Understated and classy.

Anyway, there was Jesus, resting in His manger right where He belonged. His scale was off; He was a little too big for His makeshift bed. Although He was a bit stiff and mature-looking for His age, my heart knew that He was real. It seemed like He was trying to tell me something. I was 12, and desperate for the Meaning of Life.

To be fair, several adults had previously introduced Jesus to me. Prayers before bed, Sunday School flannel board figures, and craft time at Central Baptist Vacation Bible School had all brought Him around to me. Also, I knew that God was real. Mama had made that very clear. Every time I lied to her, she would raise her eyebrows and simply state, *God knows the truth* and there was no doubt in my mind that He did. My conscience confirmed it. Like her mother before her, she was not about to spoil her children. But those times with Jesus had just been introductions in passing, like meeting someone at a party. This was different. This was just between Him and me.

There He was, with hands outstretched, lying upon the plastic straw. His swaddling cloths were gone and he seemed eager to start blessing people. I longed to be blessed. There was Mary: SO lucky to have a baby! I wanted badly to trade places with her. There was Joseph: protective and stoic, sort of in a mild state of shock. There were the well-dressed wise men, two of whom had colored skin. Their postures echoed what I felt in my heart. The shepherd was also too big to fit so he stood in the outside back. I thought he looked like King David (the only other Bible character I knew). The angel sat on top, looking ponderous and stupefied. She didn't appear to be singing any hallelujahs. The cardboard star was covered in glitter. There was also a camel and a dog and a sheep: all the elements needed to recreate this most unlikely story.

I really just wanted to be there in that little stable. That was the whole issue. But like Alice in Wonderland, I was way too big to fit. Regardless, the nativity set spoke loudly: God can work magic in unexpected places. I believed that if I could arrange the just-right tableau—the one that had really existed 1,967 years ago—I would be transported out of the emptiness here in this House. So I endlessly fiddled with the figurines. If Jesus did have the solution for my growing angst, I had no idea how to access it.

I lay there for hours under the 15-foot tree in my Ladybug nightgown seeking peace from a miniature cardboard stall. The pale green carpet carried me out like sea foam to an ocean of tranquility and dreams of livestock, babies, mysterious stars and foreign men in caftans. Time would reveal that I was, in fact, indelibly changed; but it would be a long while before I found that tranquility again.

The Holy Spirit works in strange ways.

We had been in the House for three years and the parties had pretty much ceased. The House wasn't fun anymore. The novelty was used up like crumpled Christmas wrap. My mom, brother and I all felt it. How could that have happened? It had been such a glorious achievement in the beginning, especially for Daddy. But now his boredom was plain and infected us all. The man was bored with middle-class life and was endlessly restless for female attention. The House had brought him lots of that in the beginning. Now he had to find other means. The thrill of the accomplishment had created a need for more and greater thrills, leading to misplaced affections.

I couldn't decide how I felt about him. We enjoyed so many things together: baseball and playing the Hi-Fi and dancing and making decorations; going to the symphony and plays and movies; our Cincinnati trips. But then he would detach and become cold and unresponsive when questioned. There was to be no questioning.

My personal angst was becoming unmanageable. Mama was nobly working to steer me through the minefield of adolescent ugly-duckling-hood and mood swings. She tried everything: expensive haircuts, shopping trips, ballroom dancing classes, electrolysis. Nothing worked. My teeth were an orthodontic disaster, my fashion choices were disastrous and I had nowhere to go. I had been the subject of some persistent teasing. Nothing assuaged my sense of failure.

There could only be one explanation. I simply was not meant to be. *But Janet, that's just not true* attested my mother. *Your father and I carefully planned you.* Whaaattt...? No!! Just....no.

Suicide was starting to look very attractive when I hit upon another idea with more of a future and a lot less messy. I would become a nun. *But Janet,* Mama matter-of-factly replied. *You're not even Catholic.* She was so diligent about appealing to logic. *Long-suffering* seems applicable. I didn't say this to her—the concept would never have made it past her Presbyterian sensibilities—but I knew that problem could be easily fixed.

I didn't arrive at this nun idea on my own. I doubt if I'd ever met a nun. But I had seen one very beautiful nun at the movies: Audrey Hepburn.

She proved to me and all the world that the necessity of makeup was just a myth. Her gown-like habit was so virginal and regal, with miles of flowing swishy fabric. (Just like Mary's, of course!) She never had to worry about her hair or teeth or electrolysis. She was

3

completely given over to noble, selfless causes. I concluded that self-denial while living was far more attractive than self-denial by death. Mama had told me when I often asked if I was pretty, *Pretty is as pretty does*. I linked this truth to the gorgeous nun in the movie and I had myself a plan.

But the best part of all was the wedding ring. She was MARRIED to JESUS! Oh, the rapture of it all. Only Jesus could be the perfect husband. He would never lie or cheat on me or disappear without explanation, or abandon me at a social function, because for one thing, he was, after all, invisible (by that time). And he would never expect me to engage in that disgusting procreative activity.

There was one small hitch. I was deeply perturbed (spoiler alert) by her disavowal at the end of the movie. How could this be? Was she divorcing Jesus? *Why did she do that?* I demanded from my dad. (Mama grew flustered at philosophical or theological questions.) *Because she grew tired of following bad orders from her superiors* he told me. Well, even Audrey Hepburn could make a mistake. I would gladly follow any orders for the privilege of sweating in the jungle and saving lives next to a handsome doctor. The only problem was I had to wait a few years until I was 18 and could sign up.

But here I was at age 12 and clueless about how to access what Jesus had to offer. I needed help in a big way for my growing anxiety. Real-life boys had long been a huge attraction but I had an accessibility problem there also. I was wildly attracted to boys. I had suffered debilitating crushes, one after another since at least third grade. But the interest was not reciprocated. They definitely were not interested in me in spite of my eagerness. Maybe it was the wardrobe, or the braces. Whatever the case the boyfriend outlet wasn't working and the nun option was years away. By eighth grade I would discover the much more immediate comforts of vodka, gossip, and rock & roll.

That night under the tree I was alone in the House of course. Mama and Daddy were at the plant dinner dance, meaning that the next day would probably be horrible. Just now I have no idea where my brother David was; it seems like he was never there.

He was strangely distant to me. There was something not quite right; there was a barrier. Was it gender? Jealousy? He was Mama's darling, but Daddy's...not so much. It hadn't always been that way. In our old house they were best of friends, constantly building with the Erector set and Lincoln Logs and Tinker Toys. They washed the car and rode sleds down the big hill out front. They watched Highway Patrol and David dreamed of guns and getting the bad guys and bazookas and real army fatigues. As with me, Daddy had had many moments of precious fatherhood with my brother, too.

As David grew into adolescence whatever bond was there began to dissipate. It became clear that he couldn't do math. His grades were mediocre, causing my father a constant source of grief. Mediocre grades and math struggles were completely foreign to our gifted mechanical engineer father.

The need for help with schoolwork was equally foreign. Daddy took David's struggle as a personal insult, as if he were actually trying to not follow his example. Daddy had earned his way through college with scholarships. He was an only child who didn't need help. His own parents were nothing but proud. He simply could not relate to or respect someone with so little aptitude for academics.

So anyway, David wasn't home. I suspect he was either next door at Ronnie's, tinkering with the motorcycle; or possibly at the twins', taking target practice with the BB gun; or he could have been at the other next door, at Gerald's, looking at Playboy. I didn't miss him. I didn't want anyone to interfere with my visit to Bethlehem. I needed those few hours to fantasize a world without pain.

At Ronnie's house (actually his aunt's and uncle's) a red-haired girl, just a little bit younger than I, had recently come to live as a foster child. She walked with a severe limp as if one leg was shorter. I was worried about this. When I asked Mama about it, she took a long pause. Hesitating, she told me *No one knows why. There is no physical reason.* This left me stricken and confused.

I wasn't afraid to be home alone. Our Beagle Priscilla would certainly let me know if anyone approached. Even though the House annoyed me at several levels—it just didn't look like any of my friends' houses—I had plenty to console me. There were all the special cookies, like pecan-stuffed dates wrapped in cookie dough, baked and frosted; and orange-cream cheese-toll house. There was homemade candy, like fudge and divinity, both made with black walnuts from the backyard. There was music: over and over I listened to the Walter Schumann singers on the living-room Hi-Fi. And finally there was TV: just as the Macy's Thanksgiving Day parade was a sacred marker for that holiday, so the Andy Williams special and Mr. Magoo's Christmas Carol gave my Christmas its aura. These things soothed my soul and helped me escape.

And there were always gifts to wrap. Even though I could never quite equal my Grandma W's creativity—she was always working together tiny little things to make magic on top of our gifts—that didn't keep me from trying and enjoying the effort. This was the same grandma who would make tailored suits on her sewing machine for my Barbie doll. Like her, to make something beautiful with my hands thrilled me. Grandma passed that thrill on to Daddy who passed it on to me. Understanding this thrill, he would set up a card table in the family room beside the piano specifically for me to use for wrapping.

I dreaded what would almost certainly come the next day. The Day After the plant Christmas party was usually the worst day of the whole year, and come to think of it, it's a miracle that Christmas wasn't ruined because of it.

Here's the way it would go. Mama would start getting excited about the party early in the fall because it was a huge social event with dinner and dancing and many people from Daddy's plant. She would carefully pick out the Vogue pattern and fabric, and work many long hours on her outfit's construction. Her execution was flawless and professional. Shoes and handbag were also carefully chosen. She wasn't a perfectionist; she just had a passion for excellence. She wasn't a raving beauty but her taste was impeccable. She carried herself with grace and dignity. She was fabulously glamorous without being even slightly vain. Her beauty came from an authentic place—she was an ordinary woman, exulting in the art of design and a job well done.

The big day would come and she'd have her hair styled at the salon where it would be washed, cut, rolled, dried, teased and sprayed. Every year her look seemed more sophisticated than the last. My parents would play Christmas records on the Hi-Fi and drink scotch & water while getting ready. At the big reveal there would be oohs & ahs all around. It was the pinnacle of festivity and Mama would appear, beaming and confident. I would be filled with awe, thinking that surely this year things would be different and they would have a marvelous time at the "ball." How could Daddy have eyes for anyone but her?

And yet without exception, the next day David and I would awaken to palpable tension. Mama would be at the breakfast table completely withdrawn. She would drink her coffee through pursed lips, not saying a word. Pea-soup silence engulfed the House. Silence can be far more toxic than fighting. Ugly silence indicates death in a relationship. Attempts to engage with her would fall flat to the cement slab floor. She was deeply troubled and had exhausted all of her coping mechanisms. She was angry and bereft. We tiptoed around and stayed out of her way.

I would develop a sick feeling in my stomach and lose my appetite.

Daddy would have nothing to say either. He would never defend nor deny his actions. In the afternoon when he finally would take off for the drugstore or some other unnamed errand, she would respond to coaxing, but he had to be out of the house first. She would then tell the specifics of how Daddy's admiration and attention usually had lasted only as far as the entrance to the banquet hall. Some years he would become fixated on a specific other woman; other years it was other women in general.

But every year it was the same. They would arrive at the party, choose places at a table and Daddy would disappear on a flirting rampage, leaving Mama to sit nobly in her beautiful dress, making small talk with strangers and occasionally being asked to dance by some sympathetic other husband. All the hours of preparation would just make the wound that much deeper.

Why did she keep going back, year after year, and subjecting herself to the same humiliation? Why not just pull the plug on this nightmare? Evidently hope really does spring eternal. She knew they were a perfect couple; she knew his intelligence and she gave him the credit to eventually figure it out. The House where I lay on the carpet under the tree was the tangible proof. Some couples make great music together; my parents made a beautiful House.

I was struggling to maintain my love for Daddy and my sympathy for Mama because, after all, she let him get away with this baloney. I didn't know whom to be angrier with. My life was a little dinghy in very rough waters.

To be honest Daddy definitely was winning this ignoble race. I wanted to love him and I tried to love him. I knew it was wrong *not* to love him but I was utterly disgusted by his treatment of the one person on earth I loved the most, the person he had pledged to love until death. I also knew deep down in my uninformed, adolescent psyche that the same Jesus who lay on the straw expected me to not only love my father but also to honor him. But it was impossible. Just simply impossible.

Chapter 2

My parents met in the fall of 1951 in Oak Ridge, Tennessee at an unremarkable cocktail party in someone's apartment, which was one of many hundreds. They were two single fish in an ocean of them in this smallish town.

Mama was 27 and carried a panache which belied her humble origins. She grew up in Lancing, TN, in a tiny hollow of the Cumberland Mountains, constrained by geography and an impossible-to-please father. She was the firstborn of three in a family where the mother had generally been the breadwinner. During the Great Depression her mom, Grandma Pembroke, had been an elementary school teacher; Grandpa P was an itinerant painter/carpenter, often traveling as far as Detroit for work. Between jobs, he single-handedly built the house they lived in, which originally lacked indoor plumbing.

He struggled with alcoholism, epilepsy and a nasty temper. He would disappear on drinking binges for days or weeks at a time. He once did time in prison for shooting at a man in a drunken rage, probably over politics or a poker game. After his rehabilitation stint he chose to make the world a better place by eliminating starlings with a .22 from the back porch. This also saved his birdhouses, perched on 30-foot poles along the outer edge of the garden, for friendlier species.

The garden occupied the entire backyard. The rich black soil and abundant rain guaranteed abundant produce. Gardening wasn't a hobby; it was a necessity if they wanted to eat anything not sold in a can or box. They grew corn, cantaloupes, tomatoes, squash, green beans, and flowers, adding beauty and grace to their fairly no-nonsense existence. Grandpa grew cannas and Grandma, zinnias and peonies.

In spite of Grandpa's belligerence, he remained steadfast in loyalty to Grandma come what may. But this was not without a selfish motive; anyone else would have kicked him out years before.

When he grew too old to drive to the bars and too infirm to work, he spent his waking hours on his recliner in front of the radio, control knobs just inches away from the fingers of his right hand. He endlessly adjusted the tuning back and forth between his beloved Cincinnati Reds baseball games, the news, and bland elevator music. He gave up the boxing matches after deciding they were all rigged. He did not give up politics, however, in spite of being equally convinced that it was rigged by politicians who were all corrupt.

But this was no grizzled, grumpy old man. He found redemption through a warm fuzzy place in his heart for small children. He was therefore universally adored by his 10 grandchildren. When speaking of Grandma he always told us that the prettiest girl had miraculously decided to marry the ugliest man. Which was not entirely untrue.

Grandpa P eventually grew very sick but chose to unceremoniously discharge himself from the hospital where he was being treated for colon cancer. He didn't care much about getting well. Doctors were all corrupt. Better to just stick around the house. Grandma was left with no choice but to make the best of it, which she did until he passed at 72.

She never spoke a disparaging word about her husband.

Grandma P had come from a family of seven daughters and two sons, which gave my mother a large network of extended family. Grandma persevered for many years driving 54 miles roundtrip to teach elementary school in Rugby. Her reward in later years was the position of Postmaster, right out her back door. (The post office was about 50 yards away). When not at work she canned the vast quantities of produce from the garden; she read books; she sewed dresses on a foot-treadle machine in the dining room near the coal-burning furnace, where lace curtains softly breathed in and out at the mahogany-framed windows.

She came from a long line of devoutly faithful teachers. In her closet were huge books of law and the Bible. Out of the two choices for church in Lancing she followed in her forebears' footsteps and chose the sedate Presbyterians...the Frozen Chosen. The Baptists were too loud, too long-winded, and far too expressive.

She was a woman of few possessions who wouldn't hesitate to throw anything extraneous into the furnace: books she disliked or had finished, gifts she didn't want or need, worn out clothing. She would suffer no encumbrance of stuff. She wore her thin salt-n-pepper hair long and wrapped into a chignon at the base of her head. By the end of her busy day, many wisps would tickle her cheeks and forehead. When something amused her, her cheeks glowed a girlish pink. She never owned a pair of pants.

She kept her opinions to herself—in the few situations where she actually had opinions. She was soft-spoken and painfully shy. When a mail fraud investigation came to her district she almost suffered a nervous breakdown. After the perpetrators were identified and prosecuted she was left traumatized and even more withdrawn. But she never grew cynical. In fact, it was just the opposite. It was not in her being to harbor animosity toward anyone. She met her difficulties with silent faith and fortitude and only grew sweeter, more childlike, and more content as years went by. If the meek are to inherit the earth she will be wealthy indeed someday. She was the picture of humble power under control.

For special occasions she made chicken n' dumplins and pot roast with egg noodles, all in their own gravy, that were savory and satisfying. The substantial texture of the dumplins and noodles made the store-bought variety seem measly. On ordinary days they ate pan-fried pork chops or chicken and pole beans, or just pinto beans and collard greens, always with sides of fresh cornbread from a cast iron skillet (containing no sugar, ever) and sliced homegrown tomatoes in season.

Every night after dinner, if the TV signal was strong, she tuned into Hollywood Squares. After Hollywood Squares we would sit on the back porch and rock as the sun set behind the hills, the fireflies came out to perform, and the crickets began to sing. Sometimes there were pole beans to string. Often there was a faint scent of smoke in the air as the neighbors burned their paper trash. Organic trash was composted, before composting even had a name.

Their house was adjacent to the new six-room elementary school and its playground abutted their garden. On school days, the shouts and laughter of the children elevated the mood at Grandma's house; their gaiety and collective innocence lingered into the nighttime and made our sleep deep and peaceful. Never was there a drop of alcohol in their home because of Grandpa's history, but it was utterly unnecessary. This was the sweetest, purest place on earth.

As preschoolers, my brother and I each joined a grandparent in their matching double beds with white chenille spreads. Their room was decorated with a dark bureau and only the sheerest of curtains; curtains for privacy were not needed as their bedroom looked out to the schoolyard. I was allowed to sleep with Grandpa until I was six; at that age, I protested stringently this policy, to no avail. At night after we got into bed we laughed and told jokes until everyone drifted off. Mama would be close by in the adjoining room. They always rose before dawn and Grandma put the coffee on, cut cantaloupe and scrambled eggs.

Grandma P did not dispense affection, really. At least not the way kids expect. The first time I stayed overnight without my mother I thought I would surely die of grief, but no hugs were forthcoming. I nibbled at my dinner and lost interest in my favorite cousins who lived close by (technically first cousins once removed, being Mama's first cousins but who were my same age due to gigantic families). I shuffled around listlessly all day, occasionally looking at my library book or playing solitaire or gazing at photo albums. I meandered to my uncle J.B.'s store to get a Nehi and a moon pie. I watched the trains go by.

Grandma saw my suffering but remained gently detached, believing that sympathy would be an unnecessary indulgence. Sympathy might foster self-pity; coddling was not in her game plan. She knew that my condition was simply a rite of passage. She only appeared indifferent, however. By going about her business with diligence and calm she showed me how to walk by faith. During my college years, her home became a respite from emotional pain and instability for both me and my mother.

Decades later Mama and I took my fiancé Louie to her home. As suppertime approached Grandma began preparing her latter years' go-to meal for company: fried chicken. She was struggling to butcher a whole fryer when Louie stepped in, and gently taking the knife, he said *Here. Let me finish that for you.* She took a little breath and backed away from the cutting board, blushing and giggling. Surely that kitchen had never seen male hands preparing food. From that point forward Louie could do no wrong—he had earned a place of nobility in her world.

At 90 she had a stroke when her pipes froze in the dead of winter. She survived but it wasn't discovered for a few days, which revealed a nightmarish scene. At that point she had the choice to live with one of her children or go to a nursing home; she adamantly insisted on the latter, to Mama's deep dismay. She simply couldn't face the idea of being dependent on anyone. She had lived alone for 12 years. She met my young children and quietly passed at age 92.

As sweet as it was for me as a grandchild, growing up in this household was no picnic for Mama and her siblings. Dating was strictly forbidden and Grandpa did not tolerate differences of opinion. His tyranny and high expectations, imposed hardest on Mama as the eldest, fostered a strong urge to escape. She left home at 17, more than ready for college. (Soon after, her sister Martha was sent to live with an aunt in Knoxville when encounters with their father grew volatile.) An extended relative—her father's brother's wife, Luola Spangler Pembroke, also a schoolteacher —was eager to give Mama a leg up and chipped in with her expenses; but Mama mostly paid her own way by working in the kitchen of the boarding house where she lived. She was a capable cook because she had daily started dinner while Grandma worked. She studied Home Economics for three years, working and generally enjoying life; then a somewhat bizarre opportunity presented itself.

About halfway between Lancing and Knoxville, where she was attending UT, a huge mysterious construction project was underway. Hordes of people were being hired of all skill and education levels. In 1944 Martha went first to work there then persuaded Mama to join her. Wages were handsome and so were the men, although they were far outnumbered because of World War II.

Oak Ridge had been around only a couple years at that time. It sprang to life virtually overnight as the home of the Manhattan Project. The work was top secret even to the multitudes working there. It's almost incomprehensible that anyone—let alone tens of thousands of people—would give their lives, loyalty and effort to a job without knowing the product or outcome. But such was their faith in their government; such was their gratitude for a reliable and decent wage; such was the urgent need to bring the boys home. Most of all, such was the outsize evil which had to be stopped at any cost. They were told only that their work would bring the war to a swift end and that was reason enough.

Mama and her peers had been raised to work hard and obey authority. They had survived the Great Depression. Because they had known dire hunger and poverty they didn't demand the luxury of second-guessing. With sons and brothers and husbands dying every minute on two fronts, they didn't pause to ponder the wisdom of blind trust. In August of 1945, the project's objective was globally unleashed: the first atomic bomb was detonated with the potential to vanquish all of humanity. The war did indeed come to a swift end at that point, just as predicted.

In 1951 when my dad came to town there was no need for blind trust. The Cold War had begun and the weapons industry was booming. It was deemed patriotic to build weapons in the face of enemies that now had the same. The Oak Ridge plants were still hiring in droves. By then, Mama had been there seven years and had certainly been to hundreds of social functions like the one where they met. Cocktail parties, dances in gymnasiums, and every manner of organized entertainment were ubiquitous, meeting the social needs of hordes of newly transplanted citizens.

She was a young woman of well-developed tastes and skills. She knew how to tailor a suit and manage suitors. She could manage money. She loved to dance and travel, and had toured the states by bus with Martha as far west as California. The mutual support these sisters had developed at home was put to good use as they endured eccentric roommates, bad dates, and bad bosses.

My father came from the University of Cincinnati with his degree in Mechanical Engineering and a bent for performance. He had gone to a high school the size of a community college that provided plenty of opportunity for showing off. His good looks and powerful bass voice opened doors into glee clubs, choirs and variety shows where the girls were plentiful and adoring. Fraternity life at UC was just more of the same. When he arrived in Oak Ridge to begin a career, he had no trouble catching my mother's attention.

Daddy's mother was an ultra-rare divorcee. And, there was a definite mystery about how long Grandma and Pop Wehner had been married; no wedding anniversary had ever been mentioned. They let their only son draw his own conclusions. And so, he too had skeletons in the family closet, in spite of his own supposed stellar accomplishments.

Like Mama's father, Pop was absent for long periods at a time, being a railroad engineer. Male bonding with Daddy didn't really happen. Like Mama's father, Pop, too was a drinker. To supplement his income he served as the caretaker for the apartment building where they lived in Cincinnati. He spent most of his at-home hours in the basement of the building drinking beer, chain-smoking and listening to his beloved Reds' baseball games. To help make the tiny apartment seem larger he brought the outside in with a bird-feeder just outside the window by their two-person dining table. It provided endless entertainment and company.

Pop was diabetic and had not one natural tooth in his head. He drove Grandma crazy by refusing to wear his dentures, give up his candy or pull up his pants. (He just might have invented sagging.) Grandma learned early to put all of her dreams and efforts into her son; Daddy learned early that moral support would only come from Grandma's side of the equation. Between her and Pop's two childless sisters, Aunts Myrtle and Pearl, Daddy cut his teeth on female attention. It was his oxygen.

Pop died in his mid-60s of emphysema and lung cancer. We came to remember him for the unexpected gift of amateur photography. The basement was, after all, more than just a repair shop: it made a perfect studio and darkroom.

This basement was below a Moroccan/Spanish-revival building pretentiously bearing the name "El Capitan" in an old established neighborhood near Delta Avenue. It was nestled among giant trees and gingerbread houses which awakened every romantic bone in my body. It was white (so-called) stucco with dark stairways, back stairways, and arched doorways. On the backside of the building the paint continually peeled in giant flakes. (This might have been due to the climate not really being suitable for stucco, or it might have been that it wasn't really stucco.) It had a huge dark lobby that smelled of cedar with stone tiled floors and an arched, diagonally-paned window facing the street. In the entryway, where the tile work had inlaid multicolored broken glass, a porcelain fish spit water endlessly into a basin.

This building was my very own castle complete with fake turrets. I could be any princess I chose, awaiting Prince Charming in the lobby to dance all night. This fantasy, of course, preceded the nun idea.

Their apartment was furnished perfectly to scale. There was a tiny black lacquered drop-front desk with little cubbies holding various jeweled secretarial items. Grandma Wehner collected mounted butterflies under glass; many of these were on display atop the TV and stereo or hung on the wall. Their small walk-in closet was jammed with her colorful gypsy-ish (her word) wardrobe, a raccoon coat, and mothballs. The dresser held piles of costume jewelry and scarves. She was tiny, energetic and tirelessly jolly.

Her intense energy came from within and without; she was an avid coffee-lover. But oddly she detested dealing with the grounds. The mention of coffee grounds brought a pained grimace to her face. So she put up with instant.

She loved the movies and late-night TV, especially Johnny Carson. She never missed Johnny. Her affection for him was only exceeded by that for Jack Paar, his predecessor. This was the same TV on which I saw the Beatles' first appearance on Ed Sullivan.

She never missed a Sunday at the sizable Knox Presbyterian church.

In her later years, after Pop's death, she developed a romance with a man 30 years her junior who lived directly across the hall. He was recovering from some kind of breakdown. We were unsure about the nature of the relationship until we saw them hold hands and heard them call each other *Sweetie*. It was adorably shocking.

There would never have been money for college had Daddy not earned it. No problem there; his work ethic was solid and he had Grandma's high energy. Immediately upon graduation, he took the job in Oak Ridge. He was eager to earn a living, work hard, and play hard. All that activity left him physically and emotionally hungry, being far from home and the doting females who had raised him.

Mama could fill this bill with one hand tied behind her back. And she was so much more than a good cook, having invested in stylish new furnishings. Perhaps to defy her rural upbringing she

17

chose contemporary urban items such as Heywood Wakefield's Dogbone dining room table, chairs, and occasional tables. It set the stage perfectly for Daddy's one valuable possession: a high-quality framed print of *Report from Rockport* by Stuart Davis. The architectural images and angular lines in *Report* suggest buildings going up and the busy traffic of the suburbs. The sleekness and energy of these pieces would later come to be known as *atomic period*; perfectly fitting for a couple who found each other and made their living in the town that made *nuclear* a household word.

They had matching refined, good taste which was neither garish nor pretentious. It was an informed taste; the kind that develops from intelligence and cultural observation rather than money. They shared the same likes: almost all genres of music, well-made clothing, travel, cities, Abstract Expressionist art, baseball, literature, hard work, and movies; and dislikes: pretentious people, racism, country music, and too much TV.

They were high energy, stylish, confident people who appreciated design. Mama made interesting recipes that were healthy, having studied and been raised with good nutrition. (Neither of them was ever overweight and she never dieted a day in her life.) They subscribed to *Newsweek*. They loved to play records. He loved photography and taking pictures of her. She loved to dance; he was a great dancer. He was a hard worker and a good Presbyterian, or so it seemed; she was his muse, his friend, his lover and his steady support system. She may have found her way to his heart through his stomach but she would never feed his—or anyone's—ego. He failed to notice this in the beginning.

Their attraction was also physical, of course, and they recognized a certain irresistibility in that area. They took the high road in this regard—more or less—and legitimized what might have been considered illicit in those days. All that is to say, they married quickly.

The wedding was in January following their meeting in October, in Mama's apartment with very little fanfare. Mama wore a powder blue suit with Chanel jacket. The cake was about the same size as her hat which had a tiny veil covering her eyes. Daddy looked just like a 22-year-old Don Draper in his dark suit with boutonnière. There was no guest list or bridesmaids, no bouquet or processional, no organ or rice-throwing; only a pastor and his wife, the four parents, the honor attendants, and the cake. In the pictures they are both beaming, oblivious to whatever might be missing.

Daddy's youthful confidence had camouflaged his questionable maturity. But marriage has a way of quickly undoing pretense. Very quickly. For their honeymoon, Mama, for lack of alternative, agreed to let him drive the 600 miles to New Orleans. His car was not exactly up to the task. It sputtered and lurched the entire way. There was a flat tire incident. Upon arriving at their destination they ran out of gas in front of some swank hotel. Daddy pushed the car into the valet area; Mama tried to look nonchalant and figure out just exactly who was this man she was with and why she was there with him.

What could have been their undoing instead served as a baptism by fire. She did get over it (although he never lived it down); she was ridiculously loyal and their commonalities were too many and too obvious to be considered a coincidence. The currents of Providence had swirled these single fish to the right place at the right time for the forging of a family.

Before long, Mama became pregnant and reportedly they both were thrilled. She stayed on the job until she was about five months along and then turned to full-time homemaking. Her days were spent reading books—Dr. Spock and murder mysteries and Betty Crocker—and trying new recipes. There were bridge games, bowling and the sewing of maternity clothes while Daddy went back and forth to Oak Ridge. She put dinner on the table every night for him and the occasional surprise co-worker or visiting engineer. In March, 1953 David was born via Cesarean section.

In midcentury days it was common for people, especially apartment-dwelling housewives, to monitor their neighbors' comings and goings. In polite society this was regarded as a form of public service. That way, there would always be someone to call emergency services, if needed. The Garden Apartments where my parents lived were no exception; there was one particular lady self-appointed to the job. She had a loyal streak for other women and a passion for honesty.

When Mama had been home with baby David for a few weeks this neighbor paid a visit. Over coffee and cake she delivered her report—with Mama's best interests in mind, of course. While my mother had been recovering in the hospital from the C-section, my father had been observed entertaining another woman at their apartment.

Chapter 3

What was my mother's response to this news? The confident young woman defaulted into the silent submission that she had learned from her intimidating, abusive father.

When baby David was about a year old my dad decided that Oak Ridge was just too small for comfort. Most of the neighbors were also co-workers, and nosey. So they bought a tiny house in nearby Knoxville.

This first house had only one real noteworthy detail: fabulous tongue-in-groove paneling on one wall of the living room. Actually, make that two noteworthy features: there was also an odd little space in the garage. On the side toward the house, cut into the wall there was a long, narrow—perhaps 4'x10'—closet-type area where my dad put a slender workbench and his tools, all in perfectly labeled little boxes. We called it the Cubby Hole. Daddy's engineering mind gave him razor-sharp attention to detail and an aim for perfection. Tasks like jewelry repair and gluing tiny broken things back together really got his juices flowing. He loved a good glue-repair challenge. He could spend hours in the Cubby Hole gluing and repairing. It was a forerunner of the now-popular Man Cave.

After a few months, Mama became pregnant with me. I was born in April of 1955, the same year Disneyland opened and suburban America was busting out all over. Bulldozers and concrete mixers would soon lay out the Interstate highways and fulfill the meaning of *one nation, indivisible*. This project brought a whole new roll and rumble to the land and practically begged people to plan road trips. It was virtually in our backyard there on Westfield Drive.

I think I had a very happy childhood. If moderation is the key to happiness, then the city where I grew up had a lot to do with my childhood happiness. Knoxville could be called the capital of moderation. It is neither too big, too small, too liberal, religious, commercial, political nor metropolitan. It is seldom too hot, too cold or too boring.

Knoxville's moderation dates back at least to the Civil War: Confederate and Union loyalties were evenly divided. It never had a plantation economy and many families had members on both sides. In 1794 the University of Tennessee was founded there, helping to attract free thinkers and out-of-towners (aka Yankees). That, along with the much-later influx of defense workers to nearby Oak Ridge, kept the typical Southern provincialism from taking too great a hold. A mixed-bag mentality prevailed.

Nevertheless, in the 1950s, convention ruled the day. This was the age of hats, gloves, and common decency. No one left home without these things.

Westfield Drive was an isolated street, away from the subdivisions but within the city limits, where 14 houses were built in two rows facing one another straight on. Ten of these houses had kids; in seven of those, the kids were preschoolers like us. The high visibility layout kept everyone on their best behavior and created an insulated realm in which the kids roamed freely. The parents played bridge together and the non-Baptists openly shared cocktails. This world was a fortress.

There was always someone to play with and mud somewhere to play in. Mud is the stuff that blissful childhoods are made of. Lots of mud comes from lots of rain, of course, which also meant lots of huge green trees reaching up to the sky, and a storybook-size creek at the foot of the street. I know of one perfectly realistic fringed Dale Evans cowgirl suit, with boots, and at least one pair of brand-spanking-new white Keds which were sacrificed to the mud god who lived at that creek. When the Interstate project came through, the creek overflowed its banks regularly and flooded the Kempwoods' house and lawn. In response they took up a new American pastime which would become enormously popular: they sued. The neighbors didn't quite know what to make of it. Until they won, that is.

So the trees were huge and the forest behind our house was huge and our backyard was huge. (Funny, it looks like a postage stamp in the photos.) And the June bugs were really huge. My brother and I, buck-naked and damp from our evening baths, used to flick them off the front screen door as they flew toward the lamplight. The summer nights' gentle warmth made bathrobes unnecessary. Behind us, the sounds of the faraway Reds baseball game coming from the radio assured us that God was in His heaven and all was right with the world. My parents would sit at opposite ends of the sofa and rub each other's feet, reading *Newsweek* or novels. Daddy would clip the movie reviews and place them in a file folder under the socks in his sock drawer. The house was too small for anything as mundane and unsightly as a filing cabinet.

In the mornings that followed David and I were allowed to watch TV if we were the first to get up. Usually, this was even before the TV programming began. You'd be amazed at how interesting a TV test pattern can be when no grownups are around and you're the one in control.

After the test pattern came the hillbilly band with their plaid shirts and slide guitar, singing Hank Williams and Buck Owens tunes; music that was rarely heard in our household. Yet, it was somehow comforting. We gravitated to it. This show was sponsored by the legendary local groceryman-cum-politician. I thought he looked just like my Grandpa P. Eventually breakfast was ready, eaten, and then off we'd go in search of mud. David was my first and best friend.

Birthday parties were the pinnacle of our social schedules and they were rather formal affairs. The little boys wore bow ties and suspenders; the girls, frilly dresses with crinoline petticoats. We played pin-the-tail-on-the-donkey and ate homemade cake with homemade cooked white frosting. My cake unfailingly had balloons on it, fashioned from Lifesavers candies. All of the kids on the street were included; unfortunately for my brother, they were all girls. The only boys were at least five years older than David, so his guest list did need to tap into classmates when he started school.

Our house was always filled with music and aromas from the kitchen.

Being enamored with all things mechanical, Daddy insisted on the latest in sound technology. Early on he invested in a beautiful *stereophonic* record player (the Hi-Fi) with cabinet speakers taller than me. The tuner brought in the baseball games; the turntable enabled Mama and Daddy to listen to show tunes and jazz, movie soundtracks and classical, big bands and folk.

I grew up knowing all the words to *Oklahoma* and *Carousel, The Music Man* and *Brigadoon, Bye Bye Birdie* and *West Side Story*. In these movies, the girl always loved the guy in spite of herself; he was invariably some kind of louse. By the end of the show, his infatuation and her goodness combined to move him to rehabilitation.

A close second for sing-along-ability was the Kingston Trio, especially that song about a man stuck on the Boston subway system because he lacked the nickel required to get off. It seemed he would *never return*. Daddy explained to me that this was making fun of the badly designed fare system. This may have been the very first politically insurgent popular tune, appealing to anyone who had a lick of sense. The lyrics said his wife would bring him a sack lunch every day; I couldn't figure out why she didn't just sneak a nickel in with the sandwich.

Believe it or not, given the state in which we lived, Country & Western music was explicitly exiled. Daddy fancied himself far too urban and sophisticated for it. The simplicity of it was an affront to his complex brain; the emotions too raw and exposed. Mama didn't put up any resistance. It reminded her of her toxic home of origin. Naturally this made it all the more attractive to my brother and me.

But if ever there was a soundtrack for my preschool years it would be Dave Brubeck's *Time Out,* particularly *"take 5"* of course! There are no bad days in Dave Brubeck's world. The music dances with itself, perfectly capturing the hip optimism of the time. Its quirky time signature puts a stamp of joy on your soul. The wry humor of the wrap-around keyboard and the soulful sax transformed our household to a contemporary wonderland. What Kerouac did through fiction, Brubeck did with music; breathing life back into that vivacious American spirit which had been suffocated by decades of poverty and war. The world was our oyster.

The jazz inspired Daddy to construct sleek modern arts-n-crafts projects. He made geometrical Christmas decorations out of cardboard and colored foil, most memorably a hanging mobile and a triangular tabletop Christmas tree-like thing that was magenta and purple. His handiwork mesmerized me. He worked at the Heywood Wakefield table in the dining room alcove. I sat mute and wide-eyed watching him work against the backdrop of giant-pinecone wallpaper. I could tell he was enjoying the work by the way he would rub the back of his throat with his tongue as his fingers deftly formed the objects and folded the foil. A faint Mona-Lisa type smile lingered on his face.

No doubt he was also inspired by the art of Alexander Calder, whom he had likely read about in *Newsweek* along with seeing photos of his work. Calder made the mobile a midcentury icon. He had, like Daddy, been trained in mechanical engineering; and he came to be, like Brubeck, considered a genius in midcentury style. Great models plus great music equal impressive crafting by an engineer dad.

When it came time to hang the mobile we all took a small inhale and waited. It gently and perfectly spun in mid-air. We were amazed and delighted, but it really wasn't such a surprise. Neither of my parents would ever suffer second-rate results in a creative endeavor.

As much as I treasured these pieces they were mere consolation prizes for the best foil Christmas decoration ever invented, which the Kempwoods were the first on the street to acquire. It was the six-foot, 100% aluminum tree which magically changed color. The colors were projected by a spotlight aimed at the tree from behind a rotating cellophane disc, which was divided into four pie-shaped wedges of red, blue, green and amber. This was a real object of modern beauty, but my parents weren't buying it. They proclaimed it to be garish and commercial. It would rob attention from Daddy's handmade foil items and also the matrix of greeting cards scotch-taped to the paneling above the sofa.

The music inspired Mama to cook and daydream. She was never deterred by the difficulty of a recipe and she wasn't particularly bothered when one failed. Unlike Daddy she wouldn't repeat the process until perfection was achieved; she would just ditch the recipe itself. We'd eat the dish and be comforted by the fact that we'd never be subjected to it again. But she would never throw away food. To her, waste was a by-product of arrogance.

I grew up on spare ribs simmered in sauerkraut, cornbread (without sugar), fried chicken, Swiss steak with fresh tomatoes and onion, Beef Burgundy, green beans from my grandma's garden and spaghetti. Visitors (or *company*) usually got Beef Stroganoff made from filet mignon. On a rare fun occasion, we were treated to the newest American staple: pizza. It was made from a Chef Boy-ar-dee boxed mix, baked on a jelly-roll pan. It always came out soggy and rectangular. We couldn't have cared less. We simply folded the squares (like the as-yet-unknown taco) and licked the tomato paste and cheese strings off our fingers. We always had layer cake for any special occasion, often baked in fanciful shapes and covered in feathery coconut.

Mama gravitated to romance in her music choices. Hers were the Johnny Mathis and Nat King Cole albums. To this day when I hear the former's rendition of *Chances Are* I am a little girl again, wondering about adulthood and that mysterious way between men and women. Her favorite record, however, was the wistful and melancholy French singer. It didn't matter that the language was foreign; the singer's unrestrained longing provided the catharsis

Mama needed for the strains of childrearing and monogamy. Often, when she played this record she would take me aside, look me in the eye and whisper in earnest, *French is the most beautiful language there is. It's too late for me; you must learn to speak it.* Of course, I did.

She carried a prevailing sense of joy which came from several sources outside of homemaking. She was a master bridge player. She was a trophied competitive bowler. She indulged in two cigarettes a day in the bathroom with the window open: one before her nap and one before bed.

I don't think she suffered any ill health from it, but Daddy hated it. (However, he put up and shut up in exchange for his own guilty pleasures.) She never, ever, smoked in public and I never saw any early or late photo of her smoking (a la Jackie Kennedy). It was her Mother's Little Helper. No one knew. Bathroom only. Deep family secret. When she was in her 50s the doctor told her to quit and she did.

It might have been her way of incorporating some imagined midcentury glamour into her life. And why not?

At a very young age—maybe inspired by fairy tales or the French singer—I became infatuated with romance. In the hideaway of my bedroom the fantasies flourished. I had my very own record player for 45 rpm's; I repeatedly played the one of the lady repeatedly singing "to know, know, know him is to love, love, love him, and I do, and I do, and I do" in a dreamy and needy voice.

It was very effective brainwashing. This led to irrepressible kissing sessions with Gerry McMullen under the piano at Kingston Korner Kindergarten. Mrs. Thomas was continually exasperated with it but I think Gerry enjoyed it. At least, I don't remember him putting up any resistance. Gerry was great at kissing but Bubba Davis was the original perfect boyfriend: congenial, cute as a button, and adept at friendship. We had many fun play dates. Not long after that, the male objects of my affection became distant and unattainable, while my dreams of devotion, diamond rings, and white lace grew more intractable.

27

My bedroom also served as a great make-believe hair salon. This was where I gave Annie Kempwood her first pixie haircut. I had a dresser with a huge mirror and vanity bench where the client could sit. This bench was also useful for me to sit on and watch myself cry during times of punishment, trying to create a facial expression pained enough to guilt my mother. It was like bio-feedback for self-pity. It worked great until Mama caught me in the act and hung a sheet over the mirror. I'm certain that Mrs. Kempwood's barely-controlled rage evoked one of these incidents because in that case, any remorse I displayed would have been completely feigned. Annie's curly hair looked really good in a pixie.

This bedroom was at the end of the hallway and just next to my parents'. My doorway was under the big round clock from which I learned to identify numbers. In fact from this clock, I learned all I know about numbers, especially my personal abacus-style system for math. Addition, subtraction, multiplication, and division for me are all about picturing positions of numbers on a circle. It's very efficient. Once, as an adult, I was having my inner ears tested for vertigo. The technician asked me to count backward by sevens to distract me from the dizziness. Evidently my speed was impressive. When I tried to describe the abacus thing, he said *well I've heard that visualization is the key to any mental process you want to master*. Whatever. The point is this: apparently I am visually-oriented and that was the first discernible commonality I had with my dad.

Daddy was so visually oriented that getting ready for work was rather laborious. The tie selection process could take forever. He would gaze and think, think and gaze, and choose first one, then another and another before settling on a winner. Often he would lay out the jacket on the bed and place 3 or 4 choices alongside to discern the final effect. Advice was never solicited; only he could see the look he was aiming for. Unlike other men, he adored receiving ties as gifts.

Like every good engineer, he wore short-sleeve dress shirts in the summer. Always, the security badge was clipped to the shirt pocket, as the suit jacket would normally be hung after arriving to work. The badge on the pocket was what distinguished my daddy from all the other dads on the street and in the world. That badge proved he was mine; it had his picture on it.

The huge/tiny backyard of this house had a sandbox which Daddy built. It was situated at the edge of the property under a massive shade bush of unknown species. The bush produced perfect switches with which my mother taught us right from wrong. Time stood quite still when she would walk out there, grab a branch and break it off, strip the leaves and walk back into the house. The swipes on our calves would sting like bees, teaching us that our actions and words mattered.

Judgment is born of love and we absolutely knew that. Authentic love does not protect its object from the consequences of bad behavior.

Before we were old enough to wander off toward the mud we would ride our little vehicles around and around on the driveway for hours, or if it was raining, indoors. My brother showed a very early affinity for driving and toting things (usually me). He later became a courier for the nuclear weapons produced in Oak Ridge, a career which made great use of all his best qualities. Inside the house, he would pull me in the Radio Flyer around the circle formed by the dining alcove/kitchen/hallway. Around and around we would go, constantly, merrily on our way to nowhere.

Outside we would do the same on the driveway in the little Murray Trac tractor with Dump Trac (tricycle and wagon) which had a tiny passenger seat for a little sister. If we dared cross the 2x4 positioned across the end of the driveway we would incur a switching. We were well aware that death could possibly lie just outside the end of the driveway, whatever *death* was; at that point, we were just trying to avoid the switches.

As the years went by we not only passed the 2x4 in search of mud, but we were actually sent off to Sunday School on foot, unattended. The church was at the top of the hill and across a 4-lane highway. My brother held my hand and told me when to *Run!* Our parents didn't go to Sunday School. They had other things on their minds Sunday mornings.

We had begun attending this smaller neighborhood Presbyterian church after belonging to a hoity-toity one down the pike for a few years. Upon our exit from the hoity-toity church, my dad told the pastor that the other women had made my mother uncomfortable. She told Daddy that they intimidated her, but that was only part of the story. She didn't like those women. She had disdain for them.

They were pretentious; she was authentic...full of life and ideas even if she wasn't sure what she believed about God. If she dared to expose her internal ambiguity it might create external conflict and she avoided both like the plague. She didn't want to have to figure it all out. She saw any internal struggle over faith as rebellion and therefore morally unacceptable. If the Presbyterian church was teaching it, she was buying it.

In her defense, it was a snobbish place. It is very pretentious to this day so I hear. But we all have our failings; church is about (among other things) choosing to love others and live in cooperative harmony in spite of our failings. Mama was just always preoccupied with how other people treated her. To her dying day, she regularly declared *S/He's really good to me!* as if that's completely unexpected and the highest measure of a person's character.

But, of course, there was another, stronger reason for Mama to not like the women. They were her competition for Daddy's attention. Most likely, more than one of them had caught my father's eye and he knew that she knew it full well. So he was learning how to frame every dilemma they had as if it was caused by her insecurities; Exhibit A being his words to the pastor.

The cozier size of the neighborhood church put Mama at ease as did the pastor, who often quoted Charles Schulz. Schulz' comic strip *Peanuts* was part of the midcentury Zeitgeist. She was much happier there and therefore so was the rest of the family. I loved it there because during the sermon I could gaze out the window toward the

Interstate construction and watch the puffy white clouds. Also, once a month there was a potluck dinner with lasagna and banana pudding.

This church was a perfect fit for us. It was there that I heard about the golden calf, which made no sense to me whatsoever; but I knew that these grownups really cared about these lessons and me. Mrs. Stooksberry taught me to carry a tune in children's choir. I treasured hearing Daddy's deep bass in the choir and being able to watch him in the choir loft, fingering the hairs at the top of his ears and like me, also gazing out into the clouds. However, I believe there was an incident between him and a female choir member in the robe-changing room. I never got the details.

My parents were not afraid to send us out across the 4-lane highway for church because school walkouts had taught us how to mind the traffic. In those days walkouts were required as drills to prepare for Communists dropping bombs. Not knowing anything about bombs or death I viewed the hiking home as a lovely adventure with my neighbors and brother. We were dismissed from school early and extra treats would be waiting when we arrived home. We loved our saltine crackers with butter, peanut butter, or quartered baloney slices; but the piece de resistance was brown date nut bread from a can, smeared with cream cheese.

In my earliest years, I seemed to be terrified of any kind of animal. This took the fun out of those Easter chicks all the kids got. The real, live kind from the drug store or Woolworth's. However fun it might have seemed there was a definite downside to it. The chicks had been fed all kinds of toxic dye to make them look like chirping Easter eggs, which in turn greatly reduced their lifespans. My screaming terror over the live baby chicks kept my mother from buying them, which then prevented the horror of blue, pink and chartreuse chick corpses in the backyard. But I also wouldn't/couldn't abide any size or manner of dog, even though little Sooty was awfully cute and totally harmless. To me she was a rabid werewolf. She lasted about a week.

Age and my increase in height must have turned the tide because eventually, all that changed. One ordinary Saturday when Daddy was washing the car and our attentions were elsewhere a mottled tan/black male Beagle-mix hound wandered into our yard and quietly seated himself. He had no collar. He acted like he owned the place and we figured that he was ours to keep. Choosing his name was a no-brainer: Dino ("Deeno"), just like the loyal pet on our favorite family TV show *The Flintstones*. I accepted him with unconditional love and his loyalty proved remarkable, for a stray. Forever after we were fools for Beagles. Ultimately he disappeared the same way he came and we were devastated. He had never been neutered and females must have beckoned him to greener pastures. Or into Interstate traffic.

While these episodes are clear to me, far more prominent are the sensory tidbits that float in kaleidoscope fashion: the color and texture of the turquoise velvet dress Grandma W made for my portrait, taken by Grandpa W; the putrid odor of fresh fish being cleaned in the kitchen; the shine of magenta and purple foil on a homemade decoration; big black numbers on a clock; the catastrophe of sandbox sand in my eyes; the burnt-cookie smell of coffee beans roasting at the JFG plant in the dark cold morning as we awaited my grandparents' arrival on the train from Cincinnati. The suspense of pulling elaborately decorated Christmas gifts out of the huge brown box they had sent by mail. Tightrope tension during holiday meals with both sets of grandparents, as a result of the grandpas' drinking. Cigarette smoke from the bathroom. Blood in my panties from an excruciating bicycle accident.

Familial bedrock was the foundation on which I lived but it was, on rare occasion, broken by debilitating terror: over harmless pets; over the backyard slide because my brother had fallen from the one at school and broken his arm; over late-night monsters in the living room running back and forth; and over the unnaturally distant ceiling and unfamiliar toys in the babysitting room at the downtown department store. But the ballast of love always counterbalanced the terror.

I was loved and I loved, in my tiny way. Wardine, who helped Mama with Daddy's shirts, was just another loving adult in my world, in spite of her different skin color. She sprinkled the clean shirts with water from a Coke bottle fitted with a special cap and rolled them into tidy little oblongs just like the hot dogs from Smoky Mountain Market. She stood at the ironing board in the middle of the living room, patiently ignoring my play and yet dispensing words of affirmation or gentle correction as needed.

I never knew that all couples didn't live happily ever after or that humans had appetites beyond the kitchen or that all sicknesses didn't eventually heal. Of course, there was some very real trouble in this paradise even if I couldn't identify it or name it.

When my brother was three he was sent for a week or so on a trip with Daddy's parents on the train. This was intended to give Mama a break. But he was not the same child when he returned. There were seemingly endless trips to the doctor, which was actually a speech therapist. We went there because my brother had stopped talking. When he finally did speak it was with a tortured stammer. Mama was anguished and confused but had a steely resolve to do whatever was needed for his recovery.

Later, I dreaded being put to bed with him at the neighbors' while the parents played bridge. He was overly curious about my private parts. This curiosity once spilled over into a game of doctor with the three Mayfield girls and it caused some tension. He was punished, but I never told about my own subjectivity. He was my brother. Maybe that's what all brothers did.

Snowfall in our town was rare and short-lived so we had to act quickly to enjoy it. We had great sledding on the steep hill of our street. After suiting up we'd race out to catch as many sledding runs as we could with Daddy in the driver position (lying down, head-first) and one of us on his back. Lack of traffic due to snow also meant lack of inhibitions. These were thrilling high-speed rides with no braking from top to bottom like only a dad can provide.

Usually there was no traffic. Snow mania can make one blind to hazards, and neighbors will sometimes brave inclement weather to leave their driveways. The winter day finally came when exactly at the moment my dad and brother were in the midst of a rapid downhill run, Mrs. Mayfield pulled out, forcing Daddy to veer toward our house to avoid being killed. Right into the mailbox post which he had just days earlier set into two feet of concrete.

The post was pulled out of its place by Daddy's pelvis, which was simultaneously shattered. The neighbors carried him in to the couch where he waited for the ambulance with Dino steadfastly by his side. The doctors predicted that if he ever walked again, he almost certainly would be confined to a wheelchair in his later years.

The good news is that his walking was, in due time, restored to basically normal. However, the likelihood of full-scale ability in his senior years was anybody's guess.

Up until the sledding accident, Daddy had continued pursuing his favorite hobbies. In addition to the church choir, he participated in theatrical productions at UT and joined the Choral Society. This left Mama at home alone many long evenings, which followed the long days of childrearing while Daddy was at work. Often I would hear the sound of her frustrated voice while standing at the phone cubby in the hallway, taking another of his calls announcing his late arrival.

Once, after one of his plays when Mama, David and I were brought backstage to share in the cast celebrations I became agitated over my dad's behavior. Some strange woman was receiving the attention that should have been uniquely Mama's. My budding sense of romantic loyalty sounded an alarm. *No! Wrong! Stop!* Why was this happening? Why didn't Mama intervene? I instinctively took up her slack. I couldn't articulate my case against Daddy so I pestered and heckled and whined. I tugged on his jacket and begged to *go home RIGHT NOW*. When that didn't work I threw myself prostrate on the floor kicking and screaming. Daddy finally had no choice but to whisk the whole family out to the car. He was furious to have been thwarted and clueless about why this had happened.

On the ride home, Mama coldly and calmly explained to him the source of his six-year-old daughter's wrath. She spoke with a slight air of defiance; there was an unusual assertiveness in her voice as if she was confident that the era of silent submission would pass with her daughter's generation. She saw a light at the end of the tunnel. Just as she had accepted working full time without knowing that the project was an atomic bomb, so she had accepted her husband's errant behavior without any real push-back.

In both cases, social convention and food on the table were powerful silencers. But she knew this did not have to be the situation for wives of the future.

Come what may, at the end of every day stability prevailed. At Christmastime we sat around the kitchen table in a production line to get out the greeting cards; I licked the stamps. Santa left me Barbie and Thumbelina, my very own train case, and a custom-made bridal gown with veil to actualize my romantic fantasies. In April I blew out the candles on my Lifesaver-balloon cake; in summer we drove to Cincinnati and Lancing. At bedtime, I recited my prayers to one parent or the other, according to instruction. No matter how late the hour or how tired we were, *God bless Mama, God bless Daddy, God bless David, God bless Wardine, God bless Dino, God bless Janet.*

Chapter 4

Daddy had a penchant for being among the first to try whatever new thing was captivating the national imagination. Like Disneyland. He had been anxiously waiting for us kids to get old enough for a road trip to California and it came to pass in the summer of 1963. We planned to stop at Carlsbad Caverns in New Mexico and also to visit Mama's aunt and gynecologist husband in Tucson.

We embarked upon this trip in a white 1959 Buick LeSabre with red leather interior and a black convertible top, perfect for absorbing the sun's heat. An after-factory air conditioner was installed so that we (particularly in the back seat) might be able to breathe while crossing the Southwestern desert. We were well-contained in that car; as a convertible, it had only two doors. David and I were forced to sit still and get along; we lived for the motel swimming pool at the end of the day. I managed to cope by staring out the window and continually requesting updates on how close we were to that day's pool.

I had a brief epiphany in New Mexico. Before heading south to the caverns we were obliged to stop in Albuquerque so that Daddy could complete some business at the Los Alamos nuclear plant. (This was how all our vacations were financed.) We found our way into a Mexican food restaurant and for the first time I tasted chile sauce and tortillas made from corn masa. Those distinctive flavors, coupled with the bright colors of the waitress' garments and decor, put me into near-catatonic ecstasy. *Ye gods!* as Daddy would say. What have I been missing? I would never be content with the spaghetti at Bill's Restaurant again; but the chile and corn masa, enhanced by lard and melted cheese, wouldn't come my way again for another decade when Taco Bell appeared in Knoxville.

The caverns were absolutely fascinating for those who love bats. Which did not include me. We didn't actually see any bats but we were given the statistics at the start of the tour; I didn't hear another word after that. And I didn't really notice the stalactites or stalagmites either. I was too busy looking for sleeping bats.

The hardscrabble landscape did not escape my notice, however. There was a brutality to it; a barrenness that terrified and fascinated me. To be lost or abandoned in such a place would mean certain death for a kid. But the saguaro cactus trees were funny. They looked like big people, holding their arms up in continual surrender or supplication. I had an odd sense of connection, of found identity. The Sonoran desert was a captivating place, indeed.

At our stop in Tucson David and I bonded with more first-cousins-once-removed (also our same age) in a very big way. I had many such relatives, with both maternal grandparents coming from large families. But my parents formed an even bigger bond with their house. It was all on one level and had soaring picture windows which looked out to the nearby Catalina mountain foothills. The architecture blew every emotional fuse in Daddy's brain and Mama's too. It was an excellent example of a Southwestern ranch style home. It created a must-have situation.

A few days later we checked into the Disneyland Hotel, into a room so tiny we had to stifle our instant complaints lest we ruin the whole vacation. We forgot our outrage rather quickly, however, as a most miraculous and wondrous discovery awaited us outside the sliding patio door. An orange tree dangled real, live fruit over the wall into our minuscule patio area. This filled us with wonder and awe.

We only looked; out of reverence and humility, we wouldn't dare pick it.

Disneyland was everything I dreamed it would be. *Peter Pan* had been my initiation into Disney movies; Disneyland was nothing if not Neverland. It had mermaids. It had Indians. It had a real pirate ship like the one in the movie. It had Tinker Bell. There was no discernible danger in this place; fear was just a faraway feeling from another realm.

I secretly loved Peter. His post-puberty voice in the Disney movie made him an easy love object—this was no kid, in spite of what the storyline indicated. Tinker Bell's strapless, flirty mini-dress and pom-pom shoes must have been a constant allure to him. Her skirt would occasionally flip and show a flash of her panties. This shocked me but it seemed to be working; he would always come back to her no matter how much Wendy tried to intervene. He even had a pet name for her. *Tink* knew exactly when and how much to pout and she was very adept at the use of revenge to get his attention. I soaked it all up like a sponge. I was then ready for whatever romantic wonders the third grade might hold.

We were firmly entrenched in middle-class American prosperity with a stay-at-home mother, now a piano, and two cars. The offspring of prosperity, like all offspring, can include some bad apples; which in this case included conspicuous consumption, entitlement mentality, and Keeping Up with the Joneses. Or in our case the Flahertys.

The Flahertys were an amiable family with a lot of kids. The dad was into cocktails, smoking, joking and buying new cars. I think he sold cars for a living. Cars were the hot ticket, as families discovered they could make use of more than one. Daddy liked this man. He probably envied the financial success, but Daddy liked anyone who drank cocktails and told jokes.

Later, at the inaugural cocktail party for the House, Mr. Flaherty donned my mother's red wig, thereby cementing his identity as the Life of the Party. (Wigs were a standard household convenience item in the days before microwaves. Mama wasn't wearing it that night because her own hair had been professionally styled for the event.) Judy Flaherty, the eldest of their kids, was my favorite babysitter. She likewise knew how to have fun and would take us over to her house so she could talk on the phone incessantly while earning money. Mrs. Flaherty had big beautiful eyes and seemed to be always delighted and attractive in spite of her workload.

Their family size was on the upswing. They had five kids and counting because they were Catholic and officially disallowed from birth control. Many Catholic families had five+ kids in midcentury. So the Flahertys outgrew their house and became the first of my neighborhood homies to leave our beloved enclave. They moved into a brand-new two-story house that smelled of fresh paint and new carpet and had ample space for many beautiful things. The living room was painted a delicate yellow that gave my child's heart a warm glow. Their new house exuded Order and Dignity and I tasted envy for the first time.

How would I manage this irritation? This fear of missing out? I began to pester my dad. One weekend, standing next to his easy chair I subtly broached the subject. *When are WE going to move?* No response. *When will WE have a new house?* More silence. Then finally, *I don't know, Janet* without eye contact. He stayed glued to the newspaper. *The Flahertys have a new house. Why don't we have a new house?* Always before he had been reasonable about things I asked for. This was different; I guess I had taken up the nagging of a wife. I probably didn't instigate anything but that's the earliest memory I have of our start away from Westfield Drive. I neglected to mention the stairway to him.

He pretended to ignore me but in fact, the wheels were already in motion. Daddy had in mind to design a house of our own so that he and Mama could incorporate all their clever ideas in floor planning and establish hipster cred among their peers.

The next thing I recall in this process was Mama squealing, jumping and prancing around over finding a *lot*. You would have

thought she had won *Queen for a Day*. I was confused. What's a lot?
This couldn't be good. I thought we wanted a new house. Why was a
piece of land such a big deal? There seemed to be plenty of land
everywhere I looked.

As it turned out, the lot was perfectly suited for their dream
home, an *atomic rancher*. It was virtually flat and pie-shaped. It sat at
the very top of a steep hill, nestled in an elbow curve of the street, so
it was on the left as people drive around the crest of the hill. The
House, when finished, would be very high profile, situated smack on
the hill's apex.

An easement for the natural gas line runs along its northwestern
edge and also along the edge of the neighbors' lots, which created an
unbroken backyard the size of a football field. No one had fences in
midcentury Knoxville; the lots were so big there was no real need for
them. And there were no leash laws for dogs.

There were two huge trees on this lot. Daddy would try his best
to design around them both but to no avail. The one in the center
had to go; the big walnut tree in the back remained. It had a perfect
branch for a rope swing where I would eventually spend many hours
fantasizing and navel-gazing. Mama was thrilled to have its
prodigious crop for homemade candy; Daddy and David would have
gladly sacrificed nuts in their candy to avoid the autumn mowing
hazard they created. (Picking them up out of the grass was a tedious
job, and usually delegated to the navel-gazer.)

East Tennessee consists of rolling hills; my parents needed flat
property because their goal was to create a California rancher like the
one our Tucson relatives lived in. It was the hottest thing going in
residential design. Cliff May and Joseph Eichler had done some
serious trendsetting work in the Southwest. Builders were imitating
the style in droves wherever the landscape permitted. It also came to
be known as an *atomic rancher* for the period in which it was
developed.

Mama and Daddy were content to live in suburbia and
determined to live within their means, but they would only do it in

style. A tract house was not going to work. It had to be cutting edge or nothing.

The search for the lot was evidently long, arduous and discouraging and Mama's exuberance was justified; but since I wasn't included, to me it just seemed silly. So much for the romantic stairway. Daddy did, however, persuade the developer to grant a romantic street number to accompany the romantic street name: we would live at 1414 Clairemont Trail. Every driveway in the subdivision was ornamented with a matching black lamppost, which gave the neighborhood an upscale feel in spite of it being distinctly middle class.

My father had dreams of huge picture windows looking out to the sunrise and the Great Smoky Mountains; and interior windows, to simulate indoor/outdoor living. He wanted an open floor plan, stereo speakers wired throughout and exposed redwood beams across *cathedral* (vaulted) ceilings. He wanted his own workshop for tinkering and gluing broken things. And he absolutely would endow the house with extra-long overhangs (even though we didn't have the brutal Southwestern sun to deal with), so it would be in keeping with the style prototypes.

Mama had dreams of interior brick and a laundry room where the ironing board would always stand ready. She wanted a place where she could station her sewing machine in front of a big window, and a bedroom far removed from the kids'. The sprawling nature of a rancher would necessitate an intercom system so that she could call the kids to dinner without yelling.

So the master bedroom suite was at the opposite end of the House from the other bedrooms. It was just off the living/dining room, which allowed the master bathroom to double as the guest bath. The master suite and family room would both open out to the backyard patio, which the kitchen would also overlook, thereby further advancing this indoor/outdoor concept. From the patio, we could admire the vast swaths of green of the convergent backyards and the oranges, reds, and golds of sunset.

They wanted a formal entryway with double doors surrounded by glass. Skylights and high interior windows would be used strategically to prevent dark areas.

As an engineer, Daddy was proficient in drafting and blueprint-making, but he did lack a workspace for the project. This was just a minor challenge for him. They had recently upgraded the kitchen table by ordering a rectangular piece of trendy Formica (with nasty sharp corners), attaching stainless steel legs and purchasing four complementary chairs (which I recently spotted in a 60s era movie). So for his workspace, he simply ordered a triangular piece and installed it in the corner of David's wee bedroom. It was perfect: sleek, minimally invasive and utilitarian. Piece of cake.

So the lot and the furniture became the defining parameters for the House. Daddy would joke with everyone afterward that he designed it around the Formica table. Indeed, he did, but those with the inside scoop knew that the Heywood Wakefield pieces were the greater consideration. More importantly, the House itself was to be perfectly flat—not even a rise at the threshold entrance—with wider hallways and doors and at least one barrier-free shower, for the years when he expected to be confined to a wheelchair. The House would be wheelchair accessible throughout, decades before such an idea became commonplace and even legally required.

He had learned to power-nap during his theatrical days and for this project it came in handy. He would arrive home around 5:30, sleep for 15 minutes, eat dinner, and disappear to his drafting desk until midnight or so. All weekend he was enthralled with the drafting. Mama frequently proclaimed that she saw more of him when he was out performing than she did during this design period. He was obsessed. As overtly excited as they seemed to be, there was a definite downside. Mama and I missed him terribly. I don't think David noticed because nightly Daddy was right there in his room with him.

He literally did start by designing the kitchen eating area around the table. Next came the living/dining room combination for the

HW pieces: an alcove for the desk, brick wall as a backdrop for the buffet, large open area for the dining table. With Mama as muse, providing practical input as well as timely meals, clean underwear, and obedient children, Daddy was free to make their God-given vision become reality. And so it began.

One day I came home from school to find my mother on the phone, in front of the TV and crying. She refused to make eye contact. Finally, she said something about the President having been shot. She was frantic, distant, and in a state which I had never seen before. She was unresponsive to my pleas for an explanation. Why did she avoid me so? Didn't I deserve to know what was going on? Wasn't I smart enough?

Whatever before had made us secure and carefree was not just disrupted but would soon prove to be forever gone. Insecurity was alien to me, and troubling. I had no name for it and could find no comfort. I knew that Mama sometimes would be really angry with Daddy and unspeaking, but during those times her affection toward me was either unaffected or even stronger. But Daddy had nothing to do with this. The source was external.

Eventually, I learned from the TV and my third-grade teacher Mrs. Carter about the horror of assassination. I pondered death for the first time. What made it scary and personal were the little girl and boy whose own daddy had been killed. They weren't much younger than me. I thought Caroline kind of looked like me. I had once had her same haircut.

Not long after that our abode there on the hillside went up for sale. I don't recall a sign in the yard. Maybe there was no sign. My parents needed the money to begin construction so it was sold and out we went. I felt no regret; only excitement for a new environment to explore, a new personal space to define.

My excitement was short-lived. We found a rental house a few miles away in the shade of the Interstate. It was a nondescript rectangular box with no memorable landscaping or other distinction. It was a shelter. Our furniture sort of floated around in it. We floated around in it. I have an occasional recurring dream about residing but not really living in this house. It was a time of detachment. My roots had been yanked along with the rest of the American populace.

Life had begun to be tedious for me. By first grade, I was enrolled in ballet school and piano lessons. And I had my first visit to the orthodontist.

My upper palate was severely underdeveloped and I had what they call a Class 3 Underbite. I guessed that meant really bad. My first round of treatment included 30-minute sessions every night, at home or away, pushing out on my upper palate with a pair of Popsicle sticks. It was bad enough at home but it was torture when I spent the night at the Kempwoods. How in the world can you sing along with Mitch Miller with Popsicle sticks in your mouth? Annie proved to be loving and sympathetic. *Don't you wish you could sing, too?* she would tenderly ask.

Years before, I had received some preparation for the Popsicle-stick treatment with similarly over-long sessions sitting in a laundry tub. I had a rectal fissure—whatever that could be—and the treatment was daily soaking in hot salt water. This was barely endurable. I read books and counted minutes. I sang to myself. I played with my toes. The water got cold; Mama would add hot water. Any kind of therapy is excruciating if you don't realize a problem. I thought my bottom worked just fine.

Construction on the House began in spring of 1964. I anticipated a long and boring summer without any road trips. When school was out we faced three long months in this boring rental house beneath the freeway.

I was a fish-out-of-water without my old neighborhood and its giant trees and mud creek and piles of kids. To compensate for the lack of playmates my mom invited my step-cousin to come for a visit. It didn't work out too well. His girlish ways were curious to me. He was picky (or *picayunish*, as Daddy would say) and impossible to please. He couldn't tolerate the pulp in the orange juice. He didn't play well with either me or my brother. He didn't like us and he didn't like Priscilla.

Occasionally during the Westfield years, we would beat the heat by visiting the county swimming pool. We had to drive about 30 minutes to get to it, so it was a day-long affair. Mama would slather us in sunscreen and pack sandwiches and lemonade which we would consume at a concrete table in the shade. After lunch (or concession-stand ice cream sandwiches) we had to wait 30 minutes before we could go back into the water to swim (ie bob around and splash each other). The scent of Coppertone suntan lotion even now transports me to the Concord pool. It was gigantic and full of smarmy kids and had a smarmy changing room/restroom. The floors were oddly slippery and it smelled of chlorine and mildew, a mildly nauseating mix. I'm sure that many a little girl avoided it altogether for a more convenient solution.

By this particular summer, another public pool had opened on the opposite end of the city. Semi-public that is: a fairly hefty membership fee was charged and so it carried a certain snob appeal. All the ladies in their oversized sunglasses and wacky straw hats came to sunbathe and show off. Of course, we took the bait on this opportunity. We would go weekly to see and be seen. Daddy was no social-climber but he wouldn't miss any opportunity to be hip to the trendy, especially in mixed company.

The Ambassador's Club (ultimate snob-appeal name) pool had three diving boards of varying heights which I loved to cannonball off of. Once, when Daddy was busy talking to someone, probably female, I called out his name to get his attention as I jumped. Both he and the lifeguard mistakenly took my call for one of distress and jumped in to rescue me, causing a three-person collision. The entire pool population stopped all activity to witness the (non-)drowning. Silence descended as all eyes turned toward me. I was filled with rage at being misunderstood and humiliated because my dad's lack of attention caused the whole thing, in my opinion. I instated a swimming boycott.

The boycott held until Mama rudely signed me up for swim lessons. When I met the cute swim instructor with the huge smile and funny name, Tom LeSeuer, my shame melted away like a Brown Cow on hot cement. I was smitten for perhaps the very first time. There he was: tan, muscular, confident, friendly, and best of all—interested in me and my progress! The sense of having an advocate totally turned my head around. It was *fun* being in love! From thence forward Mama had no trouble getting me to eat the peas of the same name…or to go to the swimming pool just for fun. After all, Mr. LeSeuer might be hanging around.

When I wasn't at the pool I followed my natural tendencies to pass the time. I decided to produce *The Wizard of Oz* in the carport of the rental house. My playwriting had blossomed the previous school year and Mrs. Carter was the perfect teacher for it. She always made time in the schedule for my productions. She allowed my chosen actors the freedom to rehearse, and she even prompted the class to applaud at the appropriate times.

Perhaps showmanship runs in my genes. That same school year the owner and sole instructor of my ballet school—Miss Irma— asked my parents if I could be allowed to perform in *Alice in Wonderland* which the university was producing for elementary school children throughout the city. The UT drama department produced three plays each school year. Those were the most thrilling days on the calendar because we boarded buses and missed half a school day to see the play. But this time I would be missing a whole lot of school to actually be in the play.

I would be Tweedledum and Mitzi Morgan would be Tweedledee. It was a grand introduction to the world of adults beyond my parents and teachers. Besides being pampered and nurtured by the cast members during weeks of rehearsals and performances, I was introduced to the ecstasy of coffee. The White Rabbit gets top credit for this, as one might expect. It came as a result of my being afflicted with a miserable sore throat and cold. But the show must go on: he helped me endure it with piping hot java loaded with cream and sugar. He was my first gay friend, but of course I didn't know that at the time. I just knew that he was kind, easy to talk to, and cared about my feelings. He was my favorite grownup friend and the best nurturer among a whole cast of them.

He later turned up as one of my high school English teachers. All the high school kids equally loved him. We were both amused and impressed with the way he would teach from a seated cross-legged position, unabashedly raising one butt cheek or the other to pass gas. It was audaciously unaffected. Radical even.

The carport production gave me a great reason to corral all my old neighborhood buddies by assigning them a part. The play itself really wasn't all that difficult as we had seen the movie at least every year since birth. The real challenge was the intermission entertainment. We wanted to create our very own Boy Band which had become enormously popular. We had seen the Beatles and the Beach Boys on TV and were enthralled with them. David and a couple of friends would make great facsimiles. Tennis racquets would replace the guitars and lip-syncing would suffice for the singing, as current video stars have proven. We counted on the power of imagination to produce the requisite sex appeal.

In the fourth grade, I turned to book writing and my first idea was to chronicle the doings of a frontier-era girl similar to Laura Ingalls. This project hit the skids early when Mama blithely commented on my lack of historical research. *How do you know what she would eat for lunch? What kind of stove she cooked on? What she wore?* etc.

What a killjoy. I knew she was right but I couldn't be bothered to spend hours in the library. If my imagination wasn't good enough for those details then other projects would have to suffice, such as making clothes for Barbie or the Troll doll with the orange hair. I could sew on a million snaps and miles of miniature rickrack without doing research.

But in the residential department, my patience had reached its limit and I was antsy to see if our new house would equal or even surpass the Flahertys'.

47

Chapter 5

As during the design phase, with manic obsession Daddy went
daily after work and every weekend to oversee the construction
progress and look for errors and omissions. I am certain he drove the
contractor crazy. He constantly required the crew to re-do work that
had been finished. But finally the plumbing was all laid, the air
conditioning/heating ducts were in place, and the slab could be
poured.

Mama simultaneously worked on the interior decoration without
any professional help. She never would have employed a designer,
which she considered impersonal and pretentious, besides the
expense. She had a love of fabrics so she ordered pinch-pleated
draperies for every room. The living room sofa would be recovered
(for the second time) in a velvet stripe of gold, moss green and dark
teal. They ordered the requisite Heywood Wakefield pieces for the
living room—a desk, a buffet and two matching upholstered chairs.
She completed her china: Constellation by Castleton, with its tiny
blue atomic-looking flowers connected by fine lines that swirled with
energy.

The kitchen backsplash area was wallpapered with a yellow and
orange chicken-and-egg grocery motif; the drapery fabric had the
exact same print. The refrigerator and dishwasher were in harvest
gold. The stove was a drop-in stainless steel model before anyone
had much heard of stainless steel. On the wall above the Formica

table were two gigantic wooden utensils (fork and spoon), each measuring about 3 feet long. A wannabe-Bakelite olive green oblong tray accented the end of the longest counter.

They purchased two gold velvet easy chairs for the sitting area in the master bedroom. The plan was to have the TV on a rolling stand so that it could be wheeled into that room if the kids had friends over and were occupying the family room. They took advantage of all the extra space and purchased a queen-size bed to replace their double. Mama claimed she would never want a king; *that would leave too much space between me and Daddy* she said. She wanted to keep the beautiful turquoise and green flowered spread from the double bed, so she simply attached a wide turquoise cotton fringe along the bottom. Then it fit the queen bed perfectly while adding a trendy element.

For the family room, there was a new orange vinyl sofa to complement the bamboo chairs and piano. This sofa was terrifically stylish but horribly uncomfortable—very angular, no springs, just thick foam covered in plastic with non-upholstered squared-off wooden arms. It made into a bed, but not the standard way; so we thought it was intensely cool. It was kind of like a futon. Below the seating surface was a drawer-type mechanism that would pull out, then you lowered one of the two long seat cushions onto the drawer thing and you had a level double-size bed. Of vinyl. Now we could have friends sleep over and stay all night in front of the wood-burning fireplace. If we could get the fireplace to function, that is.

Contemporary bathroom fixtures (American Standard in green, tan and pink) and countertops (more Formica) had to be chosen. Flooring likewise must be the latest thing, so it was wall-to-wall carpeting for the living/dining/master bedroom wing, green slate for the foyer and hearth, and asbestos tile for the remainder. The tile pattern simulated little cut stones for the kitchen and family rooms. The back hallway and children's bedrooms had a similar tannish brown pattern of small rectangles alternating to gray for the pink bathroom/bedroom suite which was mine. The discovery of these tile patterns brought Mama more glee.

But I believe they most enjoyed selecting the artwork for the House. They were both fond of abstract art and Mama determined that it should all be original, making an exception for the Stuart Davis print. They knew how to go to art student showings at the university and find paintings that were edgy and affordable, like the dark dramatic Blue Fissure which was hung in the dining area between the stereo speakers. The House was a perfect gallery with its ample natural light.

For the exterior they were enthusiastic about field stone which was enormously popular; but after pricing, it proved to be cost-prohibitive. They settled on used brick which was a big letdown. On top of that, used brick wasn't very easy to come by. There was tension as they waited to see if the contractor could locate enough to complete the project.

He did, and the House was finished just in time for us to move in before Christmas of 1964. We gladly abandoned the rental with the theatre-carport in the shadow of the Interstate. Or so I thought.

Moving into a new house right at Christmastime really isn't all that fun when you're nine. Once again I was a fish out of water. This was the coldest, dampest month of the year and the floors were cold in our bedrooms. My other, real home had hardwood floors throughout. The carpet hadn't been installed yet in the living room and bare cement slab creates a distinct institutional atmosphere. Jail-like. One of the picture windows had been broken out by the contractor and a sheet of plywood was in its place. The window sills in all the bedrooms and kitchen were cold gray marble. I missed terribly the tiny intimacy of my real home which was appropriately scaled for kids.

There was nothing familiar here. How could this be OK for Christmas? It wasn't. There's a photo of David and me, in a too-small dingy white sweatshirt, stretch pants with stirrups (like the skiers wore), and stretch headband, standing on the front porch. Daddy's latest handmade Christmas decorations are hanging on the green double front doors (a pair of cartoonish angels with red foil hair and bronze foil gowns complete with haloes and songbooks). They were very simplistic—friendly, sweet, simple. Folk art, we'd say now; they said *contemporary*, of course. That descriptive of greatest desire.

In this photo I look happy. I am not. I hate the place, but Mama and Daddy are really happy so I'm trying to go along with it. Not only did it not surpass the Flahertys' or even equal it, it fell far short. How can a house with no stairs be any fun? We had definitely traded down. Our old house was cozy and warm and comfortable. Kids want cozy and comfortable, or big, expensive, new, and completed— with stairs. About the only good things I could find in it were the intercom and the fireplace.

I exhibited my displeasure by being the first one up on Christmas morning and making my way out to the tree alone, save for Pink Doggie, who was my loyal constant companion. He had jingle bells in his ears and existed in a perpetual state of reclining sleep, making the dip between his head and body a perfect head rest for reading. (I used him selfishly, but he loved me anyway.) I turned the lights on and we sat in the cold for many long minutes, staring at the inert wrapped packages. The vaulted ceiling and cement floor gaped around me. I tried to conjure up that familial sense of belonging, of tradition. When it didn't come I decided to go for the retail therapy of opening my gifts. I systematically removed the paper and bows on every single one, being careful to preserve what I could for some later use.

I was assessing the varying functionality of the loot before me when Mama's bedroom door opened. There she was in her pajamas, no bathrobe, clearly not believing what she saw. As the awful truth sank in she let out a profanity. *I got tired of waiting* I innocently offered. This had no effect. She slammed the door. After considering my situation at length, I re-wrapped everything carefully and slunk back to bed.

Not only did the retail therapy not work, but my mother's displeasure and the scourge of my self-centeredness would hang over me the remainder of the day. I felt the oddest mixture of defensiveness and shame. In that fateful moment, I had just wanted to help myself feel better. Is that so wrong? I guess so. We were not off to a great start in this House.

By the arrival of the first snowfall, we were in serious need of both actual and familial warmth. This was the occasion Daddy had waited for to inaugurate the fireplace. A plan which literally backfired.

For starters, he failed to open the flue so we got totally smoked out. Even once the flue was open we had no idea how to get the chimney to draw, so it didn't make much difference. However, I'm just talking about the smoke from dozens of wadded up newspapers stuffed under giant logs and lit with dozens of matches. We had no concept of kindling; Daddy had never been a Boy Scout. We lit the newspapers, they burned fast and big and bright (the funnies were the best display because they flared with rainbow colors), and we got all excited thinking that at last we had a fire. The paper would gradually burn up and the logs were just there—dark, cold and unresponsive, only adding to our gloom. It was a mess.

Would we ever adjust to this ridiculous House? My shame and disappointment continued to grow.

Of course, these were kinks that would make only a kid suffer. The parents had their own share of headaches in addition to the broken-out picture window. The newly ordered Heywood Wakefield arrived and the color of the wood did not match the existing pieces. Had it been different enough to create a contrast that might have been fine; but the original pieces were in a pinkish tone—*champagne*—and the new pieces were yellowish—*honey*. Being told by the sales personnel that there was no remedy, Daddy was close to devastated over this loss of visual perfection. A well-practiced apology became de rigueur for every first-time visitor.

Then there was the issue of arranging the furniture to a workable situation in the family room. Because the room wasn't designed around specific known pieces (except for the piano), it exposed Daddy's inexperience. It was basically square; a shape which has given interior designers fits since the days when cave people first moved into permanent housing.

The piano went against the non-window interior wall, which backed up to the workshop and faced the patio door. We tried it with the sofa facing the fireplace, but there was no spot for the TV. We tried putting the bamboo chairs on either side of the piano, but then you couldn't see the TV from them. We tried having the sofa face the piano, but then it got in the way of the kitchen entrance, and as you came in from the garage you would see the ugly back of the TV, not to mention that it was across the room from the closet where it was to be stored out of sight when not in use. My mother grew irritated. Daddy was even more irritated, having to own this design flaw.

Nevertheless in 1964 when we moved in my parents were generally exhilarated by the achievement. Our parents were in middle-class suburban semi-utopian bliss and David and I fell in line. We developed a strict weekly routine of piano and ballet lessons, choir practice, Boy and Girl Scouting, and steak-on-the-grill every Saturday night, with daiquiris for the parents. Daddy loved all things citrus, and he loved to grill on the patio while listening to his jazz over the outdoor speaker. The House had a very hip patio which sported inlaid wooden grid work, the latest contemporary trend for cement. After dinner we sat lined up on the orange sofa and watched *Saturday Night at the Movies*. We went to church every Sunday morning. (Safely, in the car.)

By January '65 the House was ready for a showing-off cocktail party and my parents had duly earned their bragging rights. It was the first of several parties. Introducing the House to all their friends and co-workers was a gigantic thrill for them, especially Daddy. He was confident, outgoing and showed his best charismatic side. The House would be filled with people, gaiety, drinking, and gourmet hors-d'oeuvres that Mama had handmade, all set to a Dave Brubeck/Henry Mancini/Ramsey Lewis/Wes Montgomery soundtrack. It had a wonderful flow-through floor plan: the foyer and kitchen were back-to-back, with the living room and family rooms at either end of these, so one could walk a big circle through the four areas.

The guests always seemed to be at ease and jolly. The men came dressed in turtleneck sweaters or dickies under collared shirts; the women in silk cocktail dresses and pearls. They constantly commented on what perfect ages David and I were. Which is to say, old enough to stay out of the way yet still too young to ask questions, get into serious trouble, or drive. The parties necessitated a well-stocked bar of course. All the extra cabinet space allowed it to be a permanent part of the kitchen inventory.

Within a year or two I had mostly adapted to the House. I came to love the spacious living room where Daddy taught me to swing dance, which gave the stereo a whole new purpose. In the equally spacious backyard we would play pitch-and-catch for hours and he never let me think that I couldn't play baseball someday if I so chose.

I managed to make friends in the new neighborhood in spite of its sprawling size. We rode to school on the bus every day so I got to know all the kids and their families' perks, quirks, and peculiarities. There were the six Catholic siblings whose home had a great open-door policy (the parents being too often snockered to care much about privacy); the developer's three kids directly across the street (the oldest of whom, Jenny, loved to torment the driver by walking extra slow from her door to the bus); my bookworm friend with three brothers and two PhD parents; the sturdy athletic extrovert who ended up married to an NFL punter (and raised two more NFL punters); and the friendly girl from the smaller houses down below with the super-friendly parents and much older super-friendly brothers.

As I made friends the area became wonderful stomping grounds; almost as insular as my previous neighborhood, just covering more territory. It was a fairly self-contained subdivision having only two entrances from the same road below on the southern perimeter; and no outlet, except for a back entrance to an adjacent tennis club on the western edge.

I could easily walk to and from my bookworm friend's house. In summer we picked wild blackberries in the vacant lots, made cobbler, topped it with Cool Whip, and watched soap operas while eating half of the whole pan. We discovered the joy and freedom of walking to and from the nearby Holiday Inn to patronize the vending machines. The taste of independence was so sweet that we would hang around the back stairways there for an hour at a time consuming Snickers and bags of Lays.

When her dad got wind of it he had a cow and persuaded my dad to issue a joint edict: no hotel loitering. We were completely ignorant about hookers so this seemed totally unreasonable; we were furious but her father was unfazed. I don't think my dad would have bothered to prohibit this practice, but he did his best to make it sound like he had been planning it all along.

Before long, a community pool was built within easy walking distance of the House and that provided the getaway we needed and that all teens and tweens hunger for.

My pink bedroom and adjoining bathroom with full-size tub was a dream come true. When I had to stay home, I could escape into my suite at the rear of the house, play my records and daydream about my first real crush, Billy Overby, a friend of my brother. Now I was listening to the likes of the Rolling Stones' *Get Off of My Cloud* and *(I Can't Get No) Satisfaction* and the Beatles' *I Want to Hold Your Hand*, all unmistakably trending toward self-absorption. My impressionable brain didn't miss a beat. Time would reveal a paradigm shift underway toward narcissism at the mass level. I would not be left behind.

The pink suite was also a hideaway to get lost in my books. My favorites were The Borrowers and the Nancy Drew mystery series. I read them all and counted days until each new one was available at the library. I got especially wound up when the ND cover illustration involved ghosts or the supernatural.

Anything spiritual kicked my brain into high gear. Pondering unseen worlds was my favorite pastime; Halloween was therefore my favorite holiday, beating out Christmas by a hair. After trick-or-treating was finished I would stand in the middle of the field behind the House and wait for the ghosts or witches, which seemed to be all around me, to materialize. I believed that if I just stood perfectly still and paid close enough attention I would witness a tear in the veneer of reality and see them. I knew that the material world was hiding something far bigger and it ignited my curiosity.

Fourth grade stalled my developing crushing tendency as Mrs. Peters knew how to keep my mind engaged.

In the fifth grade, Jeffrey Elliott appeared. He had started to school late in life because of either a birthday issue or his parents' wisdom, and was feeling the stirrings of puberty. Like Peter Pan, he knew something the younger boys did not, and his voice had changed. He had curly hair and a definite rooster strut. On the second day of school he looked at me as I had never before been looked at, with a gaze that lingered a split second longer than it should have and a sly smile that said he had something other than school on his mind. I don't believe I was unique in receiving this come-on; by the third week of school at least a half-dozen girls had crushes on him. I seem to recall the friendly girl from the bus came out ahead of the pack, which she would continue to do clear through high school. (She was still fabulous at our fortieth HS reunion.)

By seventh grade I was reading *Gone With the Wind* and *Wuthering Heights* and my imagination took that inevitable turn toward...procreation.

Those earlier years were happily punctuated by family movie outings and road trips.

We went as a family to all the popular movies whether they were meant for children or not. I drank in the epic dramas of *How the West Was Won* and *The Greatest Story Ever Told* and the silly globe-trotting *It's a Mad, Mad, Mad, Mad World*. But my favorites were always the ones with romance. The 1961 version of *Babes in Toyland* had a boyfriend/girlfriend dynamic, which for me was the movie's centerpiece. *The Absent-Minded Professor* had a funny forgotten-wedding subplot, and *Charade* had a great do-they-or-don't-they situation between Cary Grant and my idol Audrey.

And what to make of *Breakfast at Tiffany's?* Holly Golightly was gay and elegant and witty but she also had a blue side. She put Cat out in the rain and brushed off her tortured husband. Her urban boyfriend was wistful and debonair, but I was a little bothered by her duplicity…I just didn't know what to call it. She had no visible means of income but she did somehow get by. The way she waved her cigarette holder showed us all that she had style, poise and not a care in the world.

My mother took me to see *The Umbrellas of Cherbourg* and as a fourth-grader, it left me bemused and bewildered and definitely indoctrinated regarding what people do when they're in love. Technically speaking I had no clue what the couple was up to when they went to his bedroom; it didn't seem like it should be OK, but Mama didn't say a single word about it. I concluded that it must be OK to sleep with your boyfriend. Likewise, (in the movie) the French mother wasn't too troubled when her daughter turned up pregnant. Michel Legrand's score made the movie indelible to my schoolgirl heart. It was all beautiful and poignant and glamorous. The glamour of it easily compensated for the obvious heartbreak.

And then there was the James Bond series. All of which I was allowed to see. No one made any comment about Sean Connery's interactions with the scantily clad actresses with bizarre names like Pussy Galore. Mama and Daddy may have thought that it went over my head but they were wrong. The films of the 60s were loaded with smoking and cocktails and sexual innuendo, all presented as the epitome of glamour and I soaked it up like a sponge, even if I didn't get the *pussy* double entendre.

In midcentury sex was all around but parents were mum on the subject. My sex education consisted of finding a book left mysteriously in my nightstand drawer about periods and how people get pregnant. Later, in high school when we somehow meandered onto the subject, Mama told me that nice girls don't do that until they're married. I believed her for a while, figuring that Catherine Deneuve in *Umbrellas* must have been an exception. (She was French, after all.) Eventually I was able to more adequately cover the topic with my favorite friend whom I would meet in ninth grade.

When I was old enough to go to the movies without my parents, one of the first I saw was Franco Zeffirelli's *Romeo and Juliet* in summer 1968. Like an overstressed fuse box blowing sparks, my brain was fried by the heat of the romance. There was even an exposed breast for a split second in the wedding night scene. I came out of it in a state of shock and breathlessness. I lost sleep. Beautiful young people in beautiful clothes, speaking beautiful language and so desperately in love that one would do anything to be with the other, like scale walls and drink poison. Anything. And that bedroom scene! I would definitely have to reconsider the procreative activity. They made it look pretty attractive. I think I saw the film six or eight times.

Many years later I found a copy of the soundtrack in the hallway of a friend's apartment building, where it was awaiting trash pickup. I grabbed it, shocked at my incredible good fortune. It consisted of four long-playing vinyl records with every word of dialogue, every clanking sword and every note of background music. It still takes up space in my storage closet.

Our road trips were mostly to Cincinnati, Daddy's home. He loved going to Cincinnati and therefore so did I. We would pack a picnic lunch and eat at a roadside table, with baloney-white bread sandwiches for the kids, slathered in yellow mustard, and tuna salad or ham-and-dill pickle sandwiches for the parents. These were complemented by potato chips and cans of root beer and ginger ale. If we started out after Daddy's workday, as it got dark I would gaze up at the stars and think about how the same stars shone down on ravenous brontosauruses and T-Rexes. This was as close as I could come to fathoming eternity.

I never had to ask if we were there yet because I knew the lay of the land. We were almost there when we turned onto the Columbia Parkway and drove along the river, finally turning left onto Delta and making our way into the Mt. Lookout neighborhood, and finally right, onto their street. If I'd been walking I could have found it blindfolded.

There was much to love about Cincinnati. Grandma W made us chocolate milk in tumblers of brightly-colored hammered aluminum that would sweat heavily with condensation from the cold liquid. We were always allowed to stay up late to watch Johnny with her. (Of course we did; David and I slept in the living room on the couch and a folding cot.) My parents slept on cots in whichever apartment happened to be vacant at the time, but Daddy would come and awaken us in the middle of the night to watch the raccoons raiding the trash cans in the rear of the building. David and I loved to race through the building to and from their place, to see who could find the fastest route. And then of course I had the lobby for my Cinderella daydreams.

We had a recreational circuit in Cincinnati which always started with the massive municipal parks, Ault and Hyde. They had swing sets bigger than any in Knoxville, to be sure, which were randomly placed throughout the vast green lawns. The swings never jumped out of the ground no matter how high or hard your dad would push you, and I had to have a turn on each and every set. Each visit we had separate days dedicated to the zoo and Coney Island amusement park to ride the rides. (We never knew it wasn't the only Coney Island.) Daddy would mess with us and pretend that one or another of the sites would be left out that year, just to see how distraught we could grow before he cracked a sly grin and dropped the ploy.

We walked down a paved trail through thick woods to visit Withrow High School where Daddy went and peeked in the windows. Later, in summer 1974 I had a few dates with a guy who had gone to school there, and the father of the Catholic family on our street also had gone there. Small world, huge high school. Daddy was extremely social but I think mostly with girls. He did have one very close friend, Perry Wydman, with whom he reconnected in his last year of life by using my computer without even the help of Facebook.

In season we always took in a Reds game. I didn't care about the game, nor did I understand it; but the rituals of organ music, shelling peanuts, and shouting commands to the players became near and dear to my heart. Pete Rose and Johnny Bench were my heroes. Sadly, I also learned how the mix of beer and sporting events can wreak havoc on even the most stable playing field.

Nevertheless, Cincinnati was my slice of heaven. There, Daddy was always energetic, playful and glad to be a dad and a husband. For those brief interludes, we were a solid unit and he was devoted to us. He was 100% present. Consequently, I developed a lifelong passion for urban environments.

We had already driven to Disneyland and next we drove to the New York City World's Fair in 1965. I was the first of my friends to see the singing dolls in the *It's a Small World* exhibit (before it was installed at Disneyland), which gave me an imagined edge in global perspective. The trip would have been completely fabulous if not for two strange incidents.

During a sightseeing tour in the bell tower of Riverside Church I seized up from terror. After climbing several stories on open-grate stairs, surrounded by bells the size of Volkswagens, the top of the hour came around and the bells commenced tolling. I froze as dead in my tracks. No amount of cajoling or reassurance from the adults had any effect; I had to be blindfolded to get out. No one knew where this fear came from. Perhaps it had to do with my preschool fear of heights from my brother's playground fall. It caused quite a scene with the other visitors. My parents were apologetic and ashamed of this exposure of their kid's psychological flaw. Folks today probably wouldn't even bat an eye at some tourist kid having a panic attack.

And there was the bizarre incident of being left waiting curbside for Daddy. We were on our way to or from some unknown destination and my mother, brother and I were told to *wait right there* and he'd bring the car around. As instructed we stood there, unattended on a busy Manhattan street, at night, for what was obviously way too long. He clearly had made some clandestine side trip. We waited at least 45 minutes for him to come from the parking garage. I held my mother's hand with a tight grip and slowly became disgusted and terrified, not sure which one was more appropriate; he could have been mugged or in a crash! Mama kept her dignified cool as always, repeating *he'll be here shortly* an infinite number of times which did nothing to assuage the lump in my gut.

And that's what I recall about Manhattan.

That kind of subterfuge—aka crap—was always going on with my dad. We'd be going along having a lark of a time, all systems normal, and boom: some inexplicable mysterious behavior. But never in Cincinnati.

In 1967 we went on a rare personally financed trip, driving to Atlanta to see first-hand the architect John Portman's new Hyatt Regency. It was the original atrium hotel and a true sight to behold. We were filled with awe and wonder. David and I rode the interior glass elevators continually. The novelty and trying to keep up with him caused me to forget my vertigo for the time being. The bell tower incident seemed a distant memory.

We did actually fly on one trip. Daddy was thrilled with flying—it activated his engineering psyche—and he finagled a business trip to the nuclear facility in Livermore, California in the summer of 1968. Amazingly there was a family discount: kids could fly free with parents. We stayed in nearby San Francisco.

The Wehners would NOT miss out on the Summer of Love! It was ushering in a tidal wave of social change in every imaginable and unimaginable way. Daddy was always hip to social change. It came from reading *Newsweek* incessantly. He had an insatiable need to be informed, at least, even if it not fully participatory. He wanted us to be the first family on the block to see bona fide hippies. While Knoxville may not have been quite as provincial as the Deep South, neither was it known for diversity. And Fred Wehner would not raise any babes in the woods.

Whoa boy. As we passed through North Beach I locked the car door because black leather, long hair, and motorcycles were everywhere and I had heard about Hells Angels. But not only was Daddy not intimidated, he was thoroughly entertained. As we drove around at 15 mph trying to look ordinary he solemnly observed, *The hippies have all abandoned Haight-Ashbury now. This is their newest hangout.* Hanging out was something I knew nothing about and didn't particularly care to. I scooted down in the back seat and looked straight ahead.

My intimidation dissipated quickly however when the parents were napping and Union Square was close by, beckoning me. At 13 I was surely old enough to venture out and do a little window shopping. It was exhilarating. The store windows held indescribable treasures, but the people held the real fascination. They seemed so important. They were confident and stylish and had urgent destinations. I wanted to be like that. Perhaps no one would notice that I wasn't, just yet. I made several circuits trying my best to look sophisticated and purposeful, and grown up.

Daddy's habit of making clandestine disappearances hit its climax on this trip. One evening he left the hotel room after Mama had turned in, saying later that he couldn't sleep. He was gone for two or three hours. This was sleazy; no one could be up to any good at that hour. I fumed inside but my anger got stuffed down into my heart-bottle (with a very loose cork). If Mama wasn't going to hold him accountable, did I have any right to? Not a word was ever said about it by her or me or even David.

Upon our return to the House, I decorated my room with a fringed paper Tiffany-look lamp shade and hung neon-colored mobiles with geometric shapes. I began to burn incense. The hippies had made their mark.

It has been observed that pride goes before a fall. My parents' social circle was not really all that big and once the initial thrill of the

House's unveiling was past, the ensuing letdown was more of a total crash. By age 38 my father couldn't really figure out what to do for an encore. I think he related a little too closely to Sean Connery's 007 character. He craved action and being on the cutting edge of everything. This kind of determination, along with a staunch commitment to progressive thinking, is exhausting. You're constantly running to keep up.

Slowly but surely his attention was again pulled away from home and family as it had been before the House project. He became guarded and dodgy. He was preoccupied. The repressed marital issues crawled back out into the air where they could breathe and expand. But both parents were adept at conflict avoidance and so there was no open fighting. We had instead the quiet strain of denial.

The nightly bedtime prayers had been abandoned once we moved into the House. Perhaps it was the distance between the parents' and kids' rooms; maybe it was the distraction of adjusting to a new household; maybe it was just our ages. Priorities had definitely shifted. We continued to attend church every week but there was no discernible relationship to God. Nothing—no reference to Him in conversations; no prayers at mealtime or anytime; no evidence of a desire to know God or please Him; no admittance of any personal failure or wrong-doing; no interest in the Bible. None whatsoever.

The only Bible I knew about in our home was the one with the red cover and my name stamped on the front in gold. Our church gave it to me in September 1965 as I entered the fifth grade. It had some nice pictures even if they were a bit antiquated.

Whatever social homogeneity we had at my school would gradually be dismantled, thankfully; for me, it started with a shocking discovery in the seventh grade. It somehow became known that Louise Gold was Jewish. My friends and I were appalled and went into a state of gossip-fueled dismay. How could *anyone* not believe in Jesus? It was unthinkable. And she looked so…normal. And she was so…friendly! It just didn't add up with what our culture taught was unique to Jesus-followers. This was bigger than anti-semitism; *all* non-Christians were social pariahs.

I was definitely confused about God. If He was so big and so powerful, so important, why did no one seem to acknowledge Him? For starters, Daddy. I gradually began to suspect that he attended church so that he could bless the congregation with his voice in the choir (which would also keep his voice in good shape), where he mingled with the ladies. He would never want to be a social pariah or give anyone reason to think he was a bad parent. In our world, good parents by definition took their kids to (Christian) church.

There was some sort of disconnect going on, because whenever the topic of religion would accidentally come up at the dinner table Daddy would coolly say, after a long deliberate silence, (which preceded everything he said), *What you believe is a personal issue, not to be discussed. I live out my beliefs by being ethical in the workplace.* Whatever. We had no way to independently verify this.

Mama would silently nod in agreement, doing her best to deflect any inquiry from coming her way. She strategically kept her intelligence under wraps, often claiming ignorance on a topic to avoid engagement. She played dumb—a lot. Especially with religious issues, as she had done at the hoity-toity church (read: conflict avoidant).

I came to the conclusion that if you went to church and called yourself a Christian, that made it so. Any behavior enacted by someone who called themselves a Christian was therefore Christian behavior. This seemed a little too easy and convenient but I wasn't going to buck the system. It's an ideal position for those who want to give the appearance of being moral without actually doing it. Like having your cake while also eating it.

Overlooked was the fact that morals are the way we keep from hurting other people.

Moral confusion was gaining a definite foothold in our home. For example, in one of my soon-to-be-common fashion crises, before my first boy-girl party (or maybe it was my first and last; I can only remember that disastrous one) I was pretty desperate for a pair of white go-go boots. These had been made popular by the new TV show *Laugh-In*. My friend Francine who lived across the street conveniently owned a pair but that particular day she was out of town, rendering her boots unavailable.

Or so one would think. Daddy was undeterred; he simply grabbed the key we had been entrusted with for emergencies and told me to go help myself. He was as pragmatic as he was cheap.

I sweated bullets as I went through with this caper. It felt *really* wrong to me, but he endorsed it and I looked great in the boots. But it did ultimately ruin the fun. I sweated and fretted until the boots were safely back in their box in Francine's closet. This probably contributed to my anxious rejection of the assertive fellow who wanted to play kissy-face with me on a dark stairway.

Holidays started really losing their merry glow. Both sets of grandparents still came for Christmas dinner but the event grew into a distinct challenge for me, having learned how to recognize inebriation. By that time also the dreaded plant Christmas party would be over, leaving its wake of disillusionment.

The Cincinnati contingent, who arrived several days before Christmas, was notable for a huge imbalance in verbal communication. Grandma Wehner, deeply grateful to have someone listen to her, jabbered away every waking moment to Mama, who was the only family member with the fortitude to endure it. Mama was left exhausted by her inexhaustible chatter. However, she paid perfect respectful attention without complaint, and worked out the resulting frustration by showering compassion on Grandpa W. *He* stayed quiet as long as cold beer was available.

For him, Mama would go the distance and make homemade divinity. This required a huge scary-looking candy thermometer (scary to me because of where my temperature was usually taken) and perfectly balanced atmospheric humidity for it to set up properly. It was ridiculously technical. Also on his behalf, the main dinner always included Julia Child's oyster stuffing for the turkey.

The Lancing contingent would arrive in time for 4 pm dinner and was universally silent, speaking only when spoken to. They were not much into merry-making, having never quite recovered from the trauma of the Great Depression and Grandpa P's incarceration. Also, they were geographically insulated from the retail-driven frenzy.

What we had in the House on Christmas Day was the classic meeting of City and Country Mice, exacerbated by Daddy's not-so-subtle disdain for all things of rural origin. In their younger days he had exempted Mama from this; now it was becoming irrepressible. The man was just a snob.

All this, coupled with minimalist decorating (the door angels, the tree, the Nativity set and a few sprigs of real mistletoe, hung in the doorway between the kitchen and living/dining rooms) kept Christmas low key. And yet, by focusing on the traditions—gourmet treats, select music, the annual TV shows—I could still grab a remnant of that magical childhood anticipation.

There was an exception in the anticlimactic holiday memories and it almost trumped the dance deflation, at least for that year. In 1965 Daddy gave me my own decoration craft project: I was to make a felt banner depicting a contemporary nativity scene constructed from colorful felt pieces. It was to be hung over the fireplace. In midcentury it was vastly popular to hang handmade items over your fireplace. Eventually, macramé would take center stage.

This project appeared in a ladies' homemaking magazine. A grid overlay was provided which made it easy to enlarge the design and make pattern pieces. Daddy showed me how to use his slide rule to make it even easier. I was enthralled with it; I had been prepped for the technical challenge during years of watching him.

Daddy was uncharacteristically giddy with excitement when he gave me the instructions. The scope of it displayed his confidence in me which in turn delighted me, along with growing my inherited affinity for the tedious hand-made objects. It was tremendous fun, but mainly I just wanted to please my dad. I wanted him to be happy with me and my mom and the House, with the hope that his loyalty would return. He praised me profusely for the finished product but the loyalty remained unchanged.

My bedroom suite retreat was intended to later become guest accommodations. But now it allowed me to escape the silence of my parents' conflict avoidance and nurture my crush activity. Davy Jones of the Monkees was my first long-distance love object, and magazine pull-out posters covered the wall behind the door, which was the only place my parents would allow. I soon outgrew Davy and moved up to Brian Jones of the Stones. At some point I saw a full-page photo of him—gazing provocatively into the camera—that definitely changed my thinking about the procreative activity. Maybe, just maybe it might not be so disgusting after all. Hmmm.

I could wheel in the TV and watch *That Girl* with Marlo Thomas and *The Mary Tyler Moore Show* and dream about my future independence in an urban environment. I had a tam just like the one Mary threw into the air in the opening sequence. Weekly, when the theme song concluded with *You're going to make it, after all,* I took it as my personal motto of hope and reassurance. One day I would leave behind this cold House and be like the hip urban adults in Union Square.

My junior high years saw the crushes grow more and more consuming. Van Morrison's *Brown-Eyed Girl* set the pace for me... so wistful, so light and happy... it made me believe that romance could be happy and good and fill your heart with fond memories. He sang of *making love behind the stadium,* a phrase which at this point in my life had no impure connotation. My elementary school was adjacent to the high school, and on fall afternoons there were pep rallies at the football stadium. It wasn't hard to connect all that adrenaline and frenzy with romantic intrigue; I concluded that football stadiums must be great places to fall in love.

In the seventh grade, I was madly in love with Michael Hardy. He also had a head full of curly hair and was incredibly outgoing. (In high school, he became the class president during our senior year.) He wasn't even slightly interested in me so I chummed up with his mother for consolation. She, too, was warm and amiable; after school I would sit in her car and tell her all my problems while she waited for Michael to finish gadding about. She understood everything and never lagged in enthusiasm. She made my every word seem important and valuable.

My eighth-grade year was notable for my interlude with Tommy Parker. One morning I came into homeroom to find a strange, tightly folded piece of notebook paper sitting right in the middle of my desk. I gingerly opened it. In penciled words, he succinctly and directly asked me if I wanted to be his girlfriend. I was stunned silent. I almost forgot to breathe.

There must be some mistake, I thought. I couldn't recall that he had ever even looked at me and he certainly wasn't looking at me at that moment. Tommy was another one of those boys who, for whatever reason, was older than the rest of us. He was 14; we were 13. Word had gotten around that he had actually experienced sexual intercourse. I was paralyzed with fear.

Tommy and I lasted as long as a few phone calls and one trip to the movies, where he kissed me and I responded with a perfectly still, wide-open mouth not knowing what to do. He later apologized for slipping me the tongue, saying that he was confused about my intentions. He dropped me for Amy Stephens who seemed far more relaxed around boys. Later in the year when he tried to reconnect with me, I resisted, having decided in the interim that competing for any boy's attention wasn't my cup of tea.

Even though I had, by some stroke of luck, been placed in accelerated classes, academics were only somewhat interesting. Excelling had never been expected of me and just did not matter to me. I could put up with school because it got me out of the House and it was where the social action was.

A perfect example of this meet-the-minimum standard was the way I handled my required entry for the science fair. The night before it was due I made a poster explaining how fluorescent light bulbs differ from incandescent, and placed a fluorescent desk lamp in front of the poster for people to turn off and on. I got a C and felt very proud to not have failed.

The school staff predicted dire problems for my class because for two straight years we would be the oldest in the building. In the eighth grade, we were the oldest in the elementary school; we were again the oldest class the next year when the new junior high opened and we were in the ninth. I don't recall having extra confidence from this but we were a cocky bunch.

We were particularly ecstatic when the dress code for girls went away and we could wear pants...even jeans. The news spread like hot gossip. *Have you heard the latest? We can wear pants! Pants! Including jeans!* Skirts were instantly passé, at least for the remainder of that year.

When our new Junior High was formed another elementary school was funneled into it and I met the girl who would become my friend for life. Her name was Lucy. She was happy, easy to talk to and had a head full of gorgeous black hair. I had a thing for hair. She never made me feel inferior in any way. Her clothes were mostly name brands. She was conventional and well-behaved but also a ton of fun. She pierced my ears without any pain relief in the bathroom at her house and managed to do a perfect job of it. (She gave me an apple to bite down on.)

A large crop of snooty over-confident girls and adorable boys came with her to my school. I had a very hard time keeping focus.

But I had my pink retreat for sleepovers, hours on the telephone, and consuming primitive cocktails. Daddy had designed a handy telephone nook in the hallway (like the one in our early house) between my room and David's; the phone had an extra-long cord so it could be carried into either bedroom; and in my case it even reached into the bathroom.

Or, if I needed to have a really private conversation, I could go outside and use the phone across the street. The developer who lived there had kindly installed it at the outer edge of his lawn, in its very own tiny little house for the convenience of his construction workers.

Talk therapy was the only semi-effective way to anchor my swiftly-changing mentality and I had no lack of words. People trying to phone in often abandoned the idea after 40 or 50 or 90 minutes of trying. Even Daddy, calling from Cincinnati to announce Pop's demise, had to listen to the busy signal for at least one solid hour. Probably two.

Pop's funeral was the only time I ever saw Daddy cry. As I sat next to him and watched the tears silently trickle, it made me wonder what other emotions he might have that I knew nothing about.

In my suite, I had a new LP record player which was useful for escapism, but the radio was easier and had all the very latest. Songs like *Suzie Q, Midnight Confessions* and *Light My Fire* held a definite air of mystery and stirred strange new emotions.

By the eighth grade I had discovered how vodka could enhance this experience. Vodka was extremely useful and wonderful because it would deliciously mix with any juice or soda on hand, and the bottle could so easily be refilled with tap water. Many friends were willing to join me in this. It never occurred to us that this might be wrong in any way. It gave me a thrill; it made me happy; it made me forget my familial voids.

These things, along with my diary—kept daily from January 1, 1967 through December 31, 1971—equipped me to cope with whatever drama and trauma the world would throw my way. As expected there would be plenty of both.

Chapter 6

High school was a fantastic vehicle for social growth and not much else. I started in fall of 1970, with the tenth grade. The world was in a tumultuous state: Woodstock had made social convention look stuffy and obsolete; and yet, drugs had obliterated the artistic geniuses of Janis Joplin, Jimi Hendrix, and (very soon) Jim Morrison of that *Riders on the Storm* mystique. In addition, the dark morbid scourge of Vietnam created a moral ambiguity that I, nor any of my friends, knew how to even acknowledge, much less cope with. So we never talked about it. Never.

My worst habits were formed during these years. I was absolutely mediocre in every way and happy to be so. I never had too many friends or problems, except for the one big one.

Outside of growing confusion over my dad, my biggest problem was knowing what to do with all these debilitating crushes. It completely escaped me.

I continued to be ambivalent about academics in spite of having fairly decent aptitude. I wasn't born ambitious and no one had ever given me any reason to care about grades. I learned much later, when I was in my 50s, that my parents had declined a recommendation for me to skip a grade in my early elementary years. *We didn't want you to be separated from your friends,* Mama explained.

Likewise, no one encouraged me to reach for the sky in choosing a college. My mother had repeatedly told me as I grew up that the

University of Tennessee would be perfectly fine and Daddy didn't argue. It was local and it fit their budget and apparently, my abilities. There was no talk of earning scholarships, studying for the ACT, or creating a great resume for applications. None of that ever even occurred to me. If Daddy was willing to pay for UT, why would I bother? So I learned how to slack off just enough to maintain a B average.

But in spite of not being encouraged to excel I had a very clear mandate: skipping college was not an option. *You must be prepared to support yourself. You cannot count on being married, and even if you are, you should put your talents to good use* Daddy solemnly advised. Talents? Such as...?

For Daddy to back up this advice with financing made a strong case, because the man was tight with money. He had a strict budget for us to live by and I have no doubt it was kept to the nickel. He paid the bills from a big book of graph paper at the honey-colored Heywood Wakefield desk in the living room. He gave Mama cash for any shopping she had to do. She never questioned the finances; this would prove to be a big mistake. Another responsibility abdicated as a result of Daddy's not-so-subtle intimidation.

My only other discernible problem was striking the right fashion chord. I had an insatiable appetite for wardrobe and no way to finance it. My mother stood very firm on this. She was a child of the Depression. She would not indulge vanity. This was before the days of Southeast Asia sweatshops; most items were made in America and could be produced at home for a fraction of the retail price. So Mama made much of my wardrobe.

At least, the dresses and special occasion items. It was thrilling to pick out the pattern and fabric, and in that way I was a chip-off-the-block. It got my creative juices flowing. But as much as I loved the picking, sadly, I wasn't very good at it. Almost every creation turned out to be a bad color for me, or the style didn't flatter, or the fabric was inappropriate for the cut. At least the construction part was fairly easy; at 99 pounds and with a 16-inch back waist length, I was a perfect size 10. But in spite of Mama's flawless executions I was never quite the fashionista that I longed to be.

Many of the girls wore homemade items, but not the popular girls. There was definitely competition in this arena. Evaluating one another's outfits was one of our main endeavors. My BFF Lucy always looked great and seemingly had no budget constraints, so I had that to contend with. But she was just so sweet. She was beautiful and confident and never haughty so that took the edge off any rivalry.

The one saving grace in the wardrobe area was that jeans were becoming more and more popular. Whenever I was stalemated on what to wear I took the hippie option and wore jeans with one of the smock tops Mama had made, usually from a nightgown pattern. I learned to make do until I got my first job and my clothing budget finally expanded.

Hair was also the predictable big issue for teenage girls. I had fairly straight shoulder-length dark brunette hair. If ever it wouldn't cooperate or I didn't feel like washing it, I wore a triangular headscarf (often a folded bandana) tied in the back, under my hair, at the nape of my neck. We also had the hippies to thank for this convenience. To get that much-desired long, slightly full, look I rolled my hair on orange juice cans and actually learned how to sleep that way. Mostly face down.

Getting to and from school was the most fun thing in my life. David was my requisite chauffeur. As a senior, he had his own car but it wasn't just any car.

About the only situation in our family where father and son shared a bond was over mechanics. David had a fascination with machines and an insatiable appetite for speed. He routinely disobeyed the ban on riding the next-door neighbor's (Ronnie's) motorcycle.

So when it came time for him to drive, Daddy steered him toward a car that was extremely high maintenance. This would keep him in the garage and out of trouble. But Daddy also was an expert in garnering female attention, so he knew that a carefully chosen car would give David a leg up in that area.

They drove to Cincinnati and purchased a '37 Dodge, complete with running boards and a back seat that was at least four feet back from the front. It felt like you could dance in that space. It had the original scratchy, ugly upholstery. The hinges on the rear doors were in the back, so they opened out from the front of the car.

The front fenders were big enough to sit on and had big round eyeball headlights mounted on them, which gave a rider something to hang onto on tight corners. The car was super heavy and could spin some bitchin' donuts on the Deane Hill Country Club golf course after a nice snowfall...with four people riding on the outside: one on each of the front fenders and running boards.

It was a big, shiny, immaculate navy blue limousine that could not possibly go over 60 mph and could not possibly get lost in a crowd in Knoxville in 1971. This was nothing if not a high-profile vehicle. He once got suspended for three days because his car was seen at the local McDonald's during the lunch hour. The Vice Principal was out on an errand and there was David, parked smack in front by the main highway. The story was that the cheerleaders had put him up to it.

High-profile vehicles are indeed chick magnets and this was certainly true in the early '70s, the era of the muscle car. All the cheerleaders wanted to be driven to school in this car and David was more than happy to comply. Big D, they called him.

When I entered high school and he was required to drive me to school this created some logistical challenges. We couldn't all fit in one trip, so he ended up making two full trips to and from the suburbs every morning to deliver his lucky passengers to school. I was expected to be ready extra early for the first circuit so he wouldn't have to come all the way back to our house to pick me up.

This was ridiculous and terribly inconvenient for me because it meant I had to be ready a full hour ahead of normal. I developed some real resentment at this arrangement, which led me to develop that most effective female manipulation tool: passive aggression. Of course, men practice this also; it's just that females seem to excel at it, often being physically deficient for outright aggression. I'm pretty sure Eve was the first to discover its merits.

If I dawdled long enough then David couldn't make his two rounds and I would get to school about the same time as my own crowd. But the best part was how it aggravated him. It drove him crazy, which gave me great satisfaction. That was the whole point. (Almost certainly the neighbor girl Jenny had the same idea when she strolled out to the bus every morning.) But there also was an element of protection for my brother in my strategy. Those cheerleaders were just using him and I wanted to see him learn to say no. Just like I did with Mama.

But the holes we dig for rivals we usually fall into ourselves. This plan ultimately worked against me because I learned the satisfaction of never wasting time by arriving early to something. I would much rather be a little bit late than early. Two or three minutes should be the outer limit; but who can achieve that? Consequently, I have struggled with tardiness ever since. Powerful lessons, those from high school.

The ride home from school was another matter entirely as the cheerleaders had other activities. The car made a fabulous meet-market as there was always someone new and interesting who wanted to bum a ride. I developed my first major high school crush this way: Keith Bryan.

He was a year older than me and adorable. He had a great sense of humor, dark shiny hair, a huge smile, and a kind heart. He was confident and outgoing. His personality loomed large even though physically he did not. He had many friends but was generally a follower rather than an instigator. He seemed to be everywhere that something fun, naughty, or provocative was going down.

I invited him to a party that my (otherwise lame) social club was sponsoring. The party was forgettable, but after the party a group of us went to somebody's house where the parents weren't home. Of course. Keith and I found a barrel-shaped easy chair in the TV den, and realizing we both could fit, quickly settled in and started an uninhibited kissing fest. My thirst for affection was on full display. It was so much fun I couldn't have cared less. I jumped in with abandon; he obliged without any hesitation or condescension. The fun and spontaneity felt so mutual! I was flying high on this serendipitous development: maybe I am pretty after all! Maybe my unrequited crushes are over!

We were having a ball; but what goes up must come down, as they say. We had gone there with two of his known-to-be-wild friends and their dates. While we were discovering the joys of unrestrained kissing, they were in another room experimenting with flame-swallowing or -throwing or something insanely risky having to do with cigarette lighters. The lack of our attention frustrated them so they came looking for us. When they found us like two entwined pretzels they guffawed with laughter and immediately made the connection between myself and a certain MASH character. I had no defense against being called Hotlips—mainly because I had never seen the movie or TV show—so what could I say? It was self-explanatory. And on target.

Keith avoided me like the plague thereafter. The nickname didn't stick as I retreated into a pretty deep shell. He eventually ended up with Mitzi Morgan, from my *Alice in Wonderland* experience. She was batting 1.000 against me.

His momentary but unbridled affection had spoiled me, however, and I was in love for good. This continued for about a year, when he was involved in a minor car crash. At first he appeared to be uninjured. But within a day or two, he developed severe headaches.

Within three days he was dead. He passed on Christmas Eve of a brain aneurysm. He was 17 and an only child. It was my first encounter with tragedy. My love for him, even if utterly unrequited, had been faithful and true and well-founded; he was a budding and beautiful young gentleman.

Five or six years later I coincidentally waited on his parents in a seafood restaurant where I worked after college. They asked my name, background etc. and when I mentioned my high school they asked me *Oh, did you know our son? His name was Keith Bryan.* Tears instantly sprang to my eyes. I took a small gasp. I told them plainly how I had loved him.

They invited me to their home and shared all his baby photos with me. They were charming people with no bitterness; only gratitude for his short life. After I married, I had a dream where he seemed to come to me, and he told me how happy he was for me.

Daddy had always told me to never date anyone I wouldn't ultimately choose to marry. *You never know when you're going to fall in love and become unable to disentangle yourself* he said. So I thought my first foray into the real-love business was pretty admirable, even if it was missing the vital element of a relationship. At least I had wisely chosen the partner.

When I was older and discovered the circumstances of Daddy's birth—his mother pregnant before marriage—I thought what he might have meant was, *you might get pregnant and be stuck having to marry someone you don't really love.* His parents had a rather unhappy marriage.

But as his duplicity toward my mom became more apparent, I came to realize that unwed pregnancy had nothing to do with it. He was actually referring to himself and the difficulty of disentangling from someone you're actively sleeping with. It might cloud your judgment and cause you to marry the wrong person.

The duplicity was sickening. Every Saturday afternoon he would develop errands to run, and then he'd be gone supposedly to the drugstore for three hours. When he returned, not a challenging word ever came from my mother. The only opposition she could muster was the dreaded depressed silence. No confrontation and no resolution.

Either he considered himself to be an expert on the topic of marriage or he didn't want me to repeat his "mistake," because he also had this to say. *You simply have to learn to get along with David. Your relationship with your brother is the one most like the one you will have with your husband.* My brother and I definitely had compatibility issues at this stage. It caused my father grave concern—although I thought that might be just a little disingenuous on his part.

This second piece of advice was decidedly not good news. Just when I was thinking the procreative activity might be something I could handle, perhaps even desire, I got this information. *Ye gods,* as he had a habit of saying.

Surely there was somewhere the possibility of a lifelong romance. I had to take this word with a grain of salt; Daddy clearly wasn't the most reliable source. My hopeless-romantic ways seemed to be innate. I liked longing for romance. Why would I ever work to change that inclination? If I was doomed to marry someone like David I would need to revisit the nun option.

The lessons from the neighborhood pool lifeguard and his girlfriend (my older friend Jenny who strolled out to the bus) seemed much more authentic. Between Memorial and Labor Days I stayed at the pool from noon till suppertime. Without any parental intervention we could play Hearts and Spades for hours on end and share innocent banter about the world of romance. The lifeguard was the undisputed expert in both activities, being confident, friendly, and having a position of authority.

Top-40 radio ran a close second in the romantic-advice area, with its brainwashing ideas about love and adulthood. We played it constantly.

The music all seemed fairly straightforward with one exception. About the time of the Keith affair, The Doors' *Riders on the Storm* became popular. The cryptic, desolate, violent lyrics of the refrain…the thunder effects in the background…the echo effect on the organ…were downright spooky. I was haunted by it. It took me somewhere that I couldn't name or identify. Jim Morrison's dark voice telling females *you gotta love your man and take him by the hand,* because *the world on you depends* was so ominous. So mortal, so carnal. Was he referring to procreative activity, or something more sinister?

It made me apprehensive and yet curious. And aware that there were forces and situations for which I was definitely not prepared. It scared the bejesus out of me, but not enough to change the station when it came on. I was like the kid who covers her eyes when pornography is shown, but peeks through spread fingers.

But along with the foreboding it also somehow suggested the open road and the freedom that offered, which captivated me to the point of obsession. When I was out babysitting I would open the windows so I could hear the hum of thousands of tires on the expressway pavement. (I wasn't allowed to open the windows at the House.) The hum issued me an invitation to come explore a million unknown cities. I-40 and I-75, which merged as they passed through Knoxville, surely led to the rest of the world.

Things weren't all bad between David and me. He had great fun at Young Life meetings and he talked me into going with him. These were as much about being seen and mingling with the opposite sex as they were about Jesus. The social hierarchy seemed a little less defined at these gatherings and so they were well attended. They offered good clean fun without being boring or stuffy. The leaders were authentic and approachable. They knew how to be silly and appeal to teenagers. The YL camps were known for allowing barely restrained outdoor activities, which made them excellent for burning up excessive teen energy. They were hugely popular.

We hosted YL at our house several times in our garage. Daddy had envisioned the garage alternating into a rec room, so it was painted a trendy orange on opposing walls (in support of the UT Volunteers) and had a speckled resin finish over the concrete to make it more inviting. We occasionally set up a ping pong table. But using the House for Young Life embarrassed me—again—because it was so distinctive, so unconventional in style, and everybody would see it. It was just too far out of the mainstream. Or so I thought. But Daddy was pleased as punch to have a new group to show it off to.

Once Lucy hosted Young Life in her basement rec room which was far superior because it was indoors and nicely decorated. I recall that evening the leader, a pleasant wiry young man with wiry hair and acoustic guitar asked the group if we each knew our own culpability for our shortfall before God.

He said Jesus could fix it. He asked if we believed this; I nodded. The assent in my heart was real. If God was offering clemency I was more than happy to take it. But this transaction was like the grocery shopper who stuffs her face full of free samples without buying the product. I took the forgiveness Jesus offered but gave Him nothing in return. Not even my heart. Least of all my heart.

David also encouraged me to join him at our tiny church's youth group gatherings. Most of the kids there were from another high school so their lack of any negotiable social capital left me disinterested. But the leader of the group was a burly, insanely friendly man with longish hair who had a gorgeous, plump, disheveled wife named Sally. They were insanely happy people. He was a pharmaceutical salesman who never met a stranger and treated us kids as if we were adults. His confidence gave us the freedom to let our vulnerabilities show. He had garnered a fairly sizable following with more than a few hippie types, to which I was compulsively drawn. I gradually became a regular.

Anyone who marched to the beat of their own drummer held an irresistible fascination for me. I wanted to be like that, to have that kind of confidence. I spent many evenings at the semi-mansion home of one of the rare hippies in our school. She often didn't wash her hair and wore a headband around her forehead. Her dad was the director of the state psychiatric hospital locally known as *Lyons View* because of its address. Their home was across the street from it. (Any time my brother and I drove my mother to distraction she would proclaim *Knock it off! You're gonna put me in Lanns View*, with proper Knoxvillian pronunciation.)

This hippie friend was the only pot smoker I knew—until senior year, when the class president (none other than Michael Hardy, my seventh grade crush) came out as a pothead—and although I didn't partake, I enjoyed soaking up the mystique of her house with its presumed ghosts lurking under the 12-foot ceilings.

Pier One Imports came to town just before Christmas 1971 and they hired anyone who came through the door, to get the store set up for the holidays. This was my first job; my friends and I all jumped on the bandwagon. The store reminded me a lot of San Francisco. It smelled of patchouli and eucalyptus leaves and had lots of hippie-inspired merchandise. This was my first paying job outside of babysitting, and the semi-exotic imported stuff fueled the fire of my wanderlust. I was at work there when I learned of Keith's car accident.

High school was also great for advancing my drinking capability. The Vietnam War had created a firestorm over the legal drinking age which, as far as anyone knew, had always been 21. But if young men could be drafted and sent off to die at age 18, it was untenable to tell them they weren't old enough to buy a beer. So the legal drinking age was lowered to 18 along with the voting age. This effectively meant that one could buy beer at 16 from merchants who weren't too picky.

There were at least several drive-thru *package* stores that were so inclined and we knew well which ones they were. By 1971, when I entered my junior year I was ready and able to drink outside the House.

Of course, after the Keith debacle there were other boys. The summer of 1971 I dated a pair of polar opposites.

That spring I attended prom as the guest of a squeaky clean Mr. Manners whose mother was grooming him for medical school. He had a highly developed resume. He was polite and handsome, if not a little too self-controlled for my taste. The invitation came like a bolt from the blue. He called and I dragged the phone through my bedroom into the pink bathroom, closing both doors behind me. I consented to the date before I fully realized even to whom I was speaking.

It was a lovely evening. We might have shared a cup of wine in the car, but if so, it was too small an amount to remember. We had a couple of follow-up dates and then he went off to Brazil on a foreign exchange adventure. Learning Portuguese didn't seem to present him with any problem. For some reason, after he left, whenever I would hear the Animals' *Spill the Wine* I thought of him down in Latin America schmoozing with brown-skinned girls, even though he wasn't the type. At all. Later in life, I discovered he was my father's primary care physician.

After he left for Brazil I somehow got linked up with the closest thing to a bad boy that West Knoxville had to offer. His hair was always dirty, fairly long, and he never tucked in a shirttail (this being before the days of the ubiquitous T-shirt). He was always happy and had a big mischievous smile. He smoked, and I found this to be infinitely charming. I absolutely loved the way he tasted. So consequently I took up smoking but this had to be very clandestine because of my father's abhorrence of it. (My grandpa W had, after all, died from the practice.) Badboy didn't last long either... but long enough for me to develop a fondness for these silly beer-cooler drinks of the brand name *Hoppin' Gator.* We loved to drink two or three of these and neck in the wooded parking lot at the swimming pool. Mungo Jerry's one-hit-wonder *In the Summertime* seemed to always be on the radio.

Along with the drinking capability, I was also advancing my preferences. Read: learning to enjoy other types of hard liquor besides vodka.

For example, that same summer Lucy invited me to join her and her parents on a vacation to Myrtle Beach, South Carolina. Her father had some business entertaining to conduct and so we occupied a nice penthouse apartment where they could host a cocktail party. This necessitated a fully stocked bar. After an hour or so of drinks the grownups all went off to a fancy restaurant and we had the entire inventory at our disposal, with no one tracking the fullness of each bottle.

It just so happened that that same night Badboy would be cruising in from nearby Pawley's Island to the entertainment hub of

Myrtle Beach—the Pavilion—with his friends and family. He had suggested that perhaps we could meet up there and hang out around the arcade games and amusement rides. Of course we could! This really appealed to my sense of adventure and romance.

The Pavilion at Myrtle Beach harkened back to 1948 when young people had only live music to dance to in public places. The building exuded that same electric aura of girl-meets-boy as the high school football stadium. The anxious residue of a million tentative romances was ethereal and pervasive, but only in the most alluring way. It made you want to join that club. How could I say no to him?

I assured him we would be there and loosely agreed to meet him without a specified time, having absolutely no means of transportation. Lucy's parents asked us repeatedly how we planned to get there; she kept telling them we would walk. It was a distance of seven miles. They were a bit skeptical. I don't think they remembered the determination of smitten teenagers, especially when emboldened by alcohol. They agreed to pick us up around 10 pm for the return trip, saying sternly that they would not wait. If we weren't there on cue they would leave without us.

With all that available liquor we knew that at least one of the varieties would equip us somehow to walk the distance, so we sampled them all. The gin was delicious and refreshing; the scotch was bitter. Courage arrived on cue and we set out.

It was daylight when we began. We laughed and joked and felt no pain. Boys were waiting at the other end! (Or, boy.) Many young male passersby in cars honked and catcalled. We resolutely ignored them. At one point we did need to pee. Actually, it was at several points. This was resolved by hiding behind oversized landscaping in private yards along the way. These were big expensive upscale homes so we had to make sure no lights were on. Lucky for us motion-detector floodlights were years away from being invented.

After about two hours of walking, we had lost our humor but not our determination or energy. We arrived at the Pavilion just in time to see Badboy driving away and waving from the back seat of an overstuffed car and, in a few short minutes thereafter, to be picked up by Lucy's parents.

It never occurred to us that this was in any way less than a brilliant idea. Badboy wasn't the least bit disappointed, in fact, he probably never even mentioned it. I don't recall any further dates with him.

Lucy never lacked for dates. Her extroverted, encouraging manner was a magnet for insecure teenage men. Immediately upon entering high school, she had dates with the most popular upper-class guys. She tried out a few of them but eventually settled in with one of the twins who were David's best friends. This relationship was also sparked during drives home from school in the Dodge. What a matchmaker a classic car can be.

She was a great sounding board for pondering the changes in our maturing bodies; later it was she who convinced me I was wrong about female anatomical responses to heavy petting. I adamantly insisted there weren't any. (The sex ed book from my nightstand made no reference to any dampness in panties.) And we endlessly debated the possibility of getting pregnant without actual intercourse, which would have been a fate worse than death.

These discussions were filled with hilarity and angst, heavy on the angst. They were also a necessity if we were to learn anything; there simply was no other source of information. Even if we were the blind leading the blind. In spite of our curiosity, we guarded our virginity with zealous fervor. To give it up was unthinkable. And so birth control was a non-issue.

My rides in the classic car were over after tenth grade because David graduated. He briefly attended a small state campus but left after the first quarter. He became a mechanic for an Oldsmobile dealer. He certainly had the aptitude for this, which had been displayed many times over through constant work on the Dodge. When that car had a problem, he spent hours calling all over East Tennessee looking for parts. *Do you have an oil pan for a '37 Dodge? Yes, that's right. 1937. No? Any suggestions?* On and on, endlessly. Fixing the

84

car finally outsized its novelty so he traded it for a 1957 Chevy Bel Air…much more built for speed, as per his obsession. He had become speed-dependent by viewing *The French Connection* at least a half dozen times. It was his *Romeo and Juliet.*

I was relegated to a five-student carpool for the remainder of high school, where I learned much about the idiosyncrasies of human nature. I can testify that Dagwood Bumstead and his carpool scenarios are very realistic. Daily exposure to even the kindest of people will reveal traces of lunacy. We are all broken people with the capacity to drive one another nuts. Occasionally *Stairway to Heaven* would come on the radio and keep us silent the entire length of the commute, as we each privately sang along.

As a HS junior I developed a friendship with a great senior who was very easy to talk to and unpretentious. We passed notes to one another on the surface of the desk in the AP Math classroom, enabled by its failing wood finish. I agreed to attend homecoming with him. We had a great time but it was more valuable for the acquaintance I made with his best friend Steve, with whom we double dated.

We each looked right past our dates to see something special in the other: Steve was witty, friendly, well-mannered and completely respectful. He could actually carry on a conversation and he was brilliant on the piano.

He wasn't Keith, but Keith was dating Mitzi at that point and had long since been unavailable to me. He died just as Steve and I were getting to be an item and Steve helped me think positively about the future. My parents adored him and I quickly learned to. For some unknown reason, I felt safe with him. Safe and free to be authentic.

He was a little slow and reluctant to develop a physical relationship. When what seemed like an eternity had passed without so much as a kiss, I developed a scheme. It was Christmastime and the usual mistletoe sprig was hanging in the doorframe between the kitchen and living/dining room. As he was saying goodbye one night I pulled him by the arm over to that area. It was at least our third date. My parents' spare but appropriate holiday décor served its purpose as our lips innocently grazed each other's.

We made a very cute couple. He was my proverbial best friend. His family was welcoming and sociable. Their household consisted of parents, grandmother, Steve, and his younger sister who was named after their dad. She was wildly confident and had gigantic breasts which together made her extremely popular. Steve wasn't known for popularity. While he was kind and confident he had a definite feminine streak. I didn't care; it seemed artistic to me. But high school populations recognize such tendencies and as is the usual unfortunate case, ours responded with snark and poorly concealed labeling. To them, Steve was undoubtedly a queer.

Whatever the case, Steve proved to be reliable in every way and came to be very physically affectionate but only with my consent. He was never aggressive or pushy. He knew my aspirations and proclamation of abstinence, which he honored. But he also made it clear that he was practicing restraint. He evidently had assured his whole family that we had boundaries; they lovingly called me *Sister Janet*. Again, I didn't care. There was absolutely no condescension in it. He earned my trust and I craved his warm chest, musky cologne and reassuring strength.

I had an irrepressible urge to loiter at his places of employment, but he was patient with my insecurity. Whenever I made my appearances I got a well-practiced eye-roll but he kindly withheld any scolding. Showing up at the record store wasn't so bad because occasionally I would actually buy something. Arby's was a different story. There, at best I was a nuisance; at worst the eye-rolling cut through me like so many pounds of over-salted pressed beef. Maybe it was the 18-inch-tall chef's hat that made it so damning. Fast food outlets are not the place to distract your boyfriend with continual comments about breaking up, which I only proffered to see how he would respond. In spite of it all, he loved me and put up with me.

I think his family invented hospitality. They were always having big family dinners and going camping with their motorboat on the lake with other families and big tents pitched in a cluster on a small peninsula or island in Fort Loudon Lake.

One time they included me on such a weekend. We each had our own sleeping bag and all slept on the ground inside the tent. In the middle of the night, my pitiful insecurity reared its ugly head when I suddenly awoke and Steve was not where he had lain when we all went to sleep. I rubbed my eyes and woefully implored, *Where's Steve?* as if he had jumped in his car and abandoned us all for the city.

Turns out he had grown claustrophobic and moved his bag to the boat for more air. My nocturnal lament became the fodder of mocking the following day. His mother good-naturedly mimicked my pitiful *Where's Steve?* which then initiated raucous laughter from the group. Many multiple times throughout the day.

But nothing his family did would have diminished my affection for them. I was in awe of their camaraderie and grateful to be included. I loved these people. They smoked, drank cocktails, and made merry all year long whether it was camping season or not. Steve's father was inclusive and warm, with a big laugh and nothing to hide. He led his family with wit and style and unreserved affection. This stood in stark contrast to my own dad and so it created a great deal of melancholy in my heart. I could not reconcile the wide gap between the two personalities. It only emphasized the fact that there was something terribly wrong with my home situation.

The acceptance that I found in them gave me confidence and lowered my tolerance for dishonesty. I glommed onto them. I could tell Steve anything and likewise his mother. She knew full well that my attraction to him, and them, was enhanced by my need to escape the hostility at home. Yet she never chastised me for this nor did it diminish the authenticity of our relationship. With cigarette in hand and eyes lowered for emphasis she told me it was perfectly OK to not like my dad. This was a gracious understatement. I basically hated him.

Meanwhile, I developed an outspokenness at home to which my mother unwittingly contributed. Often I would instigate an irrational and probably hormone-fueled argument triggered by some injustice I had suffered or inconsistency I had observed. I would yell at her (never Daddy) as if it were her fault. Her vulnerability made her an easy target. I bombarded her with a wild array of grievances because I knew I could get away with it. I clearly was testing her to see how far she could be pushed. Just like I did with David. Or maybe I was hoping she would grow a backbone. I would rant on and on until I reached exhaustion.

But as she had since my infancy, she modeled God's love for me. She loved me unconditionally. In response, she would show me her exasperation but never make any consequences, which I fully deserved. It was despicable of me; to presume upon grace is an arrogant and dangerous tack to take with any relationship, including with God. Especially with God. After each verbally-abusive episode, eventually I would realize my cruelty, slink back to her and beg her forgiveness, feeling horrible shame. My repentance always felt sincere and it would carry the day without fail. She always forgave me, and sincerity definitely was the ticket.

But how sincere can it be if the offense is continually repeated? She must have seen glimmers of progress.

Whatever the case she persevered. What's more, although she had often declared me *bossy* (along with a couple of my elementary teachers), I had a sense that she secretly admired my uninhibited way of blowing off steam. She knew it could be healthy because of its honesty and pressure release; it was something she longed to be able to do.

She had an amazing discernment about what was genuine self-destructive behavior—which she never would have indulged—and what was just teenage angst seeking an outlet. She put up with it just enough for me to recognize my own error. And so her support was the very best kind: loving enough to enable self-correction. But she did come perilously close to being a doormat.

Add to my verbal boldness a (possibly genetic) tendency toward drama and my disdain for my dad came out at the dinner table, which was about the only place I interacted with him. Daddy would make some statement that was obviously disingenuous; I would challenge him on it; he would call me impudent, impertinent, or belligerent, or some other word that teenagers never use (and I really didn't know the meaning of) and send me away from the table. Perhaps he thought his superior vocabulary validated his authority. But he would never stoop to explain himself or admit to anything. It was much more effective to discredit me and divert attention away from the original issue.

Communicating with him was insanely frustrating. At home, I had always thought he was kind of introverted. But in reality he was just extremely deliberate in choosing his words. We got really tired of waiting on him to speak. It was like waiting on a king to deliver an edict; a jury to deliver a verdict. During these silences, he would assume an expression of struggle and gaze at the floor or into space. But it was all just an awkward attempt to control: he really believed that if he could choose his words carefully enough he could control the outcome of every situation. This led to lots and lots of lying because that level of control is impossible.

When I was driven from the table it was often in tears. It's a small miracle I didn't become anorexic. Mama never intervened but she did see to it that I got enough to eat one way or another.

Not surprisingly my drinking indulgence continued to grow. Getting drunk was no big deal as long as someone was there to drive and help me find a place to either puke or sleep it off. Proms and other school dances existed merely as occasions to do so. It was hugely entertaining to me, eased my pain and made me feel like I was navigating the adult realm. None of my peers were put off by this; no one spoke to me about any inherent evil or long-term consequences. Or short-term consequences. Most of them were also imbibing to one degree or another. In fact, I didn't know anyone who didn't drink. The details I overlooked in my own behavior were the frequency, choice of beverage and implications.

My senior year was anticlimactic, to say the least. Steve had started college and our relationship was now on, now off.

He admitted to me increasing confusion about his sexuality. I drove myself to the branch library and read everything I could about homosexuality in teenage men. I became convinced that he was just going through an experimental phase; our physical attraction had been quite real. It had started when I lingered in his room and watched him semi-dance to the Doobie Brothers' *Rockin' Down the Highway*, clad in only a towel as he got ready for work. He was tender, kind, and gentle of touch; he patiently developed our non-coital intimacy. He taught me how bare chests pressed together could create a private, sacred sense of the inviolable. When I nestled with him on the couch or in the back seat I knew sexual love; I couldn't be wrong about that, could I? You can't fake an erection.

Tragically a couple of decades later at my twentieth high school reunion, I learned that he had been one of the early victims of AIDS. Upon hearing the news I instantly, silently thanked God for a letter I had written a couple of years prior. I told him how grateful I was to have been his girlfriend and that it was a life experience I cherished. I wrote that I had learned in hindsight just how authentic his love had been, because at every turn it was demonstrated with respect. Knowing that he was gay did not change my assessment one tiny bit. I had no interest in rekindling—I was deeply committed to my husband at that point, and told him so. He never responded.

So after a year or so of dating, his attention became focused elsewhere and I was ready to rev up my crush machine.

I had been in Advanced Placement mathematics for tenth and eleventh grades which provided the desk-carving exchanges, which led to the homecoming date, which led to my only bona fide high school boyfriend. But it also provided, during twelfth grade, the venue for falling in love with Dwayne Doolittle.

Having thus achieved another off-the-deep-end emotional involvement with another unavailable object (Dwayne had a steady girlfriend), when calculus entered the picture I promptly dropped out.

Fahgettaboutit. It was way too mentally taxing. Dwayne could and would ignore me whether or not I comprehended rates of acceleration. I didn't miss the math one bit. However, I did miss the teacher. She was brilliant and inspirational, funny and wise. She constantly reminded us that *a $50 pair of shoes will mildew the same as a $10 pair…meaning your high-aptitude brain will rot from neglect just the same as any other brain.*

Lucy had signed up to leave school at noon for what was called Distributive Education, a fancy name for getting out of school early each day. If you had completed enough academic classes you could secure a job and be excused. I grieved her going but also envied her freedom.

In her absence, I grew close again to the bookworm girl with the PhD parents. She had a matching crush on Dwayne's best friend, so we were great pals in commiseration. We would moon away hours in her living room listening to the full-length version of *Inagaddadavida* and coloring with our Flair pens, and in her basement watching TV movies and eating popcorn.

To ease our frustration, the afternoon following graduation rehearsal we sat on the grass in the backyard of the House and drank screwdrivers while listening to the Allman Brothers Band play *Blue Sky* over the patio speaker. *You're my blue sky and you're my sunny day; Lord you know it makes me high when you turn your love my way, turn your love my way…* We each knew what the other was thinking: how much higher we would feel if those boys would just give in to our flirtations. It wasn't quite as painful for her, I think, because she would soon be heading off to Mt. Holyoke College in Massachusetts.

But I had another reason to anesthetize my pain. Daddy had decided that his first-ever trip to Europe, specifically London, was far more important than his daughter's high school graduation. Someone he had met in a bar somewhere, supposedly male, had invited him to London and off he went. He wasn't present for any of the events or festivities. If you could call them that in light of the situation.

He had become an emotionally-disengaged liar. The effect on our family was chilling and disintegrating. When you think it's OK to lie to people, you reduce them to idiots. That is, you show them that you think they're stupid and powerless because they can't stop you. It is an act of degradation; the outflow of inner disdain. Even though I would not be a silent witness or subject—I took every opportunity to confront him about his lies—we still knew we had been degraded and devalued. Dehumanized.

The summer of 1973 following graduation, I decided to have one last high school fling. I joined a busload of kids heading to Young Life camp just outside of Colorado Springs. Teenagers from all over the USA were there and the boys were of course adorable. At first, I was exasperated that (as usual) none of them noticed me as I sat around mute and aloof, trying to look attractive; but it actually turned out for the best. I was free to fall headlong in love with the severity of the Rocky Mountains. In spite of the leaders' best efforts, I don't recall any particular encounter with Jesus while I was there.

But He was working on me all the same. I broke my finger on a hike when a sudden thunderstorm required a quick descent to timberline. I was forced to sit out a few of the activities which gave me time to ponder the possibility of living in such a fantastical place.

When Mama met me at the bus back in Knoxville, we each started sobbing when we saw the other. She, because I had a splint on my finger; I, because I couldn't bear the thought of another hot gray humid day in Tennessee under the auspices my father the infidel. The seeds of my wanderlust had been planted in Colorado.

The heavenly experience at camp was soon dispelled just as my tears anticipated. As the end of summer approached and I was preparing to go off to live in the dormitory at UT, Daddy announced that he would be moving out into his own apartment.

This precipitated a horrible screaming confrontation. My mother had remained passively silent, *again*, and if she would not stand up to him then I would have to do it for her. It was no coincidence that his overseas trip was timed during a milestone in my life; I wanted him to know that I was fully aware of his rejection of me as well as Mama.

This encounter took place in the living room smack in front of the picture windows, the very spot where we had danced and decorated the Christmas tree and taken a million family photos. The spot where I had defiantly and privately opened all my Christmas presents and tinkered with the nativity set; where Daddy had taught me about the slide rule and pattern-making. Where my drunken grandfathers had partaken of a lovingly prepared gourmet Christmas dinner. The spot where you could look out on a clear day and see the Great Smoky Mountains and the sunrise. It was a repository of emotion; a place of extremes both sacred and profane.

My anger was in no way repressed or hidden. I stamped my feet and shook my hair and repeated my six-year-old tantrum, minus only the prostration. I screamed right in his face, *Who do you think you are? You are not my father if you go through with this.* I couldn't accept the fact—absolutely would not believe or accept—that anyone who had served as my father, was biologically my father, would do such a thing: leave my beloved mother and our home and his architectural triumph, this perfectly personalized House. What the hell had it all been for? This choice was a betrayal against everything I knew of as Home. He stood stoically by saying nothing in response. Except I think he mentioned that I was impudent.

At that point, we had been in the House 10 years. He thought his role as a dad was finished. Imagine, for Mama: your oldest child has grown and left home, your youngest child is going off to college, and your husband of 21 years is moving out. Empty nest indeed. And you haven't held a job in 20+ years.

Oddly enough the root of my outrage was not over my own loss—I had not been close to him for years. I had long since lost all esteem for him, along with friendship and intimacy, because of the ongoing deceit. I should have been glad to see him go.

And neither did I have outrage from any breach of a moral code. My own morals were squishy at best. I was a drinker; I was an academic slacker; I snuck into the drive-in movie without paying; I thought nothing in the least about heavy petting sessions with my (gay) boyfriend; I occasionally smoked. In the eighth grade, I had carried on my own deception during tens of hours of phone calls with a university freshman I met through a radio show game.

My outrage came from the injustice and stupidity of the rejection. We had done him no wrong whatsoever. My mother was an ideal wife for him. He was flushing a great marriage down his green American Standard toilet. How could anyone supposedly so intelligent make such a stupid mistake, and be so smug about it? What were we—chopped liver?

Chapter 7

For campus housing, I requested the oldest, most architecturally romantic dorm at UT, romantically named Sophronia Strong Hall, or Sophie Strong for short.

Providence was at work in my placement there. It was generally thought that only returning women could be assigned to it; you had to wait your turn. Women clamor for romantic settings and the waiting list was long. The dorm had no air conditioning but no one cared. Suffering in sweat made it all the more desirable. It was sort of a Blanche Dubois ethos.

I took potluck on a roommate and got a lovable, often-absent grad student with a huge smile and kind heart. When I did see her, she cheered me on to persevere and not take myself too seriously.

But after my first two quarters, I abandoned her to grab a vacancy in a room at the end of the hall on the corner, where opposing windows allowed a nice cross breeze. The only downside was an occasional car crash in the intersection just below in the middle of the night. This happened about once every couple of weeks. It could be a little unnerving.

My penchant for wardrobe led me to declare Home Economics as my major with an emphasis in Textiles and Clothing. I joined a sorority and settled into my comfort zone of mediocrity and romantic longing.

Home Economics required a year of chemistry which is perfectly logical. Whether it be food or fibers, you must understand the physical nature of whatever substance you'll be dealing with in your career. Freshmen don't realize such things, however. I failed the first chem exam and promptly said goodbye to Home Ec. Chemistry was left behind with no regrets or lessons learned. I may have been OK with mediocrity but outright failure was not acceptable.

I pulled out the catalog to see what other major might strike my fancy. As a senior in high school, I had worked in a young women's clothing store. I loved making the signage there. So I decided that Advertising would suit me just fine, not knowing that Graphic Arts was a thing. The required classes for the College of Communications sounded like lots of fun so I made the switch.

Later, I found out that 80% of the chemistry class had failed that awful exam and the professor had thrown it out. Too late! The die had been cast. C'est la vie!

Sophie Strong was full of upper-class women who knew the ropes of life in general and college life in particular. They gave me boatloads of advice both good and bad. They taught me such fun things as how to get an answer to any question by calling the reference librarian (the forerunner to Google searches), how to waste hours listening to Gordon Lightfoot and John Denver on reel-to-reel tape at the library, how to appreciate scotch and water, and how to use the dorm fire escape as a regular exit. I happily lived in that dorm through my junior year.

Miraculously, my temper fit at my dad's attempted departure actually bore fruit. He relented, and with reluctance on full display, agreed to stay put in the House.

During my high school years Daddy had told people that he was certain my dearth of dates would be rectified in college, where men were not intimidated by strong women. (This information came via Mama.) He probably intended it to mean my desirability was merely undiscovered. But I took it as a valid assessment of my overbearing temperament.

It would explain a lot. Evidently I deserved the reprimands I had received from him for speaking my mind. I must be too bossy and opinionated to be attractive to men. I never considered whether or how to fix this flaw, or even if I should try. I just hoped he was right about the dating situation.

In spite of Daddy's prediction, my crush machine continued to be hugely frustrated. The men were many and attractive but seemed inaccessible. They were so close, but so far away. There were thousands of them swarming everywhere and I had neither the skill nor the confidence to connive meeting them. They fascinated and terrified me. Whatever the case had been in high school, now I was the intimidated party.

My sorority didn't help a whit in this regard. The mixers we had with fraternities proved to be dreadful affairs that were attended by thirsty men looking to get their fair share at the keg.

I started with a couple of weird romantic forays freshman year.

First, I got fixated on the Salvadoran in my French class. He was mysterious and obscured by a language barrier; he seemed inaccessible enough to be a good fantasy object. When he actually asked for my number I gave it to him and then instantly regretted it. I had heard about the passion of Latin lovers; was I getting myself into trouble? I went straight into panic mode and with good reason. For this fellow, evidently *no* meant *please call a million times until my resolve caves in.* Which it did; I finally went out for coffee with him and it was abundantly clear that his goal was blue-eyed, American children. Stereotypes or no, his fearsome, unrestrained passion singed the tips of my eyebrows along with my psyche. I beat a fast retreat and employed my roommate to make excuses until he finally stopped calling.

Next, I was seduced by someone who was utterly unavailable and not my type by several measures. The entrapment technique was slow, careful, methodical, and 100% effective. I thought I was safe and cherished in spite of being 100% exploited for gratification and kept in the closet. Technically our relationship did not involve coitus.

97

But it was nonetheless steamy, hot and misleading. I longed for us to be a committed couple. This lasted a few secretive, tortuous months. Then I realized that I had been manipulated, and that this involvement might actually be preventing me from meeting Mr. Right. As if I would recognize him or know what to do with him if I did.

During the summers of 1975 and '76 (following sophomore and junior years) I decided to pursue my dream of living in Colorado. I secured employment long-distance at a YMCA conference center near Granby. It was six miles to the southeast and just west of Tabernash.

I had heard about the job from a high school chum who gave me a brochure. It sounded heavenly, and what I had dreamed of since my first visit. Supposedly the live-in staff experience was designed to promote Christian growth and camaraderie. It was described as highly organized and offering an opportunity to meet other young adult Christians from around the country, to grow in faith and character.

Around the middle of June 1975, I arrived in Granby from the Denver airport via Greyhound bus. The bus stop was in the parking lot of a seedy motel. I stepped out with my trunk and suitcase into snow flurries. The camp director had promised that someone would meet my bus, but there was not a soul in sight. I found a pay phone in the lobby to call and see what was up. My tension abated slightly when a friendly voice assured me a ride would come right away.

After what seemed like an hour of pondering exactly what I had gotten myself into, a purple GTO vroomed up and a shaggy-haired gent got out to help with my luggage. He was an incredibly friendly soul; with good humor, he introduced himself as the camp's token Jew. As he whisked me off to my summer adventure our conversation centered on partying opportunities. I began to realize that the recruiting literature was a little bit, um, idealistic. If not downright misleading. *Whatever*, I thought. I can do partying.

The pay was very low, below minimum wage, supposedly because it included room and board. *Room* consisted of three bunk beds (two stacked, one single) in a 15' x 20' room that was underground below a roller rink. These bunk rooms lined both sides of a long dark hallway with a community shower/bathroom and pay phone at the end. We called them the Bays. Each held eight rooms, and men and women were segregated, of course. During rink operating hours the staff who were trying to relax in their bunks were treated to continual reverberating *kabooms* from falling skaters. Lighting consisted of a bare bulb hanging from the ceiling.

The *board* part of the deal consisted of meals served in plastic trays with little compartments, and half-pint cartons of milk.

Being the last to arrive in my assigned room, I got the lower bed of the stacked pair for my own. This meant that I couldn't sit up on my bed or even read from the overhead bulb. I called Mama collect from the pay phone within 30 minutes of arriving, and asked her to send my tiny reading lamp. I also let her know I may need to come home soon. Like before the lamp even arrived.

The meager accommodations, however, had the happy consequence of forcing us to get out and go as often as possible. There was a rec room with a pool table adjacent to the Bays where we could flirt and socialize. But mostly I spent off-work hours hiking and hitching rides with other staff to Denver for urban thrills.

And the sunbathing was par excellence! The high altitude UV rays cut the tanning time at least in half from what I was used to in hazy Tennessee. There was a huge meadow nearby on camp where we could spread our towels and laugh, gossip, or sleep, or just have that rare chance to be alone with our daydreams. However, we did need to wrap bath towels around our heads to prevent horseflies from attacking, as the shampoo fragrance attracted them.

For further amusement I paired up romantically with homeless drifters. I found one for each summer. They were well-meaning fellows; harmless and utterly without address, which made them easy to abandon just before Labor Day. They were both adorable and kind.

The first of these (summer '75) was the quiet, shy type, and rather handsome; surprisingly so in spite of his having only one set of clothes. He must have washed them nightly because he was always immaculately groomed. He had short, clipped hair, was clean-shaven, and smelled faintly of aftershave. His manners were impeccable, even though he resisted removing his ball cap for meals per the urging of the staff chaplain. He claimed to hail from a gated community somewhere in the greater Los Angeles area.

The second (summer '76) was kind, patient and respectful, as my Steve had been back in high school; but this fellow was definitely heterosexual. He too was handsome and had a (rare?) combination of flaming red hair and mild-mannered disposition. He was introspective and often declared that the world was *perfect*. He took his time building my trust and wooed me to conclude that virginity was an overrated status.

Birth control was off my radar screen because my periods came to a dead halt while I was at the camp. Perhaps the 9,000' elevation caused my body to choose oxygenation over ovulation. Who knows? For the time being, I dodged the consequence this negligence could have created; but that only fostered delusional thinking. I let myself believe I couldn't get pregnant because I also had symptoms of ovarian cysts (according to my gynecologist uncle). Symptoms, however, do not equal a bona fide diagnosis.

As obvious as it may have been to others, I was oblivious to the fact that I only allowed myself romantic vulnerability with high-mystique individuals unable to return any lasting emotional investment. I was like a gerbil alone in a cage running and running, chasing romance on a wheel to nowhere.

Despite that fruitless pursuit some very real roots of identity were being put down during those summers in Grand County. I was free to have fun and make mistakes; to grow, learn, and just be. Free from my dad's reprimands, from academic burdens, and from my ever-present nagging sense of inadequacy and obligation. Free from meeting expectations, the strongest of which were my own.

After dark, I spent hours walking the dirt roads of the camp which had no traffic or lighting. Traces of campfire smoke wafted around me. In several places I could walk a quarter mile or so and not see anything but unbroken tracts of lodgepole pines tickling the stars. The wind shuffled through them and I was in perfect peace; blessedly dwarfed by nature and the Divine. I didn't fear bobcats or coyotes, bears or mountain lions. I could practically feel God's breath in my ear. I knew He had me right in His sights. I luxuriated in this security, even if I felt no compulsion to otherwise respond.

It was all so delightful that I went back for a two-week stint over the '75 holiday break. The insane cold didn't bother me a whit. I slept on the floor in a sleeping bag between my best buddy from the previous summer and her roommate. They had a nicer lodge room, being year-round employees. It was my first time away from the House for Christmas and I loved it, in spite of an anguished call from home on that day. David wanted to report that Mama couldn't stop crying. I only felt vaguely sorry about it. My friendship with my buddy deepened and years later she would stand witness at my marriage.

In my third year of college, I began my advertising classes. I was invited out on a date with another red-headed fellow who came to class barefoot and kept his sunglasses on indoors. There were only a dozen or so people in the class so he had caught my eye. It would seem that my derriere, enhanced by Navy surplus khakis, had caught his eye; he certainly didn't care about my creative slogans. His smoking reminded me of Badboy.

I agreed to have a drink with him. When we went over to his apartment afterward it turned out that he was a collector of Nazi memorabilia. Which I immediately suspected as being simply for shock value. His emotional remoteness seemed put-on like a costume.

There was never a second date. However, during a senior class field trip to Opryland in Nashville, he was one of a couple of guys who thought I might enjoy running down the hotel hall in my jammies to sleep over with them. Of all the nerve.

The other one of these nervy fellows was actually a very decent, respectable guy with whom I had already been on an overnight date, to a so-called formal event of his fraternity. Absolutely nothing inappropriate had transpired. We had a very sweet time in our chaste sleeping encounter. He was a perfect gentleman. Good natured, kind, good looking, and completely boring to me in spite of our common interests. He even invited me one evening to come out and play pitch-and-catch at one of the campus parks. What a sweetheart! But he was just too well-adjusted to be appealing.

That field trip to Opryland did have one other memorable moment. It had recently been expanded and upgraded to include a massive hotel, theme park, and gigantic show hall. This hall replaced the tiny Ryman Auditorium, which had housed the Grand Ole Opry radio show for decades.

We were given a tour of the hall. As I and my classmates walked out onto the stage, listening to our tour guide cite marketing statistics, I was overcome by a sense of foreshadowing. It felt familiar, as if someday for certain I would be standing in front of an audience in a similar setting. This idea was ridiculous to me. I didn't have a lick of talent for singing or dancing. I dismissed it outright but did not forget it.

Once I was asked out by a gorgeous pre-med student. His phone call was completely unexpected. It probably had to do with my derriere and the khakis. He had seen me with one of my suitemates, who dated his frat brother. He drove a silver-blue Aston Martin convertible, so he took me to the drive-in movie and brought along a bottle of Liebfraumilch. In the back seat, he went into shock that I intended to remain a virgin until marriage (this was before the Colorado red-head).

The only other time I saw him was during another sexless four-person sleepover, this time at his apartment. We all drank heavily and conked out. The mutual friend who arranged this quasi-date did so in a well-meaning attempt to get him to reconsider me. To no avail. The next morning we let our hangovers wear off by listening to Jackson Browne's *Late for the Sky* several times. Trust me: *Fountain of Sorrow* is not the song you want to hear when you know you've been rejected. It was worse than rubbing salt in a wound. It was absolutely funereal.

At the start of that same year, the accessibility of men began to take a turn for me. I became a Little Sister for a fraternity. Little Sisters have the happy job of providing a buffer for overbearing testosterone levels, evidently, and served to make the men seem virile and attractive to recruits. We were the hospitality factor, sort of like geishas. Except without the sex. In this particular case, anyway, it was not about sex. At this frat house Little Sisters were rather revered, like biological sisters, and not to be exploited.

I earned this position by virtue of my willingness to constantly loiter there, which was not hard to do given the free and delicious meals. I had gained an entrée to the place through my participation via my sorority in a joint song-and-dance production for an all-campus variety show, *Carnicus*. Several of the guys became my great friends and consistently invited me to stay for dinner. Which I was all too happy to accept, not only because of the price. Technically, a Little Sister was allowed one free meal per week; but so few of them ever showed up that I was allowed to have their forfeits.

The cook was an oversized black woman named Greta and an undiscovered master chef of Southern Soul cuisine. I learned to watch the weekly menus for her summer squash casserole to appear. The kitchen steward was a particularly close friend to me…platonically, because he was gay. As a Little Sister I gained a passel of delightful gay companions with whom I had many memorable drinking escapades.

Emotionally safe drinking escapades. I went to many formal dance parties in homemade gowns with men who were kind and mannerly, if not marriageable. I put to very good use the swing dancing so diligently practiced in the living room of my beloved House.

As has been noted, when I did manage to fix my sights on men of the right orientation, I always gravitated to the outcast. I dreamed of finding some Mr. Aloof-with-Fatal-Character-Flaw who would become fixated on me and, inspired by my faithfulness and devotion, leap into character rehabilitation. Just like in the midcentury musicals. The idea of romance had my soul solidly in its clutches but I only wanted the unlikely long-shot, minus any passion-fueled persistence or Nazi memorabilia.

During my college years, I had as little interaction with my parents as possible. Daddy was the #1 object of my distrust. And Mama, whom I loved dearly, just seemed so impotent in dealing with him. She was zombie-like in her complicity. I found I couldn't dialogue with her. She was brainwashed.

I did see them once a week, however. Every Sunday morning without fail, even with the worst hangover, I got dressed for church and stood out behind my dorm with my overstuffed laundry bag, where Mama would pick me up. Mama, Daddy and I would all go to church together, then have lunch somewhere quick and easy. I would do my laundry and hasten back to the dorm.

I felt a major disconnect from most of the people at church. The pharmaceutical salesman had gone off to seminary and the leaders of the young adult Sunday School class were far too nice for me for me to relate to. They were prim, proper, and clean cut; the embodiment of square. Never was heard a disparaging word from them. Every week I would sit in the class and think of how boring they were and what a misfit I was. I don't recall learning a thing. Why I kept up this routine is baffling, except that I must have somehow sensed that it gave Mama moral support. There were also the forces of habit and that inescapable social convention.

During these years I don't recall learning anything new or happy about my parents. They seemed to be getting by from week to week.

There was some serious tension over Daddy's not-so-subtle encouragement for Mama to get a job. He felt it might cure her self-esteem issues. I did my best not to even think about them in general and him in particular.

The beautiful modern ranch House became a place of dread during those days. A dismal, invisible cloud of impending doom gathered below the redwood beams.

There was one major family event during my college years: David got married.

When he grew tired of the Oldsmobile dealership, and Steve McQueen's *Bullitt* character got the upper hand in his psyche (after lurking there almost a decade), he became a Knoxville policeman. In the line of duty, he met an attractive red-headed nurse in a hospital emergency room, and they wed in the autumn of 1976.

The wedding events were a bit stressful. For starters, there was no alcohol at the rehearsal dinner. This left Daddy, Mama and me incredulous. I couldn't imagine any life event, least of all anything wedding-related, without the joys of alcohol. But far worse, there was an atmosphere of hostility in the room amongst the bride's large extended family. People appeared to be barely speaking to one another. The three of us, as the only contingent from the groom's side (outside of a couple of groomsmen), felt like a big square peg trying to fit into a round hole.

I later learned that the bride's father was an alcoholic. Evidently, the accompanying issues had not been fully resolved. This was a lame excuse to me. I firmly believed that life without alcohol was not worth living and that an alcoholic should just learn how to control him/herself in settings where others would be partaking.

The wedding itself was anything but fun.

The reception was to be a breakfast party before the ceremony so that guests would not have to wait around while photographs were being made. That seemed like a fun new idea. Except when the time came for the breakfast to begin, the bride decided she wouldn't be in attendance. She claimed to have suddenly realized that it might be bad luck for her groom to see her before the vows. I heard later that actually there had been a squabble with her mother. So it wasn't really a reception. This was not a good sign. People awkwardly stood around drinking orange juice until time to go into the church.

As a bridesmaid I walked down the aisle bawling like a baby from whom candy had been taken. I continued to cry my eyes out during the ceremony. My brother was deserting me and I would be left alone with my dysfunctional parents. There was no doubt in my mind about this. He was gone. The bride had no siblings herself and did not seem inclined to gain any new ones or share his attention.

For my senior year of college, I moved to an apartment which was much closer to the frat house and the sumptuous free meals. It was also across the street from the aquatic center with twin Olympic-size pools, indoor and outdoor, where I and my roommate could work on our tans during spring quarter.

The only problem was that it happened to be the same building where my pediatrician had had his office. The antiseptic smell of the linoleum in the hallway was exactly the same, 15 years later. How could this be? It set me on edge daily. I had learned early in life the meaning of the word *injection,* and visits to his office were filled with dread that even free Dumdum suckers couldn't overcome. So there was that.

My bookworm friend from childhood was my roommate. She had ditched the Ivy League school after our weekly phone calls autumn of freshman year helped her identify her true feelings: she despised the place. The academic competitiveness was like a stranglehold choking the life out of her. College should be fun! SEC football games, drinking, and carousing! She came home for Christmas break and refused to return. Coincidentally, sometime in the years that followed she became a Little Sister at the same frat house as I and she likewise loved the free meals. Our apartment kitchen got very little use.

For the most part, everything was great at this apartment in the beginning, but anxiety about my imminent exit from the cocoon of college starting getting to me. I became a nervous wreck. I developed acne for the first time in my life and my fingernails splintered and broke below the quick. During Christmas break at the House, I would take hour-long baths. Not even the Walter Schumann singers could cheer me up, or my little Nativity set. I was morose and broke into sobs at the drop of a hat. Daddy dropped a couple of hints about therapy.

Things really went downhill from there. In January my parents would be celebrating their 25th anniversary and I knew that David and I should organize some sort of party. His new wife, however, was oddly uncooperative. She downright refused to be involved, which put a serious damper on things. The best I could manage with their lack of enthusiasm was dinner for the six of us at a nice restaurant. It never occurred to me that my parents also might actually be avoiding the issue.

Then came my accident. I was hit by a car crossing the street in front of the apartment building. I wasn't badly injured—no broken bones, but bone-deep vast purple bruises that made every twitch excruciating. Getting around campus was an exhausting ordeal, as I awkwardly maneuvered the shuttle bus steps with a pair of crutches.

I got little to no sympathy from the frat men. I had a reputation for being vacant and absent-minded (seen by my more charitable acquaintances as deep-thinking), so they openly teased me about being a danger to myself. Additionally, I discovered that codeine makes me nauseous. Very nauseous.

I was shaken and miserable, but the incident was not without value. In addition to thickening my emotional skin, the trauma of the sudden impact led me to recognize the fragile, fleeting nature of life on this planet. Can be gone in a flash, so to speak.

In April I was ready to have some fun celebrating my 22nd birthday. I started by having a couple of happy-hour cocktails in the lounge of a lovely campus restaurant with the frat steward and his best friend. After a while I excused myself to use the pay phone to call Mama to finalize dinner plans.

When she answered, her voice sounded oddly flat. She dispassionately stated *we won't be coming to pick you up because Daddy is in the driveway with a moving van.*

He was supervising the movers who were loading up his belongings and he would then be gone. He was picking and choosing which furniture and art pieces he would take. He took the gold velvet chairs from their bedroom and an abstract collage from the foyer, among other things. Mercifully he didn't take the Heywood Wakefield pieces and custom-built Formica dinette set. How could he, when the House had been designed around them?

The alcohol did me no favors at this point. My already fragile nerves were destroyed. I started uncontrollably wailing. My gentlemen friends went into protective mode so I wouldn't call too much attention to myself. They lovingly put a coat over my head and with arms around my shoulders whisked me out of the bar and back to my apartment, trying to minimize my hysteria.

I called David, who was on duty at the time. He came to the apartment in his uniform and allowed me to sit on his lap while I alternately cried and screamed *why?* which was a stupid thing to say or even wonder. We both knew why.

The conflict avoidance had taken its toll. No one was really in charge in this marriage; neither one held the other accountable. Daddy was free to check out. There was to be no discussing the situation and certainly no marriage counseling; no opportunity for anyone to scream in his face about marital and family loyalty.

He had a girlfriend. He was deep in the throes of an affair, so he just wanted to make the departure as clean and quick as possible...on a weekday when I was at school, perhaps on a day when I would be preoccupied and too distracted to challenge him. My birthday.

Daddy's girlfriend lived in the same apartment building as David and his wife. Many times they had seen his maroon Buick Opal parked in front of her place on Saturday afternoons. Hence their refusal to feign celebrating an anniversary.

Sexual obsession drives people to inhuman, cold-hearted actions against anyone or anything that gets in the way. It is an addiction in every sense of the word. And so my father quickly and coldly walked away from the House: his modest masterpiece, the classic atomic rancher that had been so faithfully designed and realized.

In order to curtail anyone who might question his judgment he wrote a ten-page manifesto on my mother's unsuitability as a wife, and why he could never be expected to love her or live with her any longer. It was laughably self-absorbed and condescending; so narcissistic that it backfired on him. By writing it he proved his own unsuitability as a husband and it laid down a permanent record of how misguided he was. In future decades my friends and I would howl over it over glasses of wine.

Later, when rehashing for the millionth time the whole drama of his moving out, I asked Mama *How could he do that on my birthday? Why? Maybe he didn't know it was my birthday.* Mama said *No, he absolutely knew, because he had the Lifesavers for your birthday cake in his shirt pocket.* She had asked him to pick them up for her at work.

My college career was drawing to a close and I was looking pretty empty-handed.

I had a series of job interviews which all looked very promising—the interviewers seemed to love me—but produced no offers.

Academically I was in fairly good shape; my only C had come from the visiting Columbia professor who saw right through my last-minute essays. But my mediocrity and ambivalence couldn't be disguised. When I asked the dean of the College of Communications for a reference letter, he declined, and let me know in no uncertain terms that I wasn't his idea of a good representative for the college. I guess showing up for class and being everybody's best friend had been a poor strategy.

So the four years went by with barely a worthy date or any intellectual breakthrough. I drank and caroused and went to Ft. Lauderdale and Key West on spring break, and paid 50 cents to see

Jimmy Buffett in the UT College of Music auditorium. I went to dances and keggers with gay men. My romantic triumphs consisted of two separate one-night episodes of heavy kissing, once in an Aston Martin and once with a handsome stage actor who was mesmerized, I think, by the effects of a push-up bra I was wearing. We had met when thrown together as members of a wedding party.

I had made strong ties during summers in Colorado and longed to live there. I was about 90% sure upon graduation that I would never have a serious career in advertising, having learned from a couple of internships and multiple field trips that I despised the profession. In 1977 it was still every bad thing that the recent hit TV series *Mad Men* depicted it as being in the 1960s.

So much for affordable college degrees.

Before leaving college I did have one last dramatic episode. Near the end of spring quarter, I received a going-away gift from Above while visiting a charismatic Christian group on campus. I happened to be at the right place at the right time to hear from God.

Some long-time members of my church led a group for young adults. They had three daughters who were in their early 20s. This couple was progressive and fearless when it came to faith. They had seen their middle child's fiancé spontaneously healed of an inoperable grapefruit-sized brain tumor.

I was lonely and without direction, so for tradition's sake, I met with their group a few times. One week they gave us each $25—a small fortune in those days—and told us to do something creative with it on God's behalf, and then report the results to the group.

At the time I had a job selling ads for the campus newspaper. One day I took a call from a religious group that wanted to advertise their prayer meetings. I called on them, was fairly impressed with their authenticity, and offered to pitch in my $25 toward their ad. They were a little bit shocked but received it in the spirit with which it was given.

Shortly after, I attended one of their meetings. It was in a store-front location on campus and there were easily 60-80 students in attendance. I reluctantly took a seat on the front row because that was all that was available. The people there were pleasant and friendly and seemed really calm. We sang a few songs and some prayers were said and then the speaker for the evening was introduced. He was said to have some kind of prophetic ability. I had no idea what to expect, but I was eager for some kind of hope or direction. A couple of times he pointed to someone in the back on the other side of the room and the person stood up. I have no idea what he said or what the response was; I wasn't paying very close attention. Or, it might just be that what happened next obliterated all other details about the evening.

The man pointed his finger right at me and asked me to stand. I sheepishly looked behind me, certain that I could not be the intended object. I stupidly said *Who, me?* and finally stood when he nodded. He was plain spoken and his voice did not waver. *You are in a very dark place emotionally. You have had three major disappointments recently and you know, but you will not acknowledge, that God wants you to focus on Him. He is calling you back to Himself and you are not listening.*

I was dumbstruck. I could not deny that this was true. Within the past six weeks I had been hit by a car, rejected by my college dean, and had seen the dissolution of my parents' marriage. I shivered and quietly took my seat.

Afterward, several people congratulated me on getting this special word. I didn't really see it as a happy thing. I had to admit that it was uncanny but I didn't know how to respond or what it meant for me. I couldn't materialize it or internalize it or comprehend it in any way.

I continued to meet with the group a few more times. For good measure I asked them to baptize me in the washtub in their back room, not being entirely sure that infant dribbling would do the job. They conveniently outfitted me in farmer's overalls for the event. They liked to be always ready when the mood...er, Spirit struck someone. I was grateful and excited. I was starting to fit in a little bit so I decided to attend one of their weekend retreats.

Because it was the end of the quarter I was just about out of money, but I managed to eke out the fee for it. During the opening assembly Friday night, when the baskets were passed for collection, we were instructed to take money out of the basket if we needed it. After being vigorously elbowed by the women I had carpooled with, I did—but just a little bit. Unconventional! But so far, so good. I was trying to stay open-minded.

As the hours went by however a feeling of apprehension started creeping in. I noticed that their founder/leader wore lots of flashy jewelry and drove a Corvette. I thought this didn't really jive with Jesus' teaching of self-denial, but I let it pass. Everyone seemed to respect him. In fact, the people seemed to be inordinately loyal to him and all the leaders.

On the last day of the retreat a major shoe dropped. The time came in the program for engagements to be announced. *Hmmm.* I thought, *they surely don't mean marital engagements.* Yes, they did.

Marriages were semi-arranged within this group. Each young person, when feeling the twinge of attraction to a specific someone, would report it to their assigned mentor. The mentors would have regular meetings to see if any couples had coincidentally indicated one another. After prayer, if the mentors both felt peaceful about the pairing, it would be announced for the first time publicly at the monthly retreat.

At the announcements this time there was vigorous applause and a giddy couple came forward and took their bows. Neither individual had any advance warning.

I quietly moved on to other pastimes. But I never forgot the words of the prophet. I just didn't have the common sense or humility to say *God, I trust you. Show me what you want...what I should do next. I need help here.*

The summer that followed was bleak. I moved out of the apartment and back to the House. I got a job at a new seafood restaurant as a waitress and had to take one final class to graduate.

For both Mama and me it was a time of mourning. Our main activity together was sitting on the patio in the evenings while she would cry and cry and cry. Copious amounts of crying and letting the tension flow out with the tears. It might have been depressing except for the cleansing it afforded her, and vicariously, me also. It was effective therapy for her and actually a sign of emotional health, I think now. I have heard that stress hormones are shed in our tears. Sit & cry, sit & cry, gaze out at the oversize trees and sunset, listen to the crickets sing, and watch the fireflies flicker for mates.

In spite of our mourning, we found serenity on that patio, which faced the conjoined backyards. This was where we had played flag football; where I had watched for witches; where we had polished the Dodge; where I had thought through my problems on the rope swing attached to the walnut tree. Where I had walked a million times to my bookworm friend's house. Mama and I belonged to each other and to the House. We were soldered together by our uncertainty about the future and the pain of abandonment; we were grounded by place.

She was no longer a complicit zombie. The heartbreak jolted her into vibrant life and recovery; it initiated her healing. She eventually mustered the strength to enroll herself in typing classes to refresh her skill and enjoy a change of context.

On the patio we tried to understand the abruptness of it all—which actually wasn't so abrupt, as it had been coming almost from the start. During those evenings she gradually told me of all the telltale incidents she had chosen to ignore. About the time she called Daddy's office when he was supposedly away on a business trip, only to have him answer the phone. About the lady who had called and asked her to tell Daddy to stop harassing her with his flirtations. About the woman from his singing group who called to report that he followed various female members out to their cars after practice. And of course, about the observant neighbor from their Oak Ridge apartment days after David was born. I did my best not to scold her for her passivity. I silently vowed it would never happen to me.

In later days, with Mama's memory loss, she couldn't remember whether he was living or dead; but she always remembered that he left her for another woman.

When Daddy left for good he moved into an apartment several miles away overlooking the Tennessee River. He had been stashing money away unhindered for years for this second household. Ironically the girlfriend didn't last long. He later told us that he had asked her to type up the terms of the divorce (for some unknown reason) and when she saw what he intended to provide for my mother, she made her exit. But this did not shock him into any kind of remorse. He was beyond pleased with himself to be a bachelor.

At this point, with the details revealed in his manifesto, I officially despised him. As in, could not stand to even be in the same room with him. The thought of him literally nauseated me just as it had during my childhood and teen years when he scorned Mama and rebuked my questioning.

In mid-July when I completed my degree I made no plans to participate in any kind of ceremony for graduation. No fancy announcements were mailed to family friends since my family was basically disbanded. There was no cap & gown, no celebratory dinner, no photo op. Daddy gave me a small sum of money which was enough for a down payment on a car; Mama's mother Grandma P cosigned a loan for me.

My brother was as usual well-informed on which of the newest cars were selling well and he recommended the Volkswagen Rabbit. He helped me find a cute shiny red one with low mileage and I became mobile.

It was small enough to be gas-efficient and liftable by a half dozen mischievous frat brothers. One night after an impromptu party I prepared to drive myself home, but the car was not where I had left it. I calmly prepared to phone the police when one of the scalawags walked me out back to find it on a lawn near the pool. They were sorely disappointed that I didn't panic and make a fool of myself. It seemed I was outgrowing my space-cadet phase. After what I had been through, a stolen car felt like nothing.

The car turned out to be a cute piece of junk. The transmission failed on me in the middle of Kansas. When the carburetor went out, no one could rebuild it and the only suitable replacement was a high-performance version designed for racing. Shortly before the car finally died six years later in a fender-bender, flames were seen blowing out the rear. Occasionally I still have a nightmare about that car.

I had absolutely no career prospects. The only thing in my life that I was certain of was that Knoxville was not where I was supposed to live out my future. So I got it in my head to move to Colorado. I didn't have a specific destination in mind connected to a job opportunity or friend; I was just going to move. It was the kind of nutty idea that only blind, naïve youth would concoct. Someone with nothing to lose. I can't even imagine how that must have added to my mother's misery—to know your kid is going to pack up and drive away without any kind of a plan, except to land in a certain state. I could have gone back to the Y camp but that just seemed too much like an admission of failure. But Colorado was definitely where I wanted to be. I was compelled.

Neither Mama nor I knew this at the time—I think we were both basically biblically illiterate—but that is exactly what Abram did in Genesis. He knew he was supposed to leave behind his homeland, his society, his social network, position, vocation, extended family, and just go. He was compelled, and when you are compelled there's no use fighting it. This was certainly the case for me. Perhaps it was just youthful ignorance because Abram probably had a closer relationship with God than I did at the time. *Maybe* he did; scripture doesn't really confirm that. But by whatever means, he did hear and obey God's mandate to leave.

But then something fairly miraculous happened. One of the jobs I had been earlier rejected for was to be a live-in advisor at the sorority house at USC in Los Angeles. I was ill-suited for the job, not

being much of a role model and never having lived in a sorority
house. Nor did I have any ambition to attend graduate school. I had
applied for the position because the first of my summertime drifter
boyfriends (summer of '75) had been from LA, and I figured if he
were there, I would sooner or later run into him. It sounded like a bit
of much-needed intrigue. I didn't know there were eight million
people in the greater metro LA area. Not that it would have mattered.

I got a phone call from an official in my sorority; it seemed that
the young woman chosen for USC had bailed out and now the job
was open again. They asked if I was available and I said *sure*. They
asked if I would be content to just take classes if I could not get
admitted to a program at this late date, and I said *sure*. My tuition,
fees, book expenses, room, and board would all be paid by the
sorority in exchange for bringing my seasoned experience as a
sorority woman into residence at their house. Of course I would
drive there, so Mama decided to come along for the ride and then fly
back.

When my dad got wind of it he decided to horn in on the action.
He had no intention of letting me move to the very place he had
always wanted to live without his involvement. I was disgusted. He
was *not* invited to this party and he was planning to crash it anyway.
He relished the idea of poking around Los Angeles. But the thought
of him being within ten feet of my precious mother made me break
out in a sweat. Reluctantly I gave him the address and dates, and
began to calculate how I could manage not to be with the two of
them simultaneously. Saying *no* to him never occurred to me.

By the middle of August 1977, the Rabbit was packed and I was
on my way.

Chapter 8

So in August, 1977, Mama and I jumped on I-40 less than a mile down the hill from the House and took it all the way to Barstow, California. We spent a night each in Oklahoma City (12 hours) and Needles, California (14 hours further) and arrived in Los Angeles on the third day. The Rabbit performed like a champ. I was elated.

And yet. As we crossed the state line the lyrics of Hotel California kept circling in my head like some kind of warning. *You can check out any time you like, but you can never leave.* It was more than a little disturbing. As had been the case when I first saw the Southwestern deserts as a child, I was attracted to but also intimidated by the brutal, impersonal, jagged landscape. It was mesmerizing.

This much is for certain: I never looked back.

We made it to the sorority house at the University of Southern California without any problem and I was as mesmerized by the glass and concrete skyline of downtown LA as I had been by the desert. But I was not even slightly intimidated by it. Outside of downtown, which stretched westward along Wilshire Boulevard, it was like one big suburb laid out conveniently on a grid pattern. Hilly East Tennessee had no grid patterns; the simplicity of this concept had me in awe. Who knew cities could be so logical! And so easy to maneuver!

The neighborhood where the sorority house was located was rather dicey and unsafe but I didn't know any better. I didn't know a thing about the Watts riots. Civil unrest had conveniently been omitted from my high school Civics and American History curricula, along with other unpleasantries like Japanese internment camps.

I was greeted as something of a celebrity having come from an old, fairly traditional Southern university, but I think it was actually my accent that garnered the attention. It was not particularly esteemed; it was more of a curiosity. There was some thinly veiled snickering, which I ignored. I was too ecstatic to care: I was free! of my hometown and the domestic heartbreak there. We made our introductions and polite conversation and then got Mama off to her hotel. She hid her exhaustion and melancholy so as not to spoil the excitement.

The next day she rode around the city with me to various KMarts to buy the few supplies I didn't bring. Then I took her to the gigantic LAX airport. There were no tears. She was quietly unselfish, displaying the same stoicism of her own mother. Besides, I would be flying home for Christmas.

The day after that Daddy showed up, conceding to sidestep Mama. I minded my manners and pretended to be glad to see him. He made sure the sorority house was not adjacent to anything seedy or shady. I didn't care if he was worried but I played along. It seemed like the height of hypocrisy to me, that he should at this late date sprout a protective instinct. We went out for Mexican food, had a drink at the top of the Omni hotel, and then he too was gone. I heaved a big sigh of relief.

Back at UT, when I announced to my buddies on the newspaper staff that I would be going to USC without a declared major, a co-worker convinced me that a Master's in Business Administration should be my goal. From USC, he said, it would be like pure gold in my hands. I had little or no interest in business. But that didn't matter; for me, it was about the thrill of the chase. And anyway it was as close to a game plan as I was ever going to have.

I was a hound on the trail. The front desk lady at the business college looked up from her typewriter long enough to tell me that admissions to that program had been closed for months and I didn't have a prayer. I chose to camp out in her office for several days, anyway to see if she could be worn down, bribed, or present someone with whom I could plead my case. I was intrepid in those days. She and I got to be good friends. But it still didn't work. She was used to such tactics.

The Annenberg School for Communications had recently opened a second location at USC (the original being at the U of Penn) and was offering a Masters in Communications Management to pretty much anyone who could afford the tuition and could pass the GRE. They didn't mind my lack of a letter from the dean. I had absolutely no clue how prestigious this institution was and really didn't care. They welcomed me with open arms. I and my crush machine were back in business. This time, I might actually grow my brain.

The young women at the sorority house were kind and intelligent, if not a little bit naïve. They were a privileged bunch but not as arrogant as sorority girls are often rightly depicted. They were sweet and quickly got over my accent. Our particular sorority was established in the South but this chapter was fairly new—so, misplaced confidence hadn't set in. They looked to me for reassurance and conventional wisdom about Greek life, of which I had none. I looked to them for fun and insight about the city, such as where the best Mexican food was, where to get my hair cut, how to deal with the traffic, and how to get to and from campus.

It turned out that a beater bike was the best way because the terrain was completely flat, and expensive bikes were quickly stolen. Of course, I didn't own a bike of any quality and had no money for one; so I spent the next nine months borrowing first one then another from a couple of the more patient gals. The benefits of the job were tilted in my favor from the outset.

The lifestyle appealed to me, except it could get a little bit lonely, even in the midst of a sorority house. USC is a commuter school perhaps because of its less than-ideal-location. The women all went home Thursday afternoon after their classes and returned late Sunday night or Monday morning. Making friends in my program at Annenberg was difficult because classes were all in the evening to accommodate working professionals. Most of them weren't there to socialize.

So I slept late every day. I would race into the kitchen three minutes before the cook was scheduled to leave and place my order for two scrambled eggs smothered in Jack cheese. Jack cheese was a novel delicacy for me. To the best of my knowledge, we didn't have it in Tennessee; just like Mexican restaurants. As I ate breakfast I would read the LA Times from front to back and marvel that I had the time and opportunity to do so, and that such a feat of journalistic brilliance was at my fingertips.

The movie ads especially intrigued me with the way they featured huge quotes from critics. It seemed that the larger the font, the louder the critic was shouting.

I actually ended up with a little too much time on my hands. I had all day every day to get my assignments done. When not at the library studying, I would hole up in my room and avoid any drama that might lurk in the hallways. I was no good at arbitrating the women's confrontations; I was too opinionated.

I put my headphones on and listened to Chuck Mangione's *Feels So Good* and Steely Dan's cosmopolitan-vibe *Aja*. Best of all was the Doobie Brothers' just-released, moody, jazzy, impossibly-apropos *Livin' on the Fault Line*. I embroidered and read books and relished the solitude.

To fill the empty weekends I drove down Sunset Boulevard with the windows down, flipping radio stations in constant search of a more singable or poignant love song, while allowing myself to be transported by giant neon billboards and the scent of night-blooming jasmine. I was living an escapist's dream.

It didn't take me long to develop my first crush. An old friend from my Colorado summer job lived in one of the 'burbs not too far from campus. She invited me to parties and introduced me to several nice young men.

When I indicated my interest in one of them she quickly put the kibosh on that idea because he was Hispanic. This confused me because I thought he was white and the same race as me. I knew of only two races in this world, white and black. My high school had a half dozen or so black kids whom we all included. They were no threat to us; their ethnicity was just part of their identity.

But this was not a race issue for her. She told me it absolutely would not work because of the cultural chasm. What did I know? I wasn't picky. So I heeded her advice and turned my attention to an underemployed swim instructor who played the flute and liked to take pictures.

About that time I discovered a much bigger problem than too much time on my hands: I had no spending money or the means to pay my car insurance. My compensation from the sorority involved no cash and I had no savings, and neither of my parents was willing to offer me a monthly stipend. Mama had been hired as an administrative assistant, and while she was able to make ends meet, she was in uncharted territory financially. Daddy saw it as a parental obligation to discontinue financial support upon college graduation. Of course I knew all that. I just made no preparations for it.

Daddy also took me off of his health insurance policy. I discovered this during a visit to the emergency room after a falling particle became lodged in my eye at the library. Mentioning that detail to me had slipped his mind; or, more likely, he assumed I was responsible enough to know better. Hardly: I barely even knew what health insurance was. UT had free clinics for students and it had never come up for me before.

So several months into life at USC I was scouring the job postings at the student union. Because my classes were all at night, I thought *What the heck? I might as well get a full-time day job.* It did not occur to me that this might be taking on too much responsibility and that the sorority honchos might not take kindly to it.

Many things did not occur to me in those days.

I took a job as a production assistant for an ad agency which was owned by a Jewish couple from New York City. This Southern Protestant was a bit of a fish-out-of-water (to put it mildly) and more than once stuck her foot in her mouth with vaguely anti-Semitic remarks...as a result of a home culture embedded with stereotypes. Cultural outsiders were routinely downgraded; it was de rigueur, even though my own parents would never harbor such sentiments.

My missteps horrified me and prompted profuse apologies. They kindly forgave me, and displayed parental affection toward my hangovers and lapses in manners.

However, the woman whose assistant I was seemed to be threatened by my (slowly) emerging talents. It grew uncomfortable. When I had been working there three months I got a call from a place I had applied earlier, *Los Angeles Magazine*. They needed a Traffic Coordinator. This position connects the ad sales and production departments. The job switch was a no-brainer. So at this point, I basically had two full-time jobs (grad school and magazine) and one part-time job (the sorority house).

All this should have kept me out of trouble in the romance arena. You would think. My first serious pursuit was the aforementioned flutist who was also into surfing and skiing, and lived in his parents' garage. He was part Native American and his brown skin and black eyes enchanted me.

Best of all he was mysterious and unpredictable. He took me to his favorite movie, *Star Wars,* and insisted we sit on the front row. He took my photograph (fully clothed of course). I hung out in his garage apartment and drove myself back to campus in the wee hours of the morning. Not even fear of the Hillside Strangler, who was actively attacking and killing women my age in the LA area, could deter me.

It didn't last long. Try as I might to hold his attention with seduction and my Southern accent, he gradually dumped me. I was heartbroken, or so I thought; heartbreak was actually an alluring kind of drug to me. The so-called poet Rod McKuen, whose work I had mooned over in high school, wrote *heartbreak reminds you that you're alive*. Better to have loved and lost, right? Rod made it all so legitimate…healthy, even, to exist in a state of perpetual romantic longing. As in perpetual rejection.

Like Holly Golightly, I could wave a cigarette and move on to the next object, comforted by morning-after coffee and independence. Except by this time I was waving small, feminine cigars. It made me feel subtly assertive and defiant.

Next came the strong silent blond from a family of 11 children in the upper Midwest. Perhaps having 10 siblings would cause one to be guarded with their emotions. He was marvelously intelligent and withdrawn, with a wry sense of humor. With persistence I did manage to wring some affection out of him. It took some serious patience, but eventually, I got to know him the biblical sense.

There was something about his aloofness that I found to be wildly attractive. Rather than being repelled by it I was drawn. Pursuing the attention of a distant, reluctant male was a way of life I had developed as a tiny child. I had an irrepressible urge about it. I thought that's what romance was all about. That, and nurturing male neediness.

Somewhere along the way, during the worst of my parents' dysfunction, I had stopped pondering the morality of premarital sex. My church youth leaders had never broached the subject (and I never dared to ask) so I concluded that the topic was at the bottom of the priority heap. Certainly, I had long ago abandoned the idea that nice girls must, by definition, save sexual intercourse for marriage, as Mama had admonished me. I was nice; if I wanted to sleep with my lover, that nullified her logic. End of subject.

And besides, she's the one who took me to see *The Umbrellas of Cherbourg* and never offered any word of disapproval or even explanation. Her silence indicated acceptance if not outright approval.

The gig at the sorority house did not end necessarily well, although it was an amicable parting. I missed a couple of major events (like the annual initiation ritual) because of my job at the magazine; which in turn called into question the quality (and even existence) of my influence on the life of the chapter. I did feel a little bit guilty about that. The job was contracted for one academic year and we agreed to part ways after that.

My degree program, however, was a two-year commitment so I needed to figure out a way for the second year to be funded. I applied for, and received, grant money to finish. It took more than a little finesse. My job at the magazine served as sufficient collateral for my avowal to become a true communications professional. At the time I sort of believed it myself. I probably did believe it. But that was not to last more than the nine months it took me to finish the work, at which point I would leave it all behind to become a ski bum.

For the second year of the program I moved into an apartment with a law student who was everything you've ever heard and/or believed about lawyers. She was diligent, exacting and no-nonsense. If I left my lunch bag out to grab on the way to work, she would come along behind me and put it away. But she did put up with a lot of my grief over the blond Midwesterner. She never, ever condescended with advice.

We lived four blocks from the shore in Santa Monica, just on the north edge of Venice Beach at the corner of Fourth and Marine Streets. The rent was high but worth every penny. I had become attracted to this neighborhood because of a wildly fun bar close by, the Oar House.

The Oar House décor had a whole new style aesthetic, what we now call *shabby chic*. Sawdust was strewn all over the floors to camouflage cigarette ashes and peanut shells, and to absorb sloshed beer. It's a miracle it didn't go up in flames. Wait...I think it did, eventually. Antique junk and old framed photographs were nailed to the walls. There was always a line to get in; when my friends and I would drive by to check out the wait we would rudely yell *F___ her! I did!* to make the waiting patrons feel foolish. Sometimes one of us would plant a bare butt in the car window for their entertainment. I loved to be able to walk to the Oar House and I did briefly take up with a young man who worked there. His name was Paulie and he was definitely reminiscent of my high school Badboy. It didn't last. He thought of himself as a rising entrepreneur...*if only those pesky authorities would stay out of the way* of his Big Plan, he frequently bemoaned. This made me suspicious. He never volunteered the details and I never asked.

All I knew was that when I was there, drinking beer and escaping to the pounding beats of the Stones' *Emotional Rescue,* I was unreliable for keeping any secret, especially my own. I would tell anything about my sexual history in an attempt to seduce the Midwesterner, who was still loitering on the fringes. Forget about Paulie.

I wanted to think of myself as footloose and decadent but I truly didn't have the energy to be. I was mentally exhausted after having held three jobs. I don't recall reading a single book. In the evenings after work, I walked down and took a dip in the ocean to relax. The water was not warm and enveloping like the Atlantic at Ft. Lauderdale and Myrtle Beach, but the bracing cold worked its own refreshing therapy.

And my roommate and I could scorch ourselves tanning on the beach every weekend. Every 30 minutes we would flip, and she would gently acknowledge the tear tracks that inevitably showed up because I had time to ruminate on my romantic frustration. Which was totally of my own making.

My financial picture didn't leave me a lot of options, either. High rent and car insurance had me living paycheck to paycheck. So for the summer of 1978, between the two academic years, I went to the magazine office by day, watched Johnny Carson at night, and otherwise mined all the cheap/free entertainment I could find.

I went weekly to an older neighborhood theatre that offered one-dollar double features of old movies. The bill changed every day so some weeks I went more than once. I learned how to eat peanut butter toast and 99-cent bean burritos from the local taco shop. Early in the pay period, I went to Happy Hour with girlfriends from work and made dinner of the free appetizers. I satisfied my fashion demon by shopping thrift stores and using my roommate's sewing machine. I also took up jogging in the mornings before work. This made me consistently late, so I learned to apply makeup while sitting in my car at traffic lights, which there were plenty of between home and my office in Century City. That worked out until the gas shortage forced me to take the bus and leave the Rabbit at the apartment. In my bedroom, now I was listening to Emmylou Harris and Linda Ronstadt (in her Country & Western incarnation) through the headphones, which in turn led to daydreaming about the locus of my summer jobs in Colorado.

My biggest emotional support came from a gay Mexican co-worker who earned his way through USC via scholarship. He entertained the dickens out of me. Everything he did, he did to the extreme. For example, he found his first 15 minutes of fame when the LA Times designated him as Grand Funk Railroad's greatest fan. He devoured books like street tacos, but only 19th century British authors, due to his impeccable taste.

He was a first-generation college graduate and an established curmudgeon at 21. Our attraction was avid and his friendship kept me afloat through dead-end romance and low funds. Several years later, his extreme tendencies and second 15-minutes-of-fame would enable a bizarre reunion for us.

During my years in Los Angeles God was little more than an afterthought. Had it not been for a hairdresser in Malibu and a Sunday School teacher in Pasadena I would have ignored Him entirely.

I had boldly proclaimed myself to be *born-again* to both my colleagues at Annenberg and the women in the sorority. I virtually introduced myself by using that descriptive. It led to some pretty serious teasing from the colleagues and cynical observations from the women. Clearly, my lifestyle and my profession of faith were not in alignment. Had I ever spent two minutes thinking about it that would have been plain to me. But as I had learned in childhood, I believed that any behavior I chose to adopt became Christian simply because I called myself a Christian.

Although I basically ignored Him I do have reason to believe that God was again trying to get my attention. One Saturday I had driven along the coast to Malibu to get my hair cut. It was a long drive, but someone had highly recommended this stylist and her fee was reasonable, so I took the bait. She was a great listener. Picking up on my accent she asked *how on earth did you end up in Los Angeles?* And so I used the next hour to regale her with my story of failed job interviews and the magical last-minute opportunity to attend USC with tuition paid.

She stopped dead still, dropped her arms and looked at me directly in the mirror. *Wow. Something big is going on in your life. You are living a charmed life.* She kept coming back to that comment, *you are living a charmed life.* I had never looked at it that way. The idea tickled my fancy. I thought about it a few minutes, then chuckled. *Yeah, I guess you could say that* was my only response. The concept of giving gratitude to the Bestower of such gifts never entered my mind.

I had not been talking much with God or making any effort to reach out to Him. There were a few Christians in the sorority and they had taken me to a wonderful megachurch in Pasadena, Lake Avenue Congregational. Once every couple of months or so I drove out there to fulfill some ancient sense of obligation. The distance from USC was considerable but from Santa Monica was just too far. It didn't matter to me anyway. I thought I was good with God and that He would be there for me if I needed anything.

But something remarkable did happen at that church. It was an ordinary Sunday with a nondescript leader in a seemingly insignificant class, which is very often the way God works. He sneaks up on you when you're otherwise occupied. The class was for college-age singles and there were about 100 or so in attendance. The teacher spoke about becoming a parent. *If you want to create a false persona,* he said, *you might get pretty good at it. You might even be able to fool even your spouse into thinking you're someone that you're not. But you will not be able to hide who you are and what you are from your children. They see through every pretense and they will mimic the real you right before your eyes.*

I wasn't married at the time and really had no prospects, so I easily dismissed this information. However, I knew that I wanted to be married. I didn't really want to work in advertising or a 20-story high-rise office building or be surrounded by ambitious paranoid upwardly-mobile wannabes. I just wanted to be a mother. My hormones were pumping at full capacity. I wanted to be someone's one-and-only and create beautiful things, say beautiful words in French, and raise children who would do the same. Remaining single felt unbearable.

It was becoming obvious that marriage was not going to happen in Los Angeles. I drove to work every day and looked up at the steel and glass, and drove all around the city on miles and miles of asphalt among eight million other cars. I didn't have the money or wherewithal to seek out social clubs or volunteering or special-interest groups, or even the most basic and obvious option, a church. The man I thought I loved was clearly not interested in anything involving commitment, in spite of the occasional great hookup.

I began to realize that meeting a spouse would require living in a place where there were actually multiple bachelors to mingle with on a regular basis. A ski resort sounded just about perfect.

One sad, lonely, hungry day when I was close to finishing the degree, it came over me like a wave that there was absolutely nothing to keep me in Los Angeles. This came to me almost like a voice speaking. The songs of Emmylou and Linda had swayed my heart. I got on the phone to my former boss at the YMCA where I had spent the summers of '75 and '76.

This camp in Granby was built to supplement a similar Estes Park facility. It was shouting distance from the ski area Winter Park and so had a very active winter business. The boss was delighted to hear from me and within hours my plan to move to Colorado was a done deal. I would be leaving an interesting, secure job surrounded by lively, supportive people, with room to grow career-wise, to be a food service worker at the YMCA. All with a Master's degree from one of the most elite universities in the USA, if not the world.

Maybe it was backlash: an over-reaction to having lived too long according to others' expectations. Perhaps mediocrity was attractive and comfortable. Maybe I had an inferiority complex. Maybe I was just horny. In any case, it was nuts; the same nuts as back in summer, 1977 when I first got the idea. Here I was, two years later, finally acting upon it. Back then, I had thought that going to the Y camp would be an admission of career failure. Now it seemed like the perfect escape route. Whatever the motivation, it was a consuming compulsion, just like the way some people have to scale Mt. Everest.

I was long overdue for serious fun and I aimed to have it. I just wanted to rub shoulders with global travelers, drink in the bars, dance, sleep off the effects, learn how to ski and find a husband. And not be so damned responsible.

Once again Mama came to my aid as a traveling companion. She took time off and helped me pack the Rabbit to the gills. I sold the few pieces of furniture I had and said goodbye to my attorney-to-be roommate, with whom I had shared beers, sunburns, and many tears over unrequited love. We did not make pledges to keep in touch. In an ironic twist, she had lost her agnosticism while dating a genuine born-again Christian. I drifted away from God; she found Him.

My relationship with my earthly father at this point was also dormant. Daddy sent an occasional photograph of himself, usually with a drink in his hand and his shirt unbuttoned in some party-like setting or next to a pool, always looking very carefree and jolly, amidst beautiful people. I think he had something to prove. It made me gag.

Mama and I set out on a gorgeous day in May, 1979 with the Pacific wind at our backs. Once again I did not look back.

I arrived at the Y at the beginning of the busy season for church groups and family reunions. The environment was as breathtakingly beautiful as I had remembered and several known friends awaited me, but all wasn't exactly well. I had a nagging sense of guilt about something. Consciously I was OK; subconsciously I was having cognitive dissonance like never before. I began to have a recurring dream about being lost on a college campus, at night, over-aged and unemployed.

I needed to eradicate this guilt. I quickly searched out lovers and drinking buddies to deaden the pain. In Los Angeles I thought I longed for breathing space; the truth was I was empty: spiritually and emotionally bankrupt. But most of all I was morally bankrupt. I was promiscuous; I loved to complain; I thought nothing of drinking and getting behind the wheel of my Rabbit, and I made no career plans of any kind for the immediate or long-term future. I wasted my time and my treasures, both material and immaterial. I had joined the ranks of wastrel youth. I developed a façade of being bubbly and the life of the party.

Oddly enough I wouldn't say I was unhappy. If this was depression I certainly didn't realize it. The living quarters for staff were vastly improved by this time; the Bays were for guest groups only. I lived in a dormitory with young people who were mostly undergraduates somewhere, full of hope and optimism. Their pleasant company kept me buoyed outwardly but also worsened my repressed guilt. They could afford to work underpaid menial jobs in a beautiful place because they hadn't finished their degrees. I had no such excuse. I tried hard to forget that.

A five-foot-six Robert Redford look-alike from upstate New York provided easy, fun company. He was an adorable miniature celebrity facsimile with charm oozing out his pores. He was in the midst of biking across the country; he wouldn't be around long. But I think he did write me a letter once after making it to his destination.

We worked six, six-hour days and on my weekly day off I did the same as before. I hiked tall mountains along the Continental Divide or went to Denver to window shop, see movies, and eat in cheap restaurants. The trips were frequent now because I had the Rabbit.

Our very favorite destination was Casa Bonita out west on Colfax, where you could eat processed cheese enchiladas and lick honey dripping from freshly fried sopapillas. All while watching divers go off of fake cliffs.

I had another gay friend from my earlier summers at the camp who lived in Denver and he was always upbeat and cheerful. With him, I never felt guilty about anything. His love was authentic and unreserved. I felt safe. My gay friends were so easy to be with; they were non-judgmental and affectionate.

At summer's end, I made the first extended solo journey in the Rabbit. I went home to Tennessee for a visit before ski season, when there would be no vacation time. I stayed at the House with Mama and celebrated David's son's first birthday, and had an awkward meal or two with Daddy. Mama and I, on the other hand, had become best friends.

Driving cross-country by myself caused me no fear even when I had a massive mechanical failure on the return trip. I was tooling down the expressway near Lawrence, Kansas when suddenly the car started losing power. I pressed on the accelerator and nothing happened. There was no ominous clunking or clanging to alert me that something had broken. As the car slowed, I downshifted and discovered that in third gear it would go. Within seconds I looked up and miraculously saw a billboard for a Volkswagen dealer at the next exit. This was unbelievably good fortune, because third gear soon also went away. I limped into the dealership with second gear.

I sat nervously waiting for the diagnosis. At long last, the mechanic came out looking as if his mother had just died. In a somber voice he told me the transmission had disintegrated.

Reluctantly I made a phone call to the only financially stable acquaintance I had whom I thought might feel an obligation to me: my dad...who without hesitation made his credit card available. Although I did not love him, I did know that he could be relied upon for financial protection. That was his one area of reliability. In spite of every other failure, he provided generously for Mama. I felt not the first qualm about taking advantage of this.

I left the Rabbit at the dealership and took the Greyhound bus back to St. Joseph, Missouri, to a friend's home where I had just said goodbye earlier that day. I had my work cut out for me but my brother's experience with the Dodge had taught me well. I got on the phone and locally found a rebuilt transmission. Then I did some serious work with long-distance Directory Assistance and managed to locate an intelligent-sounding independent mechanic, who also happened to be lower priced. So I had the car towed to his place. The process took a couple of days.

I left my sweet, patient friend a $20 bill to cover the phone calls and rode the Greyhound bus back to Lawrence with the transmission on my lap in a cardboard box.

As I waited for the car, I spent the day in the library at the University of Kansas. This I had learned as a child: libraries are great stress-relievers; they silently span seen and unseen worlds; they are quiet spaces filled with thoughts and thinkers and organic volumes which altogether impart a sense of immortality. I left there refreshed and recharged.

It would have been tempting to be depressed by such a setback, especially one that put me at the mercy of my father. But this cloud had a silver lining. On the very day that my car broke down, a massive blizzard, the first of the season and quite early, was heading east. I would have driven right into it at a place where there were hundreds of miles of uninhabited highway. In fact, there were fatalities in western Kansas from this storm. Mama concluded that my very life had been spared by a broken transmission. She saw God's protection. It was hard to argue against.

The winter came quickly and I learned to drive in blizzards as well as ski. I was enchanted by the brutality of it. It put me to the test. The mornings were so cold the air would fill your nostrils with tiny crackling icicles; the tip-tops of my ears would sting if I had no hat. Cars parked outside needed an electric engine-block blanket if they were going to start. These things didn't annoy me; I was delighted by the novelty.

The dorm was much livelier in winter as the staff was a more diverse group. They were far less earnest than the summer crew. There were quite a few more slackers for me to identify with. They had come for one thing: skiing. Many of them used the Y as a starter job because housing was provided. As they learned the lay of the land they moved on to better-paying jobs and more suitable places to live.

I was still slinging hash which in ski season was a bit more complicated. We got up before dawn to prepare and serve breakfast, finishing at 9 am; then we returned in late afternoon to do the same for dinner. This schedule was perfect for skiing every day or napping during midday to compensate for long nights in the bars.

The bars near the slopes aimed at being hip and urban-ish; as you went further west they grew increasingly homey, unpretentious and inviting. And cheap. You could feel like a real cowpoke holding a longneck bottle and listening to country tunes on the jukebox. Cracked red vinyl booths, cigarette smoke, low ceilings, beer lights, and pool tables were all staples… along with fake paneling and linoleum that appeared to be a few decades old. They were poorly lit and musty, with a benign gloom. Like someone's grandmother's den. And likewise we loved them; they were our home away from home. From Winter Park all the way 20 miles northwest to Granby, we knew them all like the backs of our hands.

In November a young man with thick ringlets and thicker Philly accent showed up at staff dinner one night. Not even trying to be nonchalant I leaned in and asked my co-workers under my breath, *Who's the kid with the curly hair?* No one seemed to know. Turned out he had literally come in from the highway and had been hired to dig plumbing lines in the frozen ground.

Later on that evening I wandered into the TV room, sat next to him and started some small talk. He shared his dismay over a recent discovery that his parents had moved without telling him. *Hmmm, I* thought. He must have something to hide. This gave him great mystique. My crush machine revved up.

In addition to the curly hair, he was a smoker and my tobacco taste/romance association kicked into action. He was intelligent, for sure, and an odd mix: boyish yet streetwise. He needed nurturing, too. All he had for a coat was a Levi's jacket layered over a red hoodie to endure subzero snowstorms. He was also car-less; endearingly dependent and independent at the same time. He was just plumb irresistible.

Within a few days, he celebrated his 21st birthday and I had no trouble getting him to sleep with me. It started with the proverbial sly kiss. At least six of us piled into one car to go to the bar to celebrate. This forced me to sit on his lap in the back seat. On the way home, realizing that he had nowhere to run I leaned in for the gentle contact. The rest fell predictably into place. Like shooting fish in a barrel.

Over time we laughed and drank beers with friends in the bars; we laughed and drank beers (illegally) in the dorm and had ample, indiscreet sex. I loaned him my car; he loaned me his Rolling Stones *Aftermath* album so that I could repeatedly play *Under My Thumb*. I was, beyond all doubt, under his thumb.

He didn't stay long at the Y. He and some of the other guys went to work at the ski area and moved into their version of a staff dorm, which was a mile-long trek up from the base lodge. This made our rendezvous a little more sporadic and unpredictable especially due to his lack of transportation.

Trying to get his attention became my principal pastime of the winter, second only to partying; skiing ran a distant third. Dating him was like trying to pick up mercury from a broken thermometer. In fact to call it dating would be rather generous. It was intensely romantic. We'd have soul-stirring encounters marked by abandon and indulgence, with us both freely sharing the L word (he started it, being singularly gifted in lovespeak); then he would not be heard from for days.

Or weeks, around the time of Christmas and Valentine's Day. I jumped the gun about Christmas and used a friend's sewing machine to make him a flannel shirt. When it became clear there was to be no gift exchanging it got stuffed to the back of my closet. I think I held onto it until Valentine's Day which also proved to be a nonstarter, and then I tossed it. Too bad; the blues and grays would have really enhanced his eyes.

Today there is a name for such an arrangement: I was his *booty call*. Always willing and available and expecting nothing in return; asking nothing in return. Not even a trip to the movies. Although he did take me out to dinner once, for a sour cream burrito at The Shed. My favorite.

I was challenged with this guy and had to come up with some really creative moves in the ploy to gain his attention. For example, I threw a Caribbean-themed party in my newly-acquired, over-sized private lodge room. The camp director had moved me there ostensibly on the basis of my seniority. In reality, it was probably due to my indiscretions. It was large enough to throw a big party, so I turned the heat up to 85, set up some lawn chairs and invited about a dozen or so friends to bring cold beer and wear swimsuits. When floor space got tight we danced on the bed. The morning-after must have been as much fun as the party, judging from the photos. About five people slept over.

But usually I just waited for him to call and I'd say, *Sure, you can come over.* And then I would go pick him up.

One night I heard that some of the younger women from the Y went for a sleepover at the dorm where he lived. I went berserk with jealousy. I didn't know where this emotion came from; I had never been the jealous type. Maybe I had just worked too hard to nail him down. I jumped in my car and decided to drop in unannounced, which involved that trudge uphill in butt-freezing temperatures. The walk did nothing to abate my rage.

The door was never locked. I quickly found him – sleeping alone in the large communal bedroom – and started pulling his hair and pounding on his chest. The mere suggestion of infidelity turned me into a cursing monster. It was a hellish scene. He did not reciprocate, but gently held my arms in place and with great patience talked me down off the psycho-ledge, and then used tender physical attention to complete my disarming. He may not have known where this boom cyclone came from, but he knew just how to handle it. The man had a definite way with me.

But sadly, there was something horribly amiss inside of me where no one could see it or fix it. Decadence had become a black hole sucking away my identity.

By the time the spring thaw began, my love object's absences grew very long. I decided to accept a few dates with a divorced high school ski coach, Bobby, to distract myself. Bobby's sister was married to the local CPA and *she* was more fun than a barrel of monkeys. They introduced me to *MASH* reruns. We watched TV and had great foursome dinners in his half of the duplex they shared. I thought sex with him might help, but it did no good. Neither one of us really cared about the other.

He was a super nice guy. But my heart was too broken to be worth anything. I missed my rebel with the unkempt hair and insufficient coat. I would not be consoled, not even by the bubbly sister. That was a short-lived encounter.

One morning during this ski-coach interlude, the rebel appeared mysteriously in my room. As I lay on my side deeply asleep, I got the sense of someone looking at me. I opened one eye and then the other. Directly in front of me, there he sat on the bedside chair, silent and calm. Oddly, I wasn't even startled.

How long had he been there? He said he needed to borrow my car and didn't want to disturb me. He had let himself into my locked room with a plastic card of some kind. Was my sleep really so valuable? Or was he trying to catch me with another lover?

I took him at his word, settling on the first option because my awakening had been so slow and easy. I had an overwhelming sense of protection rather than alarm, anger or fear. I cannot explain this in any way. I have never been able to sleep through even the sound of leaves falling, much less a man entering my room through a locked door.

In some bizarre way it felt like he was my guardian angel. For many years after, whenever I felt threatened or needed serenity, I used that scene as my serenity visual: him sitting in a chair, quietly watching over me as I soundly sleep.

The near-final episode with my rebel came as a result of some trouble he had. He had gone with a buddy to the post office late one night after being at the bar. The buddy had forgotten his mailbox key but couldn't stand the thought of leaving without his mail. Feeling no pain, neither one had much fear of the rule of law. Kung Fu kickboxing might provide a solution. It worked, but the whole wall of boxes collapsed and they had unwittingly committed a felony by tampering with the US Mail.

He asked me for a ride to the county seat, Kremmling, for his sentencing. En route he suggested we get married at the courthouse because the only visitors allowed were a spouse or immediate family.

He had a detailed plan of how we could live in Denver; I was to be the breadwinner while he completed college. Trying to wrap my mind around this bombshell I pictured us standing before the justice of the peace. What about my long white lacy dress and veil? What about the bouquet and rice and bridesmaids? Something in my brain said *Nooooo...it's just not supposed to be like that.*

Even more, as much as I wanted to believe otherwise, I knew it wasn't the real thing. All I could offer in response was a nervous chuckle and a lame comment about it not being a sound idea. I doubt if he would even remember it today.

The judge was lenient. The semi-felons were made trustees and let go after about two weeks of washing police cars. When he was released from jail he left for Wyoming to work the oil rigs.

Late autumn of that year he returned to the area. I saw him a couple of times during the ski season; once by my design and once by his. It would seem that our attraction had merely been repressed

137

rather than eliminated. I do think he regretted leaving from the jail without contacting me. But by the time he came back I was otherwise involved. And after that season he was gone.

But that spring of 1980, inside of three years I had at least twice been flatly rejected by the man I loved the most, and my dad was first among them. As the spring advanced the sun grew brighter and more cheerful and I grew more melancholy. The warming temps and lengthening days did nothing to comfort me. My bubbly confidence melted like the snowpack off the rooftops, dripping away with each passing day.

I would do almost anything to ease the pain. The few limits of my morals got shot to hell. I slept with several platonic friends just for the entertainment value. I was so indiscriminate that in later years when I tried to make a list of these men I couldn't even remember some of their names or whether or not we had done the deed. I was an over-educated, over-age waif without direction, without an anchor, without ambition. I was bluer than blue.

On top of all the romantic frustration, I had a horrible accident on the road at the camp. During a blinding snowstorm at night I was driving back to the dorm in the Rabbit and I collided with two of the guests. They were a middle-aged man and his son; the father's head hit my windshield and smashed the windshield to bits. They were walking in the road, which was not uncommon because there were no sidewalks; and the only car traffic was that of employees and guests. I was not cited by the responding officer and the victims recovered, thank God.

The scariest part of it for me was my seeming lack of horror. I was so emotionally bankrupt I could hardly detect any personal trauma. I was already so full of shame and regret that I was oblivious to any increase.

I continued to call myself a Christian but God was just somewhere in the back of my brain superintending Easter and Christmas. He had gone silent and I didn't want to bother Him. I pretended not to notice the disappointment of my friends who had authentic faith. They were patient with me but only to a point. When my mooning over the elusive rebel went on a little too long there was no sympathy coming my way. I found myself with a dramatically shrinking social circle.

One night at work I was mopping one of the huge dining rooms all alone. It was a task I had handled a million times and it didn't bother me; the back and forth rhythm of the mop was hypnotizing and relaxing. When I was about halfway across the room I noticed a small gleaming gold something in the rag strands of the mop. I leaned down and looked closely.

For years I had worn a tiny gold child-size cross around my neck as an emblem of my faith. There, in the strands of the mop was tangled the cross from around my neck. It had been dragged through the grime and filthy water. I had not even felt it come loose, but I knew why it was there. My eyes and my throat closed tightly. I picked it up, stuffed it into my pocket along with any acknowledgment that anything could be wrong in my life. I finished the mopping.

During those promiscuous years, without much of a second thought, I did things that even unholy people find abhorrent. Based on a chance that I was infertile I had lulled myself into a state of denial about the usual result of intercourse: babies are conceived. And yes, they were. Two of them. The first time it happened, my gay friend in Denver and I toyed with the idea of marriage; it was so mutually agreeable that I don't even recall which one of us thought of it first. (Decades later he recalled that the proposal was his…God love him.) We both loved kids and wanted to be parents.

But my need for romance was too great. I couldn't do it. I disposed of the pregnancy inconvenience not once but twice, never bothering to question how I had come to that place. My willful blindness led me to a fatal choice I would later deeply regret.

Chapter 9

I limped into summer 1980 and a new crop of undergraduates came to the Y staff. I managed to secure a much better job as the assistant to the program manager. This lifted my spirits.

She had been at the camp for years and had a very relaxed manner—she was a true mountaineer. Meaning, she loved the mountain rural lifestyle and was a solid fixture with her knowledge of the area and ability to keep visitors entertained. She wore Levi's 501 jeans and was comfortable with horses and pine cones and macramé twine. She was very patient with me. She had long straight blonde hair and looked 10 years younger than she was.

In fact, she had just married a man 10 years her junior and was basking in the glow of her honeymoon. This gave her great enthusiasm for matchmaking. She wanted to find me a spouse and she had two eligible bachelors in her local family: her youngest brother, who had purchased a bar/restaurant business after ending a career with the State Department in South Africa; and the son of her oldest brother, who was fresh out of college and managing that business along with bartending whenever needed.

At the time I was telling everyone that I would not be dating for several months at least as I recovered from my heartbreak...totally in spite of the fact that I had a strange sense that the time had come for me to be married. It felt certain. Like someone had told me so.

On a bright June day, she invited me to run an errand with her to her brother's bar which was located at the foot of the ski area. The eligible nephew was on duty that day. When we arrived, he was behind the bar wrapping a birthday gift to send to his mom. I was impressed. We all chatted and she took care of her business and then we went on our way. She had been very sly about the real mission.

A few days later I went back to this same bar after a hike, to use the pay phone. A major sporting event was being shown on the big-screen TV there. These TVs were the latest thing in entertainment and a big draw for drinking and sports fans. It was the fight between Sugar Ray Leonard and Roberto Duran. My hiking companion and I decided to rest our feet and watch the match.

Along came the nephew bartender. He was a friendly soul and not the least bit romantic, so my guard was down. He didn't look a thing like any of the men I had ever been attracted to; he was far too normal. He was short and muscular; blond-haired blue-eyed normal. Like vanilla ice cream. He casually asked me to the movies; I said *yes* without thinking it through carefully. We made plans to see *The Muppet Movie.*

As I left the bar that day, and every day leading up to the date, I cursed myself many times over. How could I lick my wounds properly if I was out with another man?

When we went to the movies we sat in the back row so that he wouldn't bother anyone with his sleeping (read: snoring). He had played a hard game of softball that day and he worked long hours at the bar, so his stamina was low. Some women might have been insulted but I was put completely at ease. I didn't need to hide anything from this man. Between dozes, he would awaken and madly kiss me.

Louie was his name and he had come to the ski area for the same main reason I did: to have some fun after the responsibility of college. His father was an engineer for a defense contractor, just like my dad; his hometown of San Diego was the same size as Knoxville when he was growing up; he was taken to a Protestant church during childhood; he even had a parent who had singing as a serious hobby. We were baby boomers and the offspring of midcentury conventionality. We seemed to be deeply compatible; we met each other's emotional needs. We were instantly inseparable.

We parted ways only to go to work. There were no ambiguous feelings or games; no guessing about whether the other was interested. When I spoke to Mama on our weekly call I told her I had a new friend. *We're just friends!* I insisted because that's what it felt like.

He had never met a stranger. In his youth, he had sold Fuller Brushes and Cutco Knives door-to-door. He was an Eagle Scout. He had climbed Machu Picchu in Peru and had survived a typhoon in Japan at the Boy Scout Jamboree. He was indeed a friendly, flexible sort.

By the end of the summer season I left the Y camp and its dormitories for good, packed up the Rabbit for the third time and inched my way toward real adulthood.

I moved in with Louie in spite of my mother's dismay. Ironically, when marriage actually became a possibility, I developed a sudden fear of divorce. Cohabitation seemed like a better idea, seeing as how my parents and my brother by this time were all divorced. I joined him in the three-bedroom house he shared with a male friend from San Diego and a nice young woman.

During the off-season in a ski resort, employment opportunities are slim, so we took a road trip to San Diego to meet his parents. They had lived there for decades, held professional jobs, and had a strong network of friends. They were quite friendly right from the start and we shared drinks, laughs, and stories.

It almost reminded me of my high school boyfriend Steve's family. They seemed to relish being open-minded and nonjudgmental, and not just about Louie and me sharing a bedroom. On the wall in their den there was a life-size graphic of a defiant woman holding up a broom with a word bubble proclaiming *F___ Housework!* So, in reality, it was a far cry from the parents' homes I had known in Tennessee.

142

As in all families there was a dark side. All might not be so well with this couple. One night they came home from a social engagement and made a huge ruckus yelling profanities at one another. Some of the accusations were disturbing. This went on for a very long time, with plenty of concurrent banging, stomping, and slamming. Finally it died down in the wee hours of the morning.

Louie's dad spewed similar invective toward him after we returned from overnight camping in the family camper, which was a shell on the back of a pickup truck. When he discovered that we hadn't stowed away some non-perishable grocery items, all hell broke loose. Lord have mercy, how those people could show their displeasure. There was a definite pattern of outbursts of rage. My heart totally went out to Louie but I stayed out of it.

This visit grew very bleak for me before we returned to Colorado. As much as I tried to project confidence and poise, I was feeling none of it. Louie's friends were big partiers and often imbibed in other drugs besides alcohol. I didn't understand the culture, I felt surrounded and overwhelmed by the unfamiliar, and the guilt from my lack of employment was swallowing me. I didn't talk to God because I could sense His disappointment.

My identity was lost. I had no idea who I was or why I was in that place. One day when Louie was out I decided to take a lame solution and swallow a bunch of over-the-counter antihistamines. I didn't really think I would die; I just wanted to pass out. Which I did not do. It just made me incoherent. Louie noticed it and asked me the cause, but he didn't panic. He knew that if I was talking I would be OK. And I was, eventually. Barely. I was relieved when we left for home.

Back in Winter Park I went to the ski area and applied for a job in the marketing department. They hired me as an agent in Central Reservations, where I could talk on the phone all day long and get paid for it. The director and my co-workers were delightful and we had a wonderful camaraderie. I was 25 and felt like I was in recovery. As winter came the job continued to be as terrific as in the beginning.

143

One of the perks of living and working in a ski resort is the free ski pass that most employers offer. Working at the mountain also meant that I had locker space on site, so there was no schlepping that awkward and heavy equipment. I developed enough skill on the slopes to really enjoy it and there was always someone looking for a ski companion. My happiness was growing.

Housekeeping with Louie fit me like a hand-in-glove. He had a three-year-old Golden Lab so we were a sort of family. Another male friend and his common-law wife, who was nine months pregnant, moved into the room newly vacated by the female. They struggled with substance abuse but the husband managed to hold a job and put food on the table. Soon their baby boy arrived and he slept between his parents on a very small double bed. It was certainly an odd and active household, but we all had that energetic lightheartedness that comes from lacking any fear of the future.

On December 8, 1980, we were lying on the living room floor watching the horrible news of John Lennon's murder. Something about this event triggered in me an uncontrolled crying fit over my dad's emotional abandonment. Between sobs I poured out the details to Louie of how Daddy had ditched my high school graduation and other events. Louie solemnly promised me that he would never do likewise.

Barbra Streisand's *You Don't Bring Me Flowers* was on the top-40 hit list at the time and it also triggered the weeps for me. I wanted to believe that Louie could be trusted, but the idea of romance being permanent just seemed ridiculous, even as inseparable as we were.

I really only had two main criteria for a husband. The most important was fidelity. I had vowed early in life that I would never, ever marry or even date a man who ogled other women, even when it just indicated normal heterosexuality. That didn't exist in my world. But this was never a problem with Louie; as the months went by he was nothing if not attentive. On the one occasion that another woman flirted with him and he semi-responded to her, I let him know that I wouldn't stick around to see whether she or I prevailed. That was the end of that.

My other standard was religion. Mama had always told me to only marry someone of my same religion, by which she meant Presbyterian. Not being too picky I asked Louie if he believed in God. He said he did and that was good enough for me.

It might seem that love would have been the biggest qualifier, especially for my hopeless-romantic brain. But conventional romance wasn't part of this mix; it was the super-glue of mutually met needs that held us together. I concluded that romance wasn't all that important or even necessary and that my ideas about it had been wrong.

The topic of marriage began to come up in conversation. The defining moment came one evening when I was taking a bubble bath and he was seated on the floor beside me. *What do you think about getting married?* he queried. I hesitated before answering; I had thought about it extensively. *There's only one small concern I have* I began. *It seems like you enjoy getting high just a little too much.* What I was saying, without even hearing myself, was that I knew he loved something more than me.

Drinking was Louie's prerequisite for any kind of fun or relaxation, to end the workday or enjoy a day off. A can of beer went everywhere with him, even into the movies. He was also an avid pot-smoker (which never appealed to me), and he cultivated plants under grow lights hidden in the garage.

My own long history of alcohol-fueled recreation had desensitized me to its dangers. We often drove home without a second thought after drinking a few hours. Even the 75-mile trip to Denver for evenings out, doctors' visits, or supermarket shopping included drinking. Always. And as inebriation broke down our inhibitions, often violent yelling, name-calling, throwing and breaking things would ensue. We thought it was clever and cute to explain it by saying *We fight hard and we make up hard,* meaning with sex.

145

There was a disturbing incident one day after a day of skiing. We had headed to the slopes that day with a friend of Louie's, who had moved to Winter Park from San Diego, looking for fun and recreation also. Louie informed me that they would be riding up the chairlift together so that they could smoke a joint. I nodded OK, swallowing the fact that I really had no choice.

I ended up riding the lift by myself the whole day. I felt demoted and left out. I expressed my feelings, which got me nowhere. I became moody and withdrawn as I attempted to process the situation and my feelings. I couldn't settle on a next step.

Louie wouldn't accept my lack of resolution. My visible displeasure enraged him. When we got to a place where we were alone, on the back service deck of his uncle's restaurant, he shoved me off the two-foot drop to vent his irritation.

My only real injury was psychological. As I lay on the ground trying to pull myself together and grasp what had just happened, I knew I had two choices: immediately pack up and leave, or forever expect more of the same.

I chose to stay. Singleness held the greater pain to me.

I had to admit that there was something I loved more than him also: the idea of being married and a mother. The following spring, at the end of ski season, I took him back to Knoxville to see the House and meet my family. We told everyone that we would be married a year hence. I decided that the risk of divorce was worth the likely permanence of marriage.

During this trip to Tennessee, we had nothing but time on our hands. We took side trips to see Grandma P in Lancing, to Myrtle Beach, and also to Lynchburg, Tennessee.

In Lancing we ate Grandma's fried chicken and visited my grandpa's brother-in-law. He had taken over as Postmaster when Grandma retired. He lovingly but directly asked *Why are you waiting so long?* to get married. It was a valid question which I absolutely couldn't answer. Had we not been living together I'm sure we wouldn't be waiting.

Myrtle Beach was a new destination for me. It was close (400 miles) and affordable. The idea had been Mama's and it was outstanding; it was the perfect antidote to months of hard work in snow and ice. Although it wasn't summertime-hot, it was moist, warm and relaxing. Colorado can be brutally dry and cold.

The big attraction in Lynchburg was touring the Jack Daniels Distillery. The aim of the tour was to develop their brand, of course: JD is a down-home, generations-old recipe involving a slow, careful process with the focus on excellence. Every stop on the tour looked like a picture-book vignette. But they take it one mind-bending life-changing step further: after you have been brainwashed that it's the most perfectly brewed bourbon available to mankind, and you've spent 60-90 minutes smelling the wonderful aroma of oak-cured sour mash, you are absolutely deprived of a single drop. There are no free samples or opportunities to buy a drink or a bottle. The distillery is located in a dry county and it is against the law. Or at least it was in 1981.

This isn't nearly as irrational as it would seem. It's that age-old psychological trick of withholding. People want most what we can't have. In order to imbibe Jack Daniels, you have to jump in your car and head for the county line.

Which is what we did, expeditiously. I don't think I ever drank a beer after that. JD-and-Diet Coke became my sole request for an alcoholic beverage at home or out. I spent the next 20 years trying to compensate for a few hours' deprivation. Likewise for Louie, although he chose regular Coke and would gladly settle on occasion for beer.

After a while, the bar-owning boss/uncle got to be a challenge to deal with. Louie repeatedly had to convince him that such things as meeting payroll were non-negotiable to have a successful business. Finally they parted ways. Louie entered the world of ski retailing in which he had experience from his college years. This tilted his schedule toward reasonable daytime hours.

147

More often than not we weathered difficulties as a team. A year or so into our relationship we had to euthanize the Lab because of extreme epileptic seizures. To live without his huge, lumbering goofy good-natured affection seemed impossible. We both cried for days. And during the off-season periods (late spring, early autumn) we had to fend off the mind-numbing boredom of being without work in a rural setting.

During these periods our unemployment benefits and food stamps were just enough to meet our basic needs. If we were careful, we'd have a little left over to rent a VCR at the local gas station along with VHS-format movies. Although we didn't really have the funds to travel (outside of driving to one or the other of our homes), we didn't miss it; we went car-camping and hiked the tall mountains in public wilderness areas right out our back door.

Louie's consistency continued without falter and that was what I wanted most. We were inseparable. His life's agenda may not have been in lockstep with mine but it was close enough. Meaning, he also wanted children.

We met for a few sessions of premarital counseling and in April, 1982 we were married at the Presbyterian church in Granby, three days after my 27th birthday. The minister was an intelligent and kind woman whose husband eventually ran off with his girlfriend. The loss was entirely his.

My parents did attend the wedding of course. I was still distant and detached from my dad but could handle his presence as long as other people were around and alcohol was flowing. Mama was gracious, accommodating and showed no traces of bitterness, much to her credit. Daddy tried to act as if they were still married and best of friends and it did secretly make me disgusted. But I gritted my teeth and poured another glass of champagne. It was a festive time.

I had a strange unexpected emotional response to being married. Possibly on the very morning after, or at least very shortly after— sometime on our honeymoon—I woke up...and lying in bed, staring at the ceiling, I suddenly realized that my lifelong romantic pursuits were over.

And my response was *Really? This is IT?* Our relationship seemed so perfunctory, almost like a business transaction. It was a fraternal love, of sorts. The effortless, daily sex had ceased months ago. Physical affection had become a bit of a routine.

And I made another really weird discovery which caught me completely off guard: non-committal men love to hit on married women. This was front-page news to me, never having been married before. I guess it could work both ways, but conventional wisdom in our area held that women there were outnumbered by men 5-to-1. (Which would explain my ease in finding a husband.) Also, resort areas are notoriously attrac non-committal types. This new reality kept me continually on edge, especially considering all the time we spent in bars.

The ego rush from this couldn't be avoided. It had me at war with my own best interests. I tried to deflect the attention, but it didn't come easy for a woman who had carried dozens of unrequited crushes since elementary school. At least, I thought I tried. My hunger for male attention ran deep.

I tried not to be flirtatious but I was losing the battle. Interested men were lurking everywhere. There was the bartender from Boston, the young cowboy from Oklahoma, the heavy-machine operator from Quebec, the red-headed horntoad husband of my hairdresser, and the competitive freestyle skier at work, to name a few.

The whole situation mystified me because I didn't consider myself to be attractive and didn't wear provocative clothing. But I must have been giving out some sort of subconscious, come-hither dog-whistle nonetheless.

One time I even had my panties stolen out of the locker while taking a Jacuzzi with a couple of girlfriends. Seriously.

By this time I was employed as a reservationist for a condo development which had racquetball courts, pool, spa, and a bar/restaurant on site. After work one night, late in the season, the three of us went into the bar area first for a drink. The place was virtually deserted. We were the only females in the building and the only people, except for the bartender and a couple of bored local guys at the bar. We exchanged pleasantries with them, had a drink and then headed into the locker room to change.

After a long, fun sit in the hot tub, laughing over local gossip and work travails—the contrast of below-zero air temp and the 105-degree tub makes for a great relaxation/stimulation mix—we returned to the locker room to dress and head home.

There was just one problem. I had removed my underwear, tights, and half-slip all as one unit when undressing; now all that remained were the tights and slip. I carefully separated all items of clothing, as did my friends with their own, with no luck. Out of 50 some-odd lockers, the culprit had found his treasure and left me bare-assed and speechless.

The next day, when my underwear didn't show up on the flagpole, I knew this was not a practical joke. One of the bar guys (the Quebecois) had flirted with me on several occasions so I concluded it had to be him. How's that for nonverbal innuendo?

Did I mention that this area also has an extremely high divorce rate? Or so it was said.

Being married eventually caused Louie and me to think more long-term about housing, careers, raising kids and so forth. Life in a mountain resort can make those things hard to come by; it's a lifestyle far better suited for the young/single/childless or retirees. The employment is sketchy, the climate brutal, the real estate expensive. At the time there was a very real shortage of such basics as libraries, cheap groceries, and healthcare. We began to see that our residence there might not be permanent.

Our employment had become more reliable but only just. Louie was now manager of a ski shop and my work was year-round. We could get help from the Feds on a mortgage so we decided to invest in a house. Driving west a good distance we found an affordable lot in Tabernash. It was long and narrow with a steep incline. It faced a broad, wide meadow and a few miles beyond that, due east, the Continental Divide. To put a house on this hillside would allow a spectacular view. It was just east of the Y camp where it had all started for me.

With the help of Louie's father and a couple of friends we dug a hole in the hill and built a basement. On top of that, we put a modular house made by Boise Cascade. These pre-fabs were affordable, sturdy and very popular. We ordered an open kitchen floor plan, the highest level of insulation available, vaulted ceilings (in memory of the House), and wood-framed windows. A wood-burning stove and ceiling fan kept it efficiently warm.

Our deck was perfect for watching the sun and moon rise above the Rockies. Amtrak's California Zephyr would periodically wind its way romantically across the field below. Our Christmas tree was always self-cut (with permit…usually) in the National Forest.

Having our own house was liberating in several ways at first. I got into serious cooking and learned how to make Mexican food at home, like Green Chile Colorado with big chunks of stewed pork shoulder, and chunky salsa. The salsa was a necessity because we consumed copious amounts of it. Just inside the patio doors, I grew basketfuls of petunias and begonias, which bloomed profusely thanks to the high-UV-level sunlight and super-clear skies at our 9,000' altitude. I stayed in shape by turning up the volume on Michael Jackson's *Thriller* album and prancing around the kitchen floor in my socks, although I did take in an occasional *Jazzercise* class at the rec center. It was my secret dream to be the instructor.

The party times in the bars just kept on coming. It was our connection to the community; it seemed like everybody gravitated to the bars, except for a few eccentric hermits, gentrified landowners, or the fanatically religious.

We supported every festival and celebrated every holiday in the bars. We entered the Halloween costume contests and I entered swing dancing contests knowing I'd never win, but not caring. On my 29th birthday, I drank champagne out of my shoe and had to be talked out of a bathroom stall by Larry, our token male reservationist and workplace sweetheart. (*The bull for the cow pasture*, as Mama would say.)

Louie always played on a softball league; we were consistently the last couple to leave the field, long after several beers and dark had fallen. He entered every locals' challenge ski race and then hung out at the bar for hours afterward.

The whole scene finally got tedious. With our house being farther out, the drive to and from the bars grew long and less appealing. It was time for a change. We had a black-Lab-mix puppy; we were finally ready for that biggest commitment of all.

There was one small glitch in our family planning. About the time we started building the house my dentist gave me some alarming news. My front upper teeth were all loose. My protruding lower teeth that my childhood orthodontist had spent 15 years working to correct were shifting forward and pushing out on the uppers. I would need braces again.

The traveling orthodontist said he would first need to undo the earlier treatment and get my teeth aligned properly with the bone. Then I would need jaw surgery to reduce the size of my lower jaw. Anesthesia and having my mouth wired shut for six weeks would be required. I couldn't add a pregnancy or newborn to that mix, so childbearing would have to wait. I cried my eyes out and then signed the contract, and another year of partying followed.

I silently wondered if being pregnant would cause Louie to see me in a more reverent light, as the mother of his children; and if the outbursts of hostility would disappear. They did not. But I was brave and determined: after the braces and surgery were all finished, in December, 1985 Michael was born in Denver, just before the worst of the winter blizzards set in.

Chapter 10

When he was born the nurses told me he was beautiful. I responded, *oh you tell all the new mothers that. No, we don't* they insisted. He did have incredibly full red lips. After he passed through puberty, his looks were always the first thing women mentioned about him.

I got to stay in the hospital a few days because I had a C-section. Louie couldn't leave work so it was just me and Mike bonding over Christmas carols on the hospital sound system. I finally had my own baby Jesus. Or, if he wasn't really Jesus, he certainly had come from Jesus. The two of us were in familial bliss.

A day or two after birth the nurses came to take him for circumcision. After a while, I heard a baby screaming in the hallway. Could that be Michael? Why was he in the hallway? I called his name from around the corner and the crying instantly stopped. It *was* Michael and the sound of my voice had calmed him like magic. I was awed. How could that happen?

Meditating on that caused a tidal wave of shame to well up in me. I was utterly undeserving of anything so dear and so trusting. What was I, but a shallow party girl who never grew up? The shame exposed a black hole where my soul should have been. As weeks turned into months, my sense of it grew more irritating until it became intolerable. I wanted to hide this hole, bury it, eliminate it but I didn't know how. The thought of Michael growing and walking and talking and observing his mother's emptiness sickened me. I would sooner die. Then I recalled the long-ago words of the Pasadena Sunday School teacher.

It does no good to bury or try to cover a hole. It must be filled. I looked at my past, and my current life, and realized that anything good or worthy I possessed came to me by very little, or none, of my own effort. I had too many grievous failures to be proud of anything. I didn't want to be the woman I was, compromising to win love and grabbing morsels of affection as they were tossed my way. Trying desperately to validate myself with my own puny resources. Participating in destructive activities and encouraging others to do likewise. I had made a mess of things.

But it had now brought me to the foot of the cross. My history was a tangled mess, or would have been without God's grace. Grace: unmerited favor. Bestowed in some measure on all people in all times; but for those who will see it, acknowledge it, and receive it, it becomes the means of redemption.

I knew that during the years when I cared very little about Him, God had continued to love me unfailingly. I wanted God to be the one in control of my life. I gladly and gratefully let go of it into his care. I accepted His offer to transfer my culpability onto Jesus.

In return, God filled my black hole with love and mercy and real life, which was enabled for me by Jesus' substitutionary death on the cross. Jesus dropped down into the black hole in me, *for* me, and He came out victorious, filling it as He came out. And so I stood on the shore of that ocean of peace I had longed for beneath the tree in the midcentury modern House.

It is said that everything changes with the arrival of a baby, but that wasn't our experience. Not immediately, anyway. Michael was such an easy baby it was hard to notice any new reality except for the fun and joy. He slept through almost anything. We took him skiing with us in a baby backpack. We took him to restaurants, we took him to movies. (We found his limit when we took him on a bowling excursion. I had to wait outside with him.) He rarely cried. He nursed or bottle-fed for great long sessions and then stayed full for three or four hours at a time. Piece of cake.

Having a baby did make life in a ski resort a little less attractive. Actually, a lot less. Layoffs, bar hopping and pervasive flirtations became annoying. I felt oddly inhibited, but not by motherhood.

Episodes of *Cheers, Family Ties* and *St. Elsewhere*—which I anxiously waited for each week, with their new "authenticity" about real life—no longer pacified me. Bruce Springsteen's *Born in the USA* album awakened in me a wanderlust that I couldn't put my finger on. His restlessness was mine, too; whatever the source of it may have been. Prince's *Purple Rain,* both movie and album, amplified a definite erotic longing. *The Breakfast Club* added to this strange spell as I saw myself in Claire (Molly Ringwald) and my old curly-haired rebel boyfriend in John (Judd Nelson). I had a nasty case of cognitive dissonance.

I could ski the black diamond runs, sort of—if they had no moguls—and had hiked dozens of trails above timberline. I had seen the Aspens turn gold eight times. I had plumbed the depths of beautiful scenery. But I couldn't face the idea of bundling up my kid nine months of the year to play outdoors. The crowning blow fell in July, 1986 when the temperature dipped below freezing for three nights in a row. The flower boxes I had so toiled over were reduced to a limp dead wad.

The hard truth was that boredom had set in. I was ready to run, with or without my spouse. I had become the square peg in a round hole. Louie kept finding new projects for our house; I kept telling him to cease and desist because we needed to move. He resisted.

That is, until the day he went into work and was told to take an unexpected six-week layoff. Simultaneously my company was sold for the third time in four years and my job would be dramatically changing. Perfect timing.

We put the house up for rent—Louie wouldn't hear of giving up his semi-idyllic homestead—and departed for San Diego, where the jobs were as plentiful as the babysitting relatives. We packed up a U-

Haul trailer, made a tiny space for Bingo the Lab in the back of Louie's mini-pickup, and struck out.

I was newly pregnant and drove our little brown Sentra sedan with 18-month-old Mike. There were several deserts ahead and we had no air conditioning in either vehicle. I managed the heat by draping all the windows with towels and sheets to keep the sun out. It didn't bother me a bit. All that I was leaving behind was thirsty men and a host of dark memories of spiritually vacuous years, including the earliest ones with Louie.

We hit a small hiccup when we stopped in Baker, California to spend the night. No, not Bakersfield; Baker. We checked into the only motel we saw that was open; it looked a bit sleazy but we were exhausted and didn't much care as long as the room had a bed and shower. We were OK with Michael sleeping on the floor with lots of blankets. Until we saw a huge water bug scurry past. And then another. And another.

Although it was after midnight, we asked for a refund and hit the road again, finally ending up in Barstow. The motel we found there was clean, fresh and had a swimming pool. The following morning as I floated in the pool, I visualized our new environment of split-level houses, smooth green lawns, backyard swimming pools, and suburban Little League. We only had about a half-day's drive ahead. I was eager to be there.

All else had gone very well on the trip, even with the heat. But when we were on the very last leg, driving into San Diego County, it took a negative turn. We had been traveling with Louie in front, me following behind because his was the slower of the two cars; this meant he had to keep me in his sights in the rearview mirror. As we got closer to his home he sped up, however, and drove out of sight.

When I first discovered I couldn't see him, I grew apprehensive. I slowed way down thinking he must have somehow gotten behind me. I watched my rear view mirror diligently but he didn't appear. Finally realizing that couldn't be right, I then sped up and drove as fast as was reasonably safe to try and catch him.

I grew frantic. He was nowhere to be seen. My terror mixed with anger and confusion: how would I handle this, pregnant and with a small child in a mostly-strange city? Louie's mother was at work; who would I call? And where? I didn't know where I was going. I had nothing in writing and wasn't even sure of the address.

As I continued south on I-15, I eventually came to an exit with a name I recognized as being from his parents' neighborhood: Clairemont Mesa Boulevard. It had to end up in Clairemont. I decided it was my best hope, so I got off and followed it west until I vaguely recognized my surroundings from previous visits. By trial and error, turning this way and that, and probably making several loops, I finally found my way to his parents' house.

There he stood in the driveway. *What took you so long?* he wondered with irritation.

This was not the way I wanted to start our relocated life. He was utterly unconcerned and shrugged off my requests for an explanation, with a slight shake of his head. Realizing that screaming or crying would do no good, I stuffed down my frustration and got on with unloading.

His parents very graciously allowed us to share their home until we could secure jobs and our own rental house. It worked out well because his dad was long-distance commuting and gone during the week. I think Louie's mom enjoyed the time with little Mike. While she was at work I prepared meals I hoped she would like.

We arrived in June, 1987; Julie was born in early 1988. Her birth was to be by C-section which allowed us control over her birth date. So we chose my Grandma W's birthday to be Julie's also.

She came with squalling, both inside (from her) and outside the house. San Diego was hit by a rare tropical storm a couple of weeks after her birth, which felled a tree in the backyard of our rental house. This was an omen. We had always talked about having four kids, but after Julie came along, the subject got dropped like the proverbial hot potato. Not that she was a terribly difficult baby, but she was fussy. It felt like we already had four kids.

Meanwhile back in Knoxville, time had marched along its way for my parents also, of course.

Mama had rediscovered the resourceful woman of her youth and was enjoying single life to the hilt. Her crying was all in the past. She went regularly to Lancing to soak up her mother's fortitude, fried chicken and back porch ambiance. The rhythmic sway of the rockers and Grandma's steadfast serenity was perfect therapy. This lasted until early 1990 when Grandma passed at 92.

In addition, Mama's outsize network of cousins, aunts, and uncles was continually on the ready to offer support and bolster her confidence. She was beloved and appreciated at work. She was invited regularly to travel with her divorced and widowed friends; her thrifty ways allowed her to afford it. She saw London and Paris and Rome. She went to Istanbul and bought Persian rugs and sailed on a cruise of the Greek Isles, tracing the Apostle Paul's journeys. She even took a job working the census and she loved it: for some reason, ringing doorbells and coaxing resistant people to fill out the form gave her great delight.

She had the run of her beautiful House and was as happy as a clam, having been liberated from the tyranny of emotional abuse and philandering. She never accepted a single date with any man, although she had offers. Her soul was satisfied.

Meanwhile, my father grew tired of being a single man. He moved his mother from Cincinnati to an apartment near his and hired a full-time caregiver for her. Grandma W remained jolly, positive and fun-loving, outfitted in colorful clothing and accessories right up to the end. The three of them drank frozen daiquiris on the balcony overlooking the Tennessee River and told funny stories about old times. But Dad was nonetheless lonely and wanted his own companion.

After ten years of bachelorhood, he married a red-headed real estate agent ten years his junior.

Dad's new wife Nancy was also divorced and lived in an older two-story frame house in a nearby small town. Her house was the antithesis of Dad's House; it was full of her own antiquish things. He was given a small anteroom off the main living room for his books, photos, and artwork. This room measured about 15' by 40' and led to the back porch. It was reminiscent of his Cubby Hole in the Westfield Drive house. He spoke longingly of building a new house for the two of them but that was a short-lived notion. She was entrenched and going nowhere.

When they first married they seemed very happy. Dad was unexpectedly compliant; she was assertive. So that worked. She made the decisions and he took care of the logistics.

He continued at the same plant where he had been hired when he first came to Oak Ridge in 1952. He'd had a handful of promotions over the years; now he was designing breeder reactors rather than weapons. I don't think he ever questioned the social or moral implications of either endeavor. He did what he was paid to do. But he also began to help his new wife with her real estate chores, where he could put his favorite hobby of photography to good use.

Nancy was an outgoing vivacious sort and displayed many traits typically associated with real estate agents. She, like Louie, never met a stranger and loved to party. Dad and Nancy were the cocktail party couple. She had lived and worked for decades in the same small town. Like Grandma W, she was jolly and wore colorful clothing with all the right accessories. They loved to go out to eat, drink, tell jokes and long stories and hang out at her country club. He expressed a mild but quickly abandoned interest in golf, which Nancy enjoyed, along with tennis. They took an occasional trip together and made some great memories.

She gave him confidence, and appropriate prompting when a word or phone call was due his children and grandchildren. She saw to it that gifts were picked out for birthdays and Christmas, which he had never done. He had never even remembered them much less pick out gifts. He began developing tiny shreds of empathy.

Early in the marriage, they came to San Diego for a visit. We were in the middle of our annual two-week hot spell. It can be stifling

159

and brutal as many people, including us, have no air conditioning. (Cool Pacific breezes make a/c unnecessary the remaining 50 weeks of the year.) Despite the challenges of a new baby, a toddler, and withering heat, we all got along splendidly. We went out to eat and had cocktails and everything was jolly.

I was relieved to have a buffer when I needed to be in Dad's company. I started to be happy for him. I was trying to keep an open mind.

As the years progressed things didn't go quite so smoothly. One year we decided to shake up what had become a tired Thanksgiving routine and took the kids to Disneyland. Dad and Nancy also needed a shake-up and invited themselves along. After some hesitation, we agreed. What could go wrong at *the happiest place on earth*?

The results were mixed. Our manic running from one ride to the next sent them back to their hotel room for midday naps, which was not at the same hotel as ours. Nancy had chosen theirs for amenities and reward points rather than location, so this took a big chunk out of the day. We really only rode a few rides together and took some photos. But Dad was a good sport about it all and I cautiously let myself have fun with him.

A few years later he would make Thanksgiving in San Diego a tradition, but without Nancy. She preferred to spend that holiday with her brothers and her mom. I think the small bedrooms of our house made her claustrophobic. On her one and only stay with us, some of her luggage had to be left in the car, forcing Dad to run in and out to fetch her wardrobe changes. Also, it's difficult to control the schedule when you're a guest.

She declined all future invitations to come back. Her only other visit to San Diego many years later would prove to be one of the most stressful weeks of my entire life. More on that later.

When we first arrived in San Diego I was terribly homesick even though I couldn't identify a home location for which I longed. I just knew this wasn't quite right. Homesickness was a whole new experience for me and a sad surprise. The only thing close to it in my emotional history was that first stayover with my Grandma P in Lancing during my tween years.

I suppose it might have been expected since I was surrounded on every side by in-laws and Louie's childhood friends. This was his domain, after all. The friends all kept saying *wow, you have REALLY CHANGED* to Louie. To which he consistently responded, *Everyone has to mellow out sometime.* This irritated the dickens out of me. I hadn't noticed any change since I'd met him; what was I not seeing? What?

The homesickness might have been aggravated by our lodging. We lived in an adequate but nondescript rental house. It had no upgrades, which was fine, and was the best of a depressing selection. We could and did make do. Buying a home was out of the question without selling the Tabernash house. The rental did sit on a gigantic pie-shaped lot with a great yard for kids; Louie planted a vegetable garden and I planted zinnias. But there was still something missing.

I took a full-time job as an employment agent for a temp service and Louie worked to build a clientele as a financial planner. I quickly became exhausted.

I lived for the weekends when I could hang around in my pajamas, drink coffee and observe my kids' adorable behavior for hours on end. And, of course, go to church, where weekly I had a nice silent cathartic cry and prayed for all I was worth. I knew that God saw my tears and that He cared, although I had no idea why I was crying. But I knew He was with me. Church became an indispensable part of my life.

Julie was only six weeks old when I went back to work and Michael was two. We decided that the best arrangement for child care was to hire a nanny to come to our house. We went through a couple of young women who wouldn't always show up and I began to panic over it.

I mentioned this to one of my temp interviewees who happened to be a devout Christian. He was very concerned; he told me he would pray about it and get his church in on this effort. I smiled and said *thanks* and went about my business. It sounded naïve to me and almost silly. God knew what I needed; why should I, or he, or they pray?

But very soon, in response to my newspaper ad came a human angel. She was in her 50s, Dominican, and rather hard to understand with her heavy Spanish accent. But she was gentle, good-humored and as reliable as the day is long. Best of all was her faith. I thought I loved God; she praised Him almost every time she opened her mouth. To be in her presence was to bask in her calm and be elevated by her joy.

She clearly was an answer to someone's prayers.

The kids never got under her skin. Her patience far outshone my own. One time I came home from work to find an entire roll of toilet paper unwound throughout the house. I didn't know what to do with my extreme annoyance. It filled my mind with fears of what other unseen, unsupervised acts had been committed. But I bit my tongue. She just laughed and said *all de chirren doing dese things! All of dem!* What could I say?

Sadly she only worked for us about a year. She developed a rare bone disease and was forced to retire. She died within a matter of months. Her obituary read simply *She was an avid student of the Bible.*

Her funeral was packed with people. It was nothing less than astonishing. The Dominicans were wailing loudly which might have been horribly unnerving, but instead it emphasized how much she was loved and reflected her own passion. There were people of many various races and nationalities. There were many prayers and hymns and praises offered up to Jesus. Arms and hands were raised in joyful appreciation. This was clearly the culmination of a life of faith well-lived.

In spite of her meager eighth-grade education, I count her as one of the greatest people I have known.

I knew I had seen a glimpse of heaven at that funeral. I longed to have a faith like hers and a multicultural environment to worship in. I had forever been bored with my own uninteresting ethnic makeup. Being white just seemed so dull to me. I thought I had the heart of a gypsy like my Grandma W and I was continually frustrated in trying to express it. My attempts at cultural appropriation through (highly questionable) wardrobe choices weren't easing my sense of missing out. I craved diversity.

About that same time I got it fixed in my mind that one day I was going to have an African-American mentor. It wasn't a specific desire, although it could have been. It was advance knowledge. Aka premonition. I have no idea how I got it; I don't recall any dream. Just like the pre-marriage understanding. I just accepted it and waited. It seemed completely unlikely as I had no friends or acquaintances outside of my own race. The diversity in my social circle consisted of my Japanese friend Mary who was American born and bred, third generation.

Meanwhile, my workplace had grown increasingly hostile. My boss was emotionally abusive and would choose a target, whom she would torment until that person had to quit, usually after collapsing into therapy. Conversations with my old friend Lucy provided some much-needed perspective. *Money comes into the household and it flows out* she said. In other words, don't lose your joy over money. I knew she was right.

I longed to stay home with my kids. After two years of working, Louie's commissions started to increase and I was able to resign. I was ecstatic in spite of the budget crunch it put us in; we knew how to make it work from our ski-resort years. Then I could, and did, stay home in my pajamas till noon all week long. When we needed an evening out, we hoped and waited for an invitation from his parents. They were often kind that way.

We didn't have cable TV or a VCR but we did own a video camera through which we could play VHS tapes. It cost us $2,000 and we bought it on credit from the Spiegel catalog in 1985 when Michael was born. And thus began our descent into credit card debt, justified by the fleeting nature of childhood. It did save us a few bucks on movie rentals; to avoid renting or buying tapes for the kids we'd set up the camera in front of the TV and record PBS shows for them to watch over and over.

In November, 1991 Louie's father died after a long and difficult illness, which exhausted his mother. She was in her late 50s. Several years later, she happily married a widower who was a business acquaintance. We embraced him and started learning the ins and outs of blended families.

When our kids grew old enough to dress themselves I decided that I should spend lengthy visits in Knoxville with my mother in her spacious House. Julie was five and Michael was seven. Lucy was there with her three daughters who were similar ages. I wouldn't have to cook as much. I wouldn't have to clean as much. After the kids and Mama were in bed, I could sit on the patio, sip Jack Daniels, and enjoy the ambiance of a billion frisky insects.

Whenever an electrical storm blew in, I could open the living room drapes all the way and watch the show through the gigantic picture windows. Wildly blowing and bending trees, huge sudden flashes of light, and ear-splitting crashes were high drama beyond compare.

Best of all there was no domestic tension to deal with. Mama's loving support was consistent. She did have a few cranky days when we'd first arrive, but she always adapted and made us more than welcome.

It became our summer ritual to go and stay there four to six weeks. I did not travel lightly for these trips. I would pack big boxes full of Legos and board games and such. It was a ridiculous undertaking which exhausted me, and more than once caused us to miss flights both coming and going. But once we got there I unpacked it all throughout the House and we settled in for long days of building, make-believe, and swimming at the same neighborhood pool I had frequented as a teen. The pool was every bit as regenerative as it had been before, and now the trees were gargantuan, creating a quiet, nestled sanctuary.

While in Tennessee we always made a six-hour side trip to Myrtle Beach for several days. Mama and I read books from 8 to 4:30 under a canvas umbrella on wooden lounges rented from the city lifeguard. The kids would spend all morning watching cartoons and eating Fruit Loops (otherwise forbidden), and all afternoon playing in the sand and eating ice cream bars from a vendor with a bicycle-driven wagon. When the heat forced us, we went into the ocean to bob around in the so-called waves, and then air-dried. No towels needed. Just like my preschool years after the evening bath.

We brought simple groceries from home and only went out for dinner. The locally-owned seafood restaurants all seemed to have a cedar scent to them which caused me to ponder bygone decades, for some unknown reason. To this day I am transported to mid-Atlantic seafood dives when I smell cedar. The only perfume I own has hints of cedar.

Before and after the umbrella hours I would sit on the narrow balcony and watch the ever-changing cloud activity, with morning coffee or late-afternoon cocktail. For me it was a mesmerizing novelty; as I've noted, clouds are a rarity in San Diego. This soothed and tranquilized me and made me think of heaven.

Atlantic seaboard weather is exhilarating in its unpredictability. The cloud show escalated when a hurricane was brewing somewhere in the Caribbean. In the days leading up to the trip, it was Mama's ritual to announce periodically *We will not be staying in Myrtle Beach in the event of a hurricane.* Just in case I might choose to do otherwise. In her defense, she was fully aware of my love of bad weather. Like clouds, San Diego has no bad weather. It can get tiresome.

After dinner, we would pick one of the many dozen miniature golf courses to hone our skills and digest our meal in an upright posture. Or, we would head to the Pavilion to partake of carnival rides and hand-dipped soft-serve ice cream cones. Toasted coconut was my personal favorite. As I feverishly tried to stay ahead of the drips, I reminisced about Badboy and marveled that the place had not really changed in 20+ years.

Many people in Knoxville expressed disbelief that I, hailing from the beautiful beaches of San Diego, would waste my time in such a tacky tourist mecca. But that was precisely why it appealed to me and to Mama, too. Myrtle Beach in the '90s was home to dozens of family-owned hotels right on the beach with low rates. It was accessible by land and budget. It was vastly entertaining: it was, and is, Middle America on parade and the best people-watching outside of Disneyland.

It was not without drawbacks of course. It was firmly stuck in midcentury with regards to development and traffic flow. Decent restaurants were like needles-in-haystacks; waits were horrendous for good or bad food; and left-turn arrows on two-lane highways were still years in the future.

Maybe it was actually the lack of progress that made it attractive. It awakened a bit of nostalgia in me. In spite of the inconveniences I looked forward to this sweet getaway all year long. I fantasized about it. It was a sacred space.

My final brief and shallow crush transpired there when at 42 I decided the 21-year-old lifeguard was far more mature than his age would suggest and was worthy of my attention. As oedipal as it might have been. I reluctantly left him behind when no one in my family wanted to add days to our visit.

It should probably come as no surprise that Myrtle Beach was the locus for the afore-mentioned serenity visual featuring my Philly-bred rebel boyfriend. Just north of our usual hotel, the Sea Dip, there was a stretch of large homes along the beach which were probably rental properties. One of these houses was white, wood-frame, with paned windows, dark green awnings and a large screened-in porch. It, along with the cedar-scented restaurants, took my mind to a simpler midcentury era when single women lived in boarding houses as my mother had done.

The serenity tableau featured me soundly sleeping in a pink nylon nightgown (like the one I owned as an adolescent), on my stomach and head turned away, lightly covered by a sheet, in a hot, humid upstairs bedroom. The hardwood floors are gleaming, the paned window is open and the sea breeze is gently blowing sheer curtains. My boyfriend patiently waits in a chair to the left of the bed, smoking, for me to wake up so we can go out for a late dinner and stroll. In the scene, I slowly arise and pull on my jeans, and hand-in-hand we wordlessly exit the white house with green awnings.

This scenario calmed and comforted me for years until I discovered a greater, far more real Serenity.

I didn't want to live in Knoxville or the Southeast, but it never occurred to me while I was there to miss Louie or our San Diego home. I was richly satisfied with my kids, my Mama, Myrtle Beach, and the respite of the House.

I slowly loosened up around my dad but it was never easy. He always insisted on picking us up at the airport and driving us to the House. During the entirety of the long flight, I dreaded that moment. The House was indelibly his—his signature was in its architecture from every angle—and yet he had walked away from it. Time had not helped me reconcile this situation.

We'd arrive at the House from the airport, ring the bell and Mama would appear with a cordial smile. He would waltz in with us as if he lived there. It galled me. This was always his way when he was around Mama, David, and me: behave as if no one had ever been hurt or rejected; life is just a song. In his world, we all forgive *and* forget.

He was dutifully attentive and we would have at least a couple of outings during every visit. His choice was to take us to the Smoky Mountains, rent inner tubes, and have lunch at a picnic area where you could also float on a shallow river. This area is known as Metcalf Bottoms. Mosquitoes and humidity could be pesky, but we grew fond of the place. Well, the kids did anyway. They knew that I was a little withdrawn around Grandpa Fred but they ignored it.

We were always invited to his home at least once for backyard croquet which I was incredibly fond of. Croquet is such a genteel game. He had a perfect yard for it. Meaning, flat. Nancy would light a half-dozen citronella candles and madly run about spraying mosquito repellant until we were afraid to inhale. Likewise, we'd cover ourselves in the stuff. Lemonade and whiskey were served and chips, if Dad could find any.

Of course we didn't conform to the conventional attire for croquet. Children and all-white clothing are not a good mix. Rules weren't strictly followed in any case as no one could really remember them. Except that Dad did know how to space the wickets. He diligently placed them by counting off paces. Once in a great while one of Nancy's adult children would join us, but they seemed oddly detached. They never seemed to know basic details like if I was married or not, what my spouse's name was, or our occupations.

During these visits, Dad proudly showed me the flyers he made for Nancy's listings and his other photographs, which were always technically strong and original in composition. Often they gave me pause with their artistry. I tried to persuade him to enter competitions but he resolutely shrugged it off. I finally concluded he didn't want to deal with the disappointment. Or, perhaps it would be awkward for him to receive any acclaim in their household.

With each passing year, his belongings seemed to be fewer in number. And he very rarely would have seen the latest popular movie. This confused and troubled me because movies had always been such a big part of his life. His identity seemed to be eroding.

I finally asked him about the movie situation. It turned out that Nancy wasn't the type to pop out to the movies after dinner or for a matinee. Her concept of going to the movies involved getting dressed up and making an evening of it. This was a carry-over tradition from the years when there was no local movie theatre in her town; residents had to travel the 30 minutes into Knoxville. Movies were reserved for special occasions. Over the years it just became too much trouble for Dad to bother with, even after many nearby options opened up.

The solution seemed so obvious to me. Just make the announcement that you're going—then go on your own. Why not?

Movies can be richly enjoyed without a companion. But I gradually deduced the answer: there would be hell to pay if he developed such independence. In my world, I would just walk away from such a response (or so I thought). To give into it is powerful reinforcement. I suspected Nancy could be very creative in her negative responses, but so what? If he would just ignore it eventually she would find it not worth the effort. He clearly was relinquishing his joys and preferences in the interest of keeping her quiet.

It was easy for me to spot codependence in someone else's marriage. So easy.

By this time my brother David had remarried, after being divorced from the red-headed nurse, re-married to her, and divorced from her a second time. They had some issues. He serendipitously reunited with the friendly, big-hearted grad student who had been my first college roommate. Back in my college days they had gone on a few dates but had gone separate ways and married other people. After a dozen years or so, when both were divorced, she called him up and they made it work splendidly.

He was enjoying his job as a courier for the Department of Energy, driving all over the country with highly sensitive materials and national treasures. He couldn't tell anyone where he was going until they arrived at their destination. It was all very clandestine, dangerous, and romantic. Very cloak-and-dagger. They drove big white unmarked 18-wheelers flanked by black SUVs.

He was a natural. He got the job because he was well-qualified. But there is stiff competition for such a job and David knew this when he set out to apply for it. He logically approached our dad for referrals to the appropriate bosses there in Oak Ridge. Dad knew many of them; he had been there for decades. But Dad denied the request by ignoring it; to his own discredit and his children's disgust. Maybe he was remembering the math homework. Ultimately it didn't matter. David prevailed on his own.

He was highly trained in anti-terrorism techniques and kept these skills sharp through war games held at a camp near San

Antonio. This career fulfilled every fantasy he'd ever had about overcoming bad guys, driving powerful engines, and serving his country. Not to mention playing with guns.

Coincidentally David and his second wife's (third marriage) home was in the same small town as Dad and Nancy's. They lived just a few minutes apart, but David reported that there was virtually no social interaction between the households. This surprised and disappointed me as it also did David, but I can't tell you why; it was all so consistent with their history. I guess we just never stop hoping for love to prevail.

David owned a motorboat and we all went water skiing frequently on Ft. Loudon Lake. The lake water was warm, green, calm and liberating, unlike the Pacific Ocean. It was also delightfully uncrowded, unlike all the recreational spots in San Diego. Louie was a strong water skier and when he joined us in Knoxville we were on the lake constantly. I preferred to simply plop my butt into an inner tube and bob around under the puffy clouds, wishing away the thunderstorms and waiting for fish to nibble my toes.

My life seemed to overflow with pleasant diversions. For our tenth anniversary, we took what would become an annual trip to New Orleans, the place of my parents' honeymoon. Not that that was any reason to go. But restaurants, bars, and unlimited music were all very strong reasons. It didn't hurt any that the completely-free French Quarter Fest was held on the second weekend of April every year, which coincided with my birthday and our anniversary. We coaxed a handful of friends to join us and a grand tradition was started.

This city ignited my imagination with its ancient decrepit buildings and lurking ghosts, but also its penchant for celebrating. The place is unrestrainedly festive; at least it was, before the ravages of Katrina. The citizenry were oddly carefree: it seemed as if there was plenty they should be worried about, like crime (the first night we were there a tourist couple was shot and killed execution-style just a block away and 30 minutes after we had walked through the area) and poverty (horribly neglected shanties not a half mile away from Garden District mansions), but no. They choose to fixate instead on parties, celebrating, and cultural expression and I was happy to let them distract me from the negatives.

It was all just so much *fun*. We ate oysters at Casamento's and the Acme; we ate trout meuniere at Galatoire's and bread pudding at Commander's Palace. We ate hamburgers at the Camellia Grill and muffalettas at the Napoleon House, washed down with Pimm's Cups. We listened to jazz at Tipitina's, guzzled chicory coffee at the Café du Monde while watching the tourists, and waited for ghosts at Lafitte's while sipping Jack Daniels. I joined Rockin' Dopsie Jr onstage at the Maple Leaf Bar on my 40th birthday. We bought inexpensive original art from the locals at the festival. We danced to Tab Benoit on the grass as gigantic freighters glided by on the river. It was simply the best of the best.

Somehow even with all the drinking we only had one negative episode during our eight or ten New Orleans trips. The flea market was on our annual to-do list and was as much about mingling with eccentrics as it was about shopping for curios. In this instance, Louie and I had gone without the others and he and I got separated, which is not hard to do when you're fascinated by cheap and often tasteless imported junk.

After making a quick once-around scanning the crowd for him I positioned myself in a central spot to wait. It was my turn to practice what I had always told Michael and Julie to do if we got separated: stay put in one place. I waited at least 20 minutes, but no Louie.

I became overwhelmed with frustration. So often Louie seemed oblivious to my welfare or whereabouts. Finally, I started back to our hotel and as I walked the tears started flowing. And flowing and flowing...letting loose a long-repressed sense of abandonment. By the time I reached the hotel, I was in a full-blown sob.

There he was, confused but nonchalant. If I were upset, I guess that was just my own problem. The hotel maids, however, were unrestrained in their hugs and words of comfort. They became my new best friends.

I got a strange feeling I should live in New Orleans or would live there someday. In lieu of living there in the immediate moment, I became a fan of Nancy Lemann books and brushed up on Louisiana history. Huey Long was quite a character; a truly colorful and scary demagogue. I determined that seeing the bullet holes in the marble walls of the capitol building in Baton Rouge, where his assassination took place, was a must-do-before-dying thing.

Escapism was my obsession. Nostalgic ponderings filled my mind. Without the distraction of a paying job, I could daydream to my heart's content. But wouldn't that be a normal response to living in my spouse's eminent domain and being financially strapped to raising kids without assistance? I coped by living for the next trip, biding my time with library books and rental movies. The library and Blockbuster Video were my sanctuaries.

And then there was Disneyland.

Disneyland was extremely effective in fueling the escapist tendency. The early '90s seem to have been peak years in Disney's attempts to offer the visitor a perfectionist imaginary world. Disneyland had been a big influence on both our childhoods, so Louie and I again/still saw it like our own Neverland. We went at least twice a year, which became five or six times as our income increased and annual passes became available. Inside the Pirates of the Caribbean I gazed longingly at the fake clouds in the fake nighttime sky. They were almost as good as the real clouds over the shore at Myrtle Beach. The fake fireflies were also pretty good and caused me to miss the backyard of the House. The Blue Bayou Restaurant was kinda sorta like New Orleans...or at least provided a reasonable facsimile.

I also dyed my hair bright red. Or *burgundy,* as David pronounced.

My heart had been reborn in Jesus and I knew God's love and mercy; the craving for male attention was starting to recede. We now owned a lovely two-story home, with a staircase, pool, and cul-de-sac location. But something was still not right. I was having my old accessibility problem and cluelessness about what to do about it. I loved my kids and husband but did not find the emotional satisfaction I had always believed would come with marriage, motherhood, and homemaking.

Escapism was my coping mechanism, but it only works until the Jack Daniels wears off and/or you finish the library book and/or you return from vacation. The morning-after never stops coming.

Chapter 11

In the spring of 1995 a Messianic Rabbi came to teach Sunday School at our church. There was something different about this man. He glowed. He was set apart. He was ethnic, and that seemed somehow vaguely connected; but I didn't know how. His heart was clearly on fire; he had a contagious enthusiasm and it was all for God. And he had a knowledge of and respect for the scriptures that even my own pastor didn't have. *He* didn't have any accessibility problem—he had a fountain of hope within and a spring in his step.

Whatever it was he had, I wanted it. Badly.

The following summer when I was in Knoxville a strange thing happened. Three separate friends, completely independent of one another, apparently randomly chose to tell me about a Bible study they participated in that had classes all around the world. They each took care to impress upon me how well-suited they thought I would be for this class.

The first to mention it was Lucy; I nodded, smiled, and shrugged it off. The next was the mother for whom I had regularly babysat in high school. The third was the athletic girl who married the NFL kicker. She was out mowing her lawn and waved me over as I drove by, just to tell me about the class. For years we hadn't done more than wave at each other in passing. That interlude finally got my attention.

When I returned to San Diego I looked in the phone book but the class wasn't listed, so I let it go with deep disappointment. I asked my little daughter Julie, who was eight at the time, to pray with me that God would send us a way to study the Bible. And we did, every night.

In December of that same year, another strange thing happened. In a hotel room in Orange County, where Louie and I were sleeping after his company Christmas party, I awoke sometime around three am. I rolled over, and waking Louie, told him I was going to write a book one day and I would help him pay the bills. This was not a desire; it was something I inexplicably knew to be true. I guess I dreamed it. But it did not feel like a dream.

I jumped up, went into the john and shut the door. Sitting on the commode lid, I wrote a tongue-in-cheek Christmas letter semi-mocking my suburban life. It flowed out of me without effort. I took that incident as confirmation that whenever the story came for this mystery book, it would be something that would flow from a seemingly outside source. The letter brought lots of affirming comments from our friends.

The highlight of this letter was an anecdote about a bizarrely answered prayer. I had been missing my gay friend from LA Magazine and had no clue how to find him. He had a very common Hispanic name. I didn't have a habit of praying for such things, but I thought I'd give it a go.

A few weeks later my husband made a strange comment as I poured my Saturday morning coffee. *You're not going to believe who was on TV last night* Louie laughed. Louie knew nothing about the prayer. He made me sit and wait as he cued up a VHS tape recording of the X-games, made during the middle of the night.

He hit the play button. There was an image of a Hispanic man panting, sweating, and running, in slow-motion, with a race number pinned to his shirt. *Isn't that your friend from the magazine?* Louie said. Indeed, there was Ric, in all his obsessive-compulsive glory, featured in a Nike ad for being a successful marathon-runner who was also HIV-positive. Encouraging us all to *Just Do It.*

His first and last names were emblazoned on the ad like a personal telegram from God. My prayer had been answered with flair and humor and left no room for doubt. I could almost see God on his throne having a good laugh.

I don't know if that's why people loved the holiday letter, but I decided to take the premonition about the book very seriously. I signed up for a couple extension writing classes at San Diego State. I was in my niche, but nothing happened. No book. And no Bible study.

The following January I went grudgingly to a social function out of obligation to a relative. I left at the earliest respectable moment. As I left, there was another woman leaving who also seemed to be glad to depart. Probably reading my body language, she chatted me up and mentioned her quest for some new community involvement. It seems she had grown too comfortable in her current service. She had been in leadership for a Bible study for many years.

I drew a sharp breath and asked her the name of it. It was indeed the one to which my Tennessee friends had invited me. It also turned out there was a class not far from my house. I enrolled right away.

These funny coincidences were becoming frequent.

The class was rigorous. The questions were deep and not easily mastered. Especially for a woman who didn't know where Israel came from, or why it even mattered anyway. All I knew of the Bible was the letters in the New Testament that told you not to be sexually immoral or get drunk, which I had easily disregarded. Oh, and of course the Nativity and golden calf stories.

So I started learning buckets of history and information about God's character, specifically what He has done for people and what He values. I would gaze out the dining room window as I studied and try to wrap my mind around how profound it all was.

The Bible cracked me up in some ways and amazed me in others. The main characters (except for Jesus) were just all so flawed. Their lives were messy and chaotic.

And God was always doing these crazy, unexpected, seemingly irrational things. Like telling a long-infertile *elderly* couple to go ahead and do the deed, because they were going to get pregnant.

Like telling the Israelites that all they had to do to be saved from a deadly snake bite, from a snake plague which God Himself had instigated, was to gaze up at a bronze snake on a pole. *"Look at it and live,"* God said. For reals.

Or like sending his prophets out on missions that He knew were going to fail. Like telling one of these prophets to marry a prostitute, and another one to burn a pile of human dung and lie with his face to the wall for an extended period.

Like telling a common teenage girl not to worry about being pregnant and unmarried…a stigma that she certainly would carry her entire life. Because that baby might just be worth the trouble.

What I really couldn't understand is why people would think this is invented, or fictional, content. Who in their right mind would create such a god? Or present as His *chosen* people, individuals who were so deeply flawed? Even including King David, who was called *the man after God's own heart,* who was a murderer and adulterer. Who would make up such ludicrous stuff?

After learning about the history of Israel, and how unique and unprecedented it is in all of human history; and how after 2,000 some-odd years, in 1948 it was reinstated just as Scripture said it would be in dozens of verses, I determined that not only was the Bible true but that I had darn sure better know what it had to say on any topic.

Perhaps the most surprising thing of all that I learned was about what God has in store. He seemed to be pretty good at knowing the future. The prophecies were dramatic, specific, and scary, and left one with a feeling that there was, in fact, a grand design to all this madness.

177

The trick is, it's a story of mercy, from start to finish. People err, and God fixes it. But if they don't take His offer of rescue…there's hell to pay, because after all, they made the choice in the first place. It doesn't matter if you believe in a literal Adam and Eve because just as surely as the sun rises, we each have chosen to ignore or disobey God at some point. Pretty early in life.

And since He created it all, He gets to make the rules; but we're born wanting to break rules. Breaking rules just makes us feel so darn powerful. We even love to break rules that we make for ourselves.

The weekly class meetings were organized into two parts: first, small group discussion where we reviewed our answers, followed by a lecture which was written and delivered by a middle-aged housewife who was in charge of the class. She was a black woman with five kids and a husband who had played professional basketball. She talked about piles of laundry and trying to get the kids to do their homework, all without a smidge of self-pity or complaining spirit.

Upon my first visit, I pondered if she might be my long-awaited black mentor. She talked about the passage that had been studied and why it should matter to me. She didn't use esoteric language or display any condescension. I soaked it up like a sponge, in spite of the lady in the pew next to me who worked on organizing her coupons the whole time.

I looked carefully around me after the lecture trying to assess if I would fit in. I was surrounded by women of every age and color and nationality. I knew I was where I was supposed to be. I took to it like the proverbial duck to water. Weekly, I answered the questions with a hungry brain and heart.

As it turned out I never developed any personal connection to that teacher; I did, however, hang on her every word. Like the messianic rabbi, she had a visible passion for her subject matter.

During the course of this class something magical and wonderful began to happen to me. I came home to San Diego. The homesickness departed. I began to know that I was loved and that my life was more than just being someone's mother or wife; that what I did, and who I was mattered, here and now, and also in the grand scheme of things.

I began to look back at the things I'd done and realize just how bad they were. Of course, when Michael was a baby I had come to see these choices as bad, but I didn't realize how self-destructive they were. The better I got to know God, the worse and worse I looked. Ironically this was not depressing; it had the opposite effect. It made God's love that much more precious. I was constantly on my knees with trembling gratitude realizing just how deep and dark was the abyss I had been plucked back from.

It also became impossible to hold any kind of grudge against anyone else, for any offense. The offenses others may have individually made against me paled in comparison to the 18-wheeler-truckload I had committed against God. My father began to seem like a more regular person. He was just another broken individual, hungry for love and validation, exactly like me.

I started telling Louie and his parents, and then my parents and all the others, just how regretful I was that I had lived with him before marriage. I wasn't wracked with guilt; I just wanted others to know that I was sorry for that choice along with a few others. Many others.

I realized that my actions and my choices actually did influence others, and could either bless or mislead them...and I began to want to please God above all else in my life. As Mama had told me when I was so small, He knows it all. He sees. The God Who Sees. And He absolutely cares. But He also knows we're helpless without Him.

My enthusiasm must have shown because I was approached to be in leadership for the following year. But there were several stipulations. It was a significant time commitment and would involve an extra meeting to prepare to lead the class. I would be asked to show leadership by dressing appropriately and by forgoing almost all alcohol.

Whaaat?! I thought to myself. *That's ridiculous. NO ONE is going to ask me to wear a dress and I'm certainly not going to give up my cocktails.* This, in spite of the fact that I generally delighted in dressing up, and had cut way back on the drinking after moving to San Diego. I politely declined.

At the end of the class year, I heard women tell their stories of what God had done for them during the study. There was a companion program for the preschoolers where the kids were actually taught the same passage that the moms were studying. More than one mother shared that she had witnessed her child experience spiritual growth.

I was dumbfounded. Incredulous. Preschoolers can spiritually grow in an observable way? This sounded crazy, but I decided to take them at their word. It all added up. During the course of the spring, I had been told that the children's leaders were praying for more children so that their classes would be full. This had left me likewise amazed. What, pray for *more work*? Who would do such a thing?

Only people who really care about the work they are doing; who care more about helping others than about their own trouble. So at every turn, my worldview was being flipped by 180 degrees.

I realized I had no excuse for not giving my children the same opportunity. They were in elementary school. Their potential for growth was even bigger and the time for opportunity shorter. The following September, I transferred to an evening version of the same class so that Michael and Julie could come with me.

It was hell, at first. Initially, kids don't want to do such things and will work hard to resist. I had to bribe and cajole and bribe some more. We always hit the fast-food drive-thru on the way home for fries and ice cream.

But when they started learning all the details of the prophecies their attitudes changed. We started talking about blood moons and earthquakes at the dinner table, and pretty soon Louie was won over also. Even though the men's class met during Monday Night Football, in January of 1997 he signed up and it became a family affair. That's why God made VCRs.

The teacher of the women's evening class was also black and had a personality the size of Mt. Sinai. Her voice was like velvet and she wore colorful flowing ethnic clothes with chunky handmade jewelry. Her hair was closely cropped to her head. She was the epitome of style but with no haughtiness. She seemed to not be afraid of anyone or anything. She mesmerized me, like the fake clouds at Disneyland. But she wasn't fake in any way. Like the rabbi and the other Bible teacher before her, her heart was on fire. She never spoke in platitudes, she never sermonized, and she never moralized. She loved Jesus like no other. She was the real deal.

Halfway through the class year, she too invited me into leadership. Her invitation was perfectly timed; I had just watched a half-dozen shows on the History Channel with some really frightening (non-biblical) ideas about the end of the world, and I decided I had better make the most of what little time I had left. California might soon be underwater.

I tossed out my objections to the dress code and alcohol prohibition, and I had a new career for myself, albeit volunteer. The leadership meeting began at 4:55 every Friday morning, but it was fairly close to my house, so I took a big gulp and agreed to it. I bought a mini coffee pot for the upstairs bathroom, one black skirt, and I was good to go.

Taking this step changed everything. Fifteen years after becoming enamored with Jack Daniels, I began to lose interest. I discovered highs that were immensely more satisfying and did not leave me sickish the next day. I volunteered to teach classes at my church, beginning each one with the disclaimer, *I am not an expert on the subject but here's what scripture has to say about* _____. My crush machine, which had subsided dramatically after moving to San Diego, thank God, finally sputtered and ground to a halt.

Life itself became an amazing romance as I learned to observe God's hand at work. He is the source of prophetic dreams, inexplicable coincidences, and unexpected beauty. Month by month, year by year I grew up by growing down… discovering with childish wonder just how big and satisfying God is and how powerless I was without Him.

In the spring of 1998, the teacher asked if I would stay after class and speak with her. All through the class that evening, I dreaded the moment. I was certain that some kind of reprimand was forthcoming because I could think of at least a half-dozen job duties that I didn't do well (or at all). I comforted myself by repeatedly thinking *God disciplines those He loves. Nothing can separate me from God's love. Nothing can separate me from God's love. Nothing can separate me...*

Instead of a reprimand, she asked me to pray about serving as her substitute. It would involve giving the lectures in her absence and giving seminars on various aspects of Christian life. I told her on the spot *I don't need to pray; God already told me that this was to be. For years I have been waiting to meet my very own African-American mentor.*

After a few stunned seconds, she rubbed her eyes and breathed a big sigh. *This is such wonderful confirmation* she said. And thus I identified the woman I'd been waiting about six years to find.

That night following our conversation a terrifying and inexplicable noise awakened me from a sound sleep. I was sleeping with Julie (to avoid Louie's snoring) and about 2 am. there came a metal-on-metal banging from the dining room directly below. It sounded like a 300-pound man was slamming a pipe with a giant hammer. Even as my blood drained and skin turned clammy, I instinctively sensed that this was the point of the thing: for me to be afraid.

In the next split second, I starting telling myself *Do not be afraid. I will not be afraid. I will NOT be afraid.* Julie slept right through it, which confounded me; and after four or five rhythmic *wham*s it ceased, and I ran back into our bedroom. Louie had bolted upright in bed. *What the hell was that?* he breathed. *I have no idea, but I'm not going down there to see!* I blurted out, as I jumped in bed next to him. Neither would he; with taut muscles, we spooned up and eventually drifted off.

Michael had slept through it also. This we could not explain. But it all seemed indicative of a battle being waged in an alternate dimension. Whatever the case, I was impervious to it.

And so my responsibility in the class grew and changed and I tried to keep up with it. It was a happy challenge; the subject matter was infinitely engaging and the other leaders and women in the class were sterling.

When I was called upon to lecture, I stood before the 300+ women in the class in a church sanctuary that was sized for over 1,000 congregants. It felt very similar to the auditorium at Opryland; I believed that my college-days premonition was thereby fulfilled.

One spring day a year later, I was scheduled to give the lecture; my mentor was confined to home, recovering from surgery. I had just returned from taking the kids to school and picking up dog food. There was a female voice on my machine asking me to call Mama at a certain hospital number in Tennessee. I didn't think much of it; there were so many relatives who were of advanced age. I called the number and asked for her. *I need you to come to Knoxville right away* she said. *No problem* I assured her, still not thinking much about it. If Mama needed me to do that I didn't even care about the reason.

David is dead she informed me. He was 46.

Chapter 12

I'm grateful she didn't say *David passed away* or something euphemistic like that. He was dead as a doornail. Abruptly and permanently. The man who was healthy and vibrant and in love with his wife, who had just called me a few days earlier to wish me a happy birthday from the war-games camp near San Antonio, who had just six months earlier finalized the adoption of a seven-year-old girl who had been abandoned by her birth mother, was dead.

It turned out he wasn't so healthy. He had a swift, lethal, calamitous heart attack following a treadmill fitness test that was required of all the agents once per quarter.

No one had any idea that he even had heart disease. The physician at work had advised him multiple times to see a cardiologist. He had declined, probably out of fear of becoming disqualified for his job. His risk factors were horrendous. But nonetheless, an autopsy was ordered because no one could fathom what had taken him down within minutes of stepping off the treadmill. He had just completed an eight-minute mile.

I called my area supervisor for the class and told her the horrible news, and that I was trying to get out of town that same day so I could not deliver the lecture. Her words of response are still with me. *God has known about this day since before David was even born* she gently told me.

Within six hours I was on a plane to Knoxville.

This was a completely new kind of pain and I did not know how to deal with it. I ordered myself a Jack Daniels and Diet Coke, and then another, and then another. The flight was smooth and easy, and all I had to do was sit back and let the numbing effect of the whiskey do its job. I stared out the window at the straight horizon under ombre sunset colors and pondered how anything could be so normal, so serene and so beautiful under the circumstances.

As usual, Dad insisted on picking me up at the airport. I walked toward him knowing that the smell of the whiskey must be preceding me by a few feet. He gave me a hug and I let him. *God help us all* was all he could say.

For the funeral Dad decided to make the obligatory photo collage for the foyer of the church. Neither my mother nor I had the wherewithal to accomplish it, so we just let him. I dropped off a few photos at his house and chatted with him and Nancy about the service. She was irritable and frustrated, as were we all; in her case, it was over the content of the service. *What's all this stuff about Jesus?* she complained. *All I hear is Jesus, Jesus, Jesus. Isn't this supposed to be about David?* I couldn't bring myself to respond.

The collage was well-designed but there was one thing odd about it. Right in the center of the poster Dad had positioned a 5x7 of him shaking David's hand, both of them smiling and proud. They appeared to be best friends. Nothing could have been farther from the truth. If my dad believed that this was an accurate depiction then he was truly in a separate reality. Mama and I just clucked our tongues and shook our heads.

I was determined to speak at the funeral. I did not want to miss the opportunity to tell people the obvious in a sudden-death situation: *Get right with God. Take inventory. Would you go to heaven if you died without making amends with Him? How do you know?* I don't think the Presbyterian pastor was too pleased. Presbyterians are big on predestination. The Frozen Chosen, as earlier noted. He suggested that I should beware of exploiting the situation.

My lecture training for the Bible class had taught me to speak to an audience of One, and I didn't think He would mind if I prompted people to consider the consequences of spiritual procrastination. So I carried through with my message.

At the close of my speech I turned and stumbled off the small raised platform they had at the podium. Everyone gasped and the pastor jumped up to catch me. It wasn't necessary; I righted myself quickly and gave a thumbs-up. Lucy said it was like God printed my words on bright pink paper, jolting people to attention.

The funeral was strongly attended as is often the case in the death of a younger person, but maybe more so for a civil servant with a high-risk job. There were dozens of police officers and men in black suits wearing sunglasses. They were young and handsome, stoic and anonymous. They didn't smile or cry. They didn't bring their spouses.

Years later this scene was repeated for me when I attended the death of a helicopter pilot for the Drug Enforcement Agency. He had been a member of the fraternity where I ate the free meals. His chopper had gone down in Hawaii as he flew over marijuana fields. My brother's way of passage was less romantic but nonetheless in the line of duty.

I stayed with Mama as long as my family could do without me. We dragged out the sizable cache of slides and the projector. We spent hours and hours laughing at midcentury images of domestic life, while sitting on the Heywood Wakefield chairs under the midcentury cathedral ceiling.

A couple of years later we received notice that David's name would be engraved on a memorial for fallen peace officers in Washington, DC. The scheduled dedication and unveiling of this memorial was on Mother's Day, 2001. Mama, David's widow, and his two daughters all planned to be there for the event. I longed to join them but it wasn't practical for me to do so; I prayed for it anyway.

God answered with His usual creative flair: Louie earned a bonus trip from his company which just happened to be a trip to DC on that very weekend.

I had not been with my mom for Mother's Day since my college years, and to stand beside her for this somber event was an amazing gift indeed. This trip became a cherished memory for life.

The autopsy showed that David had had a previous silent heart attack and also had a congenital defect of a shortened aortic artery. His death almost certainly could have been prevented with proper attention from a cardiologist and lifestyle changes. Even sadder was the fact that his best friend from kindergarten was a top cardiologist in Knoxville.

At least, his death served as a big wake-up call for Dad and me to have ourselves checked out right away.

When the nurse called me with the results of my cholesterol screening I went silent after hearing the numbers. *Ms. Dillon? Ma'am? Hello? Are you there?* she said. I gave a little cough and tried to laugh to cover my dismay. I had to find a cardiologist pronto. When I did, I discovered that in addition to a frightening cholesterol count, I had this little-known protein factor, designated as Lp(a), in quantities that were literally off the chart. It's a genetic thing. Lp(a) makes the bad cholesterol more sticky and dangerous. It was a gloomy affair.

To get myself started down the path of responsible cardiac health, I decided to hire a trainer to design a program for me. Fortunately, the perfect person was readily available: the sports physiologist who had administered my brother's final fitness tests, and was by his side when he died, could do it for me.

He was a saint of a man and as kind and compassionate as they come. The evaluation process was a series of exercises that I was to perform to my limit. As he encouraged me to *Keep going, Janet! You got this! You can do this!* there was unfiltered advocacy in his voice. It was a foreign sound to me, coming from a male. It both startled and thrilled me that a man could and did believe in me, and was partnering with me to meet my potential. This fleeting moment left an indelible imprint. Something big was missing from my life.

David's cardiologist friend wasn't taking new patients at that time, but he agreed to take on Dad out of respect for my brother. Dad was immediately scheduled for triple-bypass surgery.

It turned out that years earlier he had seen a cardiologist in his new hometown, but had dropped out when his diagnosis came back grim. Dad said he didn't like that doctor. Supposedly he didn't communicate well.

Suddenly Dad and I had a common challenge and we discussed it frequently. Through the course of our conversations, I learned that his health had indeed been a source of frustration for Nancy. She nagged him constantly to exercise more. He had retired several years earlier and now spent most of his time running real estate errands for her. Her promptings seemed to be directly related to his resistance; I'm sure she took his lack of cooperation as disrespect. It was a battle of wills.

He had had rheumatic fever as a child which left him with a weaker heart and disinterested in physical exertion. As a young father he'd mow the yard and wash the car, maybe play catch with me, or badminton, or ride a bike on flat streets; but he much preferred to sing and perform, play the stereo, fix things, go to the baseball game, go to cocktail parties, and go to the movies. This drove Nancy crazy. She was a former smoker who was committed to exercise. When they golfed, he drove the cart. His health and advancing age were starting to spoil their party.

As years went by our croquet games at their house became stiff and labored affairs that Nancy often would skip if a call from work summoned her away. On more than one occasion we'd be in the middle of a game and find ourselves alone; she would disappear to work, and Dad, into the house to look for snacks. We'd be left to finish our game unaccompanied or to make small talk with Nancy's elderly mother. It was very tempting to jump in the car and take off for greener entertainment pastures.

When Dad and Nancy did remain, there was always the risk of a disagreement breaking out between them over some undone household chore or mishandled dilemma. Depending on the hour of the day and the amount of alcohol consumed, these confrontations could alert the whole neighborhood that something was amiss in their backyard. They yelled. Loudly.

The tenor of our summer visits to Tennessee after David's death changed in many ways both obvious and subtle. The gay afternoons on the lake were all in the past. Mama's crying jags in the evening on the patio returned. The House took on a strange heaviness.

The House became a place of sadness in general, and I started to believe that the days of joy within its walls were over. It made me anxious when I was there and I had trouble sleeping. Something was not quite right.

I would awaken in the night to see light coming from around the crack of my bedroom door; the lamp in the family room had come on by itself. I would close my eyes in disbelief, only to open them again and find that the darkness had returned. Once I was awakened by the sound of a female voice coming from the same area as the lamp. Often, when returning from shopping or errands, doors would be open or closed that were never, ever left that way. Including the door 12 feet up from the floor in the garage which led to an empty attic.

Once, while sleeping in a tank top and lightly covered with a sheet, I woke to what felt like an icy finger on my back poking the soft skin under my right arm. I began to read my Bible before turning out the light to sleep…if I turned out the light at all. And the Bible stayed open on the bed next to me. My prayers for protection were fervent.

It became very difficult for me to visit Knoxville, especially after Julie and Mike entered high school and my trips would occasionally be solo. But my commitment to Mama remained solid no matter what the prevailing atmosphere in the House. Our loyalty to one another was like cement.

A few summers after David's death Mama and I took a sentimental road trip to Cincinnati. We needed to see for ourselves if Grandma W's building *El Capitan* was still standing, waiting for princes to come calling. Indeed it was and it was remarkably unchanged. The paint on the rear of the building was still coming off in gigantic flakes; the carpet on the interior stairs was still the same wiry, scratchy hunter green; the lobby still smelled musty and of old wood; and the same black iron *6* was still affixed to their apartment door. How could it be, that the place was so unchanged after 35+ years? It was as if Dickens' Ghost of Christmas Past had transported me back.

And like Scrooge, this made me unspeakably melancholy. The weather mirrored my feelings. A tumultuous thunderstorm began raging and we had to park beneath an overpass for shelter while the worst of it blew through. Behind the wheel, I barely kept it together until we were safely in the hotel room. I opened the curtains wide and watched the electrical display while Mama slept. Then the dam let loose and uncontrollable sobbing followed, as I thought about how it had been and what might have been.

This episode was not cathartic, per se. It just helped me realize the magnitude of the loss. Dickens truly knew what he was talking about.

Back in San Diego, I was faced with the challenge of managing my newly-discovered health concern. Years before, when I hit my 39th birthday, I had started going to the gym on a regular basis, so at least I had that score in my column.

I soon became a nutrition Nazi. I eliminated ground beef and virtually all cheese and cream and started eating soy hot dogs. I took Niacin in gargantuan quantities because it was the only known treatment to lower Lp(a). When migraines set in I was forced to choose between discontinuing it or cutting my own head off. My friends were a great help in my efforts, demanding that waiters have cream sauces removed and forming prayer chains to see if God would take pity on me and reduce those bad numbers.

After Dad's surgery, he did well for a while. He tried a little bit harder to go for walks, but like his father before him, he never really submitted to any diet restrictions. Maybe it was because he had never been overweight. Bright red beef was his meal of choice, in any form: prime rib on a sandwich, filet mignon at a restaurant, or T-bones on the backyard grill. He always ordered rare beef if it was available. He was glibly oblivious to the connection between his eating and his bad heart. He also never heeded the prohibition against grapefruit for Lipitor patients. Citrus was a passion he would not deny himself.

Our new commonality softened my heart toward my dad. I began to listen to him more carefully. His faltering words were few but carefully chosen. After several years of his annual Thanksgiving visits, I gradually got a disturbing portrait of his domestic situation.

I recall a heart-to-heart talk with him once when we were strolling in Balboa Park. I told him that a relationship with God was the way to withstand the drama in his marriage. *You submit to God; He supplies the strength* I counseled. Dad stared into space blankly; he could not connect those dots in any way.

I couldn't explain why or how that works, or maybe I didn't want to. So I asked him *why do you agree to buy the wine for her—don't you realize that you're contributing to the problem?* More of the blank stare in response.

I had heard the term *codependent* but had no idea what it meant. All I knew was that he was far too willing to make trips to the liquor store every few days for a half-dozen or so bottles of wine. He also diligently recycled them, so he knew the rate of consumption. He was disturbed by it, but also seemed disinterested in finding a solution. It was not optional to not comply with his wife's to-do list. He had transformed into a step-n-fetchit employee, ironically repeating the role my mother had so dutifully played for him. The tables had truly turned.

In the summer of 2002, I was asked to consider taking full responsibility for one of the classes in the Bible study. This would involve recruiting and training all the leaders, and researching/writing a weekly 40-minute lecture for a class with over 120 members.

As had happened to me so many times before, I already knew the answer from a series of obvious events which pointed me in that direction. The foretelling had been so strong in this case I almost replied *I thought you would never ask,* but I didn't want to appear impertinent.

Louie had always been eager for me to pursue interests outside the home (maybe sometimes a little *too* eager, in trade for expanding his own independence), but this commitment would interfere with my ability to take a paying job while running the household. We decided it was a worthy sacrifice. I promptly accepted, believing it was an offer I was not at liberty to refuse.

The job, of course, came with stress and opposition. Recruiting leaders was a never-ending task. Upholding guidelines was often tedious; as noted, all people love the freedom and power inherent in rule-breaking. I was required to deliver lectures that were, above all, truthful. Truth can be very brutal. People often recoil from structure and truth, even in a voluntary setting.

The opposition was wide and varied. One time a class member was so incensed by an illustration I used that I wasn't entirely sure she wouldn't show up the next week with a pistol, ready to take me out. She was a political extremist. They were always trouble. She perceived that I had made a politically offensive comment; but she was the only one who heard it, I guess. I gave the class administrator and my area supervisor fair warning.

A (suspected) poltergeist developed in my kitchen, which banged cabinet doors intermittently. Domestic harmony got difficult to maintain. Dinner menus were noticeably less creative. My energy levels and availability were significantly lower. And so forth.

But the learning that it afforded me was like a banquet for my hungry brain and I was having a ball at this feast. The women in the class were mostly diligent, appreciative and gleeful in their discovery of the real Jesus. I got to weekly hear stories of God's work in their lives: bad habits dropped, relationships restored, guilt eliminated and joy prevailing in the midst of difficulties.

In the leadership group I was surrounded by women that were unselfish, curious, good-humored, and incredibly supportive. We knew an intimacy better than family. I was living what Jesus meant when he said *I have come that they may have life, and have it abundantly*.

Drinking and escapism were both becoming distant memories. I recalled with shock my former belief that *life without alcohol was not worth living*. But I had lived long enough, finally, to have so often seen the horrendous effects of it, both inside my home and out, that I developed a repulsion to it. (With teenagers around it was a distinct liability to keep Jack Daniels and champagne on hand. Well I remembered the easy access to alcohol of my youth). I didn't need to enhance or fantasize any experiences because life itself had become an enchanting adventure. I didn't want to miss even a single hour by not being clear-headed.

All the while Dad's situation was growing worse and he was rapidly declining. One night when my family and I had all been out for dinner we came home to a blinking light on the answering machine. I pressed the button and heard a horrible screaming match between a man and woman. It was just a snippet, so the actual words were indiscernible. But there was clearly violence in the tone of each person.

A pall fell over all four of us as we stood in our kitchen barely believing our ears. It was like a scene from a murder mystery. We played the message many times trying to figure out what and who it was. About the fifth time, the horrible truth sank in. It was Dad and Nancy. He had accidentally, or intentionally, pushed the call button for my number and never realized the answering machine had picked up. With this fly-on-the-wall glimpse, I was shaken to my core.

I'm sure that no one in the small town where they lived knew of the problem. They were the smiling senior couple working as a team to sell houses. In fact, Dad had told me of a pact they had made to never let the shouting occur in front of anyone or to tell anyone about it.

In the spring of 2004, David's daughter invited us all to her storybook wedding at The Citadel in Charleston, South Carolina, where her fiancé was about to graduate. The thought of going back there put a spring in my step. We had been there more than once during our trips to Myrtle Beach, and I knew it was a visual and culinary treasure. In fact, the thought of visiting any ancient coastal Southern city gave me heart palpitations.

In spite of the expected family drama associated with weddings—my brother's first wife was on her fourth marriage to her second husband (twice to my brother and twice to this fellow), and Dad and Nancy would be there also in the presence of my mom—we had no doubt that the charm of the occasion and the city would carry the day.

All was well throughout the ghost tour the night before, the ceremony itself, and the golf club reception. Military uniforms can make any wedding ethereal; this one was no exception. We danced and stayed up late, slapped the no-see-ums that bit our scalps as we ate and gazed fondly at the near-perfect couple. Julie made a beautiful bridesmaid; Mike chose to strike a pose or several in his black suit with matching black Converse sneakers. We plopped into bed exhausted but delighted by visions of David smiling from heaven and grateful that we had nothing scheduled for the next morning.

But the phone startled us awake around 7:30 am. I groggily answered. It was my dad. *Just calling to say goodbye since you aren't up yet!* He sounded rather cheerful. *We have to get on the road quickly to get to the rental house we're sharing near Kiawah Island.* What the heck?! I knew they were going on to another vacation spot, but I had not been told about any particular deadline.

I asked him about this apparent development. He said that Nancy was stressed out about arriving early to the destination so she could supervise the assignment of bedrooms. Dad, therefore, thought it best to pack up and hit the road. I thanked him, gushed over how great it was to see them and referenced our later upcoming summer visit to Tennessee.

We took our sweet time getting up and dressed and sauntered down to the breakfast buffet just before it closed, where we had a leisurely meal with the groom, who absolutely charmed me. I couldn't believe my niece's good fortune. But of course, they both were lucky to have found one another and be so apparently stable. Before the age of 17 she had moved houses at least 11 times with her mom, attending husband, and brother. Her mother was a bit hard to satisfy. At any rate, we finished up just before noon and headed across the parking lot to meet in the lobby and plan the day.

Imagine our surprise to see Dad standing at the back of his van, both rear doors open, laboring away arranging and organizing what looked like enough luggage to stay a month somewhere. I didn't have the heart to approach him. I let our earlier goodbyes stay in place. But I was seriously concerned over the discrepancy between what he had said and what my eyes were seeing.

We went back to our room, read magazines, drank coffee and chatted about how to spend the rest of the day. We settled on a boat ride on the bay. We would meet up with my sister-in-law and niece in the lobby at 2 pm.

Mama and I were a little early, so we found a comfortable bench where we could watch the tourists coming and going. After a few minutes the elevator opened, and out came Nancy with a luggage trolley filled completely up. There was enough stuff for five people. On the top were a pillow and comforter brought from home, and a makeup mirror balancing precariously on top of those. The mountain of stuff wiggled and teetered and threatened to come crashing down. She painstakingly inched it across the lobby directly in front of us.

We witnessed this scene like having front row seats to a play. We stifled our impulse to guffaw with laughter and instead formulated polite well-wishes.

These were to forever remain poised in our throats. She pretended not to see us. She wasn't feeling any humor. It was…awkward. As my mind connected the dots, my heart did a flip-flop for Dad as I recalled his chipper and hopeful voice from the phone call more than six hours earlier.

By 2006, Dad had been coming alone to San Diego for Thanksgiving for quite a few years. That year he had a slight change in plans. He moved up his arrival date to earlier in November because Nancy was going on a six-week cruise to the Greek islands. He had told me not to make any plans for activities because he wasn't feeling very well. I reassured him that we had no expectations or plans. I wasn't thrilled to have him underfoot for the whole month but also didn't have the heart to tell him not to come.

As usual, I was a few minutes late arriving at the airport, and so I immediately knew something was amiss when he was not at the curb with his suitcase. I circled the airport a few times and finally parked the car to go inside to search for him.

I found him standing at a pay phone breathless and exasperated. He said he had been trying to call me dozens of times because his cell phone battery was dead. He had left his bag unattended by the curb, being too weak to keep it with him. I rushed out immediately to grab it—hoping it was still there, and that the bomb squad had not been called in—scolding him all the way for not trusting me and being patient.

I suggested that we walk out to the car; he asked if I could get the car and come around for him. This alarmed me. He was definitely exhausted beyond the usual. I complied but with a measure of confusion; I didn't know whether to be irritated or concerned. Unfortunately I, like his wife, always felt that he didn't put out sufficient effort when physical exertion was required.

We made it home and through dinner and he excused himself early for bed. He was very lethargic the next day and by evening seemed troubled and still exhausted. I was up extra late preparing for an early-morning meeting, and when I went to bed around midnight he was sitting on the edge of the bed. Again I felt irritated—why didn't he just turn the light out and go to sleep? Were his former night-owl tendencies still active? I impatiently asked him *what's the trouble?* He said *I can't seem to breathe.* I silently diagnosed anxiety and disrupted circadian rhythms, and got myself to bed.

After my meeting the next morning I returned to an empty house. I found a note; Louie had taken him to Urgent Care. I went immediately to relieve him of duty and began what would be a day-long wait for resolution. The physician on duty told us *I need the hospital cardiologist to come in to evaluate your father's congestive heart failure.*

I had no idea that he had this and I scarcely even knew what it was. All I heard was the word *failure.* Failure equals death, right? Failure of the heart to pump. Failure to live. Failure to breathe and talk and laugh and get better, to take photographs and come to visit on Thanksgiving.

His condition was extreme fluid retention from a weak heart not pumping things around properly. He was basically drowning. He could not lie back in bed at my house because the fluid levels would rise and limit the capacity in his lungs. It seemed he had stopped taking his diuretic because it made him have to run to the bathroom too often. His mild incontinence could be awkward if he didn't make it to the bathroom in time. His body was massively bloated to the point of being life-threatening.

But he certainly didn't have a failure to rebel. When it was finally announced about 8 pm that he must be admitted to the hospital he began shouting. *There's nothing wrong with me that a few pills can't fix!* According to him, the doctors were fools and no way would he spend his vacation in the hospital. He said all this in his most intimidating of his bass tones. I was reminded of my high school dinner-table episodes, and in a more distant, third-person way, my Grandpa P's distrust of doctors and hospitals.

I had to think and talk fast before the nurses called Security as he tried to get up off the hospital bed. *Dad, these doctors are your friends. They're some of the best in the country. They're on your side. They accept Medicare.*

Janet Dillon

Miraculously his face softened and he sat back. His muscles relaxed. After thinking about it a few minutes, he let the nurse insert the catheter and off he went for however long it would take to extract the water.

His room had a stunning view of the blue Pacific which lay beyond the Torrey Pines golf course. He was in awe of it and in disbelief that he would deserve such luxury. More than once he asked me *Do they know I'm a Medicare patient?*

In the course of all this, we discovered another disturbing condition. His upper right arm had a huge open wound where the thin skin had been rubbed away. I had not seen the sore because he always wore long sleeves. There was no Band-Aid big enough to cover it all, but he had awkwardly tried to dress it left-handedly without help. This was an intentional secret.

He slept continually but I tried to be there for the moments when he was awake. I asked him about the arm wound and he said he had fallen on the carpet getting out of bed in the night. I was skeptical, so I pressed him. The doctor also pressed him, trying to establish if he had had a blackout. It was imperative to get to the truth for proper diagnosis and treatment. Finally, he disclosed that he actually had been pushed. It had happened over a week ago, but it was still gaping and oozing. I took a picture of it for future reference.

I called his office in Tennessee to let them know he was in the hospital. During the call I made quick friends with several compassionate and concerned co-workers. Two of them had given him a ride to the airport and had been in severe doubt about whether he would even survive the flight. They sent flowers and cards and subtly let me know that they were aware of his routine daily difficulties.

At the end of five days he was released to come home with me, 35 pounds lighter. And an arm wound that was way deeper than broken skin.

198

Chapter 13

And thus began a continual parade of healthcare workers to our house. A nurse came; a physical therapist came; a social worker came. My calendar grew full of Dad's appointments.

Weekly visits to a cardiologist were required. I asked this kind and patient doctor if congestive heart failure could be reversed. He answered in the affirmative and I suddenly had a new priority. I began measuring his food, daily tracking his sodium consumption and figuring out creative ways to make the fruits and vegetables irresistible. It was just a caretaking continuation for me after chauffeuring two kids for umpteen years and managing my own dietary situation.

We canceled his flight home. He was too weak to travel and we all agreed that he should stay as long as possible to recuperate, grow strong, and reap the benefits of this host of warm bodies working on his healing. At home, he would have been alone until Nancy returned from her cruise so that was out of the question anyway.

I called her cell phone and left a lengthy message explaining the situation so that she would know the full story immediately when she was within the phone service area. I told her about how he had arrived on the brink of death, about the 35 extra pounds of water weight, and about the neuropathy in his feet making it difficult to walk. We outfitted him with ankle boots and a cane.

He was a quiet and grateful house guest. His 80%-deafness eliminated extraneous conversations. He had long ago decided that it was much easier to live in an isolated state rather than continually ask for words to be repeated. And yet as quiet as he was, he would occasionally come out with some hilarious and keenly observant comments.

Once when we turned onto Gilman Drive in the UCSD area he suddenly and loudly proclaimed *Well I'll be damned! Gilman Drive! Named after the legendary Sid Gillman no doubt.* I thought he was nuts, and I'm still not sure if he was right, because of the spelling discrepancy. But it turned out that a certain Sid Gillman was the head football coach at the U of Cincinnati when Dad was there, and later led the San Diego Chargers to the AFL championship in 1963. So it's actually possible. I'll be damned!

He had never taken the time to watch cable TV in his former life of running errands and was unfamiliar with what it had to offer. I knew that there was much male-friendly programming so I turned him on to *Modern Marvels* and *Myth Busters* among others. In the days to come when I or Louie would ask what he had watched that day, he would say *well the History Channel of course!* just as if he had been doing it for years. It was adorable.

Mostly he was content to just be alive and have no one asking him for anything. He got used to our saying grace at every meal, including restaurants, and eventually asked to be the one to speak the words. He slept with an oxygen tank at night and dozed outside in the sun during the day. We lived in a cul-de-sac near a public trailhead where a park bench was installed by a neighbor. He spent hours on that bench, basking in the sun and pondering matters both deep and shallow. At one point he did tell me he needed to see an attorney. I knew better than to encourage that activity or even slightly be involved in it, because of the likely repercussions. The only irritation he really caused me was when he got hold of tools and dismantled things to improve their design.

One day when I was frantically working on my lecture for class that same night he came into the living room and planted himself in a nearby armchair. When his staring got the better of me, I asked him *What's on your mind Dad?* I needed to get the issue resolved and back to my task. *I can't figure out why you're being so nice to me* he replied, as he fingered the hairs on the top of his earlobe.

That was a no-brainer. *Because it's the right thing to do* I patiently answered. I could tell this did not compute. *It's the right thing to do. You're my father.* More blank staring. Eventually he left me to my work. It irritated me that he should ask a question with so obvious an answer. I couldn't fathom any other reason. Little did I know.

We scheduled him to return home a couple of days before Mom was to arrive on December 19. Under no circumstance would I allow him to be under the same roof with her. She was my longest friend; my time with her was too brief to be shared with him. Especially considering the history.

Before he left he was adamant that he should purchase some Christmas cards. He had a new urgency to contact people. He didn't specify what message he preferred but he wanted the artwork to depict *something religious.* He let loose a spate of indignation when such cards were hard to come by. *Good grief. Don't they know what Christmas is about?* This kind of talk was new to me, coming from him. I didn't quite know what to make of it.

During his first week back in Tennessee Dad was scheduled to see the cardiologist, an appointment that had been difficult to obtain. Before he arrived I had left updates on Nancy's voicemail, and she did call me with appropriate concern and gratitude.

But I'm not sure the seriousness of his condition really sank in. It seemed she had a schedule conflict with her hair stylist and she told Dad that he would have to skip the appointment.

Rather than call her and ask her *What the hell do you think is going on here?* I merely took matters into my own hands. I lined up Lucy to take him in, God bless her. I spent a good half hour on the phone giving her all the details on his status so that she could intelligently converse with the doctor. Only to have it all canceled at the last minute. When Nancy got wind that outside parties had been brought into the fray, her hair appointment was suddenly rescheduled.

I talked to him every few days but he didn't have much to report. He sat on his back patio when the sun was out and claimed that he felt pretty good. I asked him about his diet; *there are always plenty of frozen entrees* he said. *Loaded with salt* I thought to myself in response. My heart sank.

Then Christmas Day came around. I got a call from him around the middle of the afternoon, East Tennessee time. His tone was hushed. *I can't believe I'm in this hell hole. We came to see this friend of Nancy's, and she arrived at the door with her hair in curlers. On Christmas Day! Of all the nerve. The place is filthy. It smells like her dog. I'm calling you from a back bedroom. I need to get out of here.* He was angry, helpless and miserable.

I could not come up with any words of encouragement. I asked him about Nancy's kids and grandkids. She had three children, all local; I was confused that they weren't with at least one of them on Christmas Day. He said their tradition was to do Christmas Eve together. There had to be more to that story; I could never choose not to be with my mother on Christmas Day.

His next call came about a week later. He had resolve and hope in his voice. *I have my plane ticket now to return!* He was jubilant. I was completely shocked. I had not invited him back and I wondered what Nancy would have to say about it. *Well, I haven't told her yet* he said. Oh no. Not again.

After speaking to Louie we agreed that he would be welcome to come for as long as he wished. His recovery, health and possibly even his life depended on living in a stress-free environment. But this time around we would have to see about legal affairs such as Power of Attorney for healthcare and so on. Who knows how long this might turn out to be? What would happen if he died on my watch? Or became even more disabled?

The thrill of making secret plans must have been embedded in his DNA. Either that or his extreme aversion to conflict was to blame. His way was to just forge ahead with plans and decisions, bypassing the messy work of negotiating with a spouse. Then, by not looking back, he couldn't see the wreckage. It was a lifelong pattern.

He did it one last time, to me at my own house. And it would prove to be the beginning of the end for him. More on that shortly.

To paraphrase Abraham Lincoln, fooling people is only successful on a part-time basis. After making his arrangements for San Diego, Delta Airlines conveniently confirmed his flight information via email. The email address on file happened to be Nancy's. All hell broke loose. His return trip was in limbo. Threats were made.

By some miracle, Dad prevailed and he arrived here January 13, 2007, late in the evening. Dad and Nancy told all their acquaintances that he needed to spend the winter in my warm climate for his failing health.

We got right down to taking care of legal matters and also had a chat about finances in addition to resuming all the doctor appointments. Specifically, we needed to know what provisions were available for long-term health care. It turned out that he did not have any insurance for that and we started to get very nervous. Dad said *No worries! I've been advised that I'll never need that.* Come again? That was when we learned about the pension.

Turns out he had a sizable pension from his years of working for a government contractor. I didn't even know what a pension was at that point. Who would ever imagine such a thing? That your job would send you a paycheck—for life? And that when you died, if you left a spouse, your spouse would get the paycheck for the rest of her life? Who invents these things? And how can I get one?

So someone needed to inform Nancy about the necessity of changing Dad's checking account to San Diego so that if, God forbid, he had a stroke or some other calamity we would be able to pay the bills and know what funds were available. He wrote her a lengthy letter explaining the prudence of such a situation and assuring her that he would still send a monthly stipend to supplement her real estate income. It was sent by certified mail.

The next thing we knew Nancy had scheduled herself to come for a visit. Predictably she called Louie rather than me regarding a hotel. She also took his advice that a rental car would be valuable.

Louie agreed that we would bring Dad to the airport to meet her plane at 11:30 pm, even though I would have been up since 5 am that morning. But he drew the line at her request for us to lead them to their hotel, which was not close by. *Rental cars are well outfitted with maps and directions* he reassured her. *You'll be fine.*

Wrong, wrong, wrong. I could have warned him about the results of such a denial; Nancy received it as a direct insult. After I dropped Dad off at the airport to meet her flight, he and Nancy basically disappeared.

I had offered to give them daily tours of all the beautiful San Diego sights and he promised to call me right away to set an itinerary for the week. It was clear that *I* was not to call *him*, which I understood.

I waited and waited and kept my schedule empty. I tossed and turned at night. My anxiety and anger grew by the day. No call ever came. I was in disbelief that my hospitality and flexibility, and that of my husband, could be so blatantly disregarded.

A couple of days before she was to leave, he finally called to see if we could make dinner that same night. His voice was flat. I knew he was merely meeting an obligation. By that time I was so disgusted I could hardly take the call. I politely declined the offer. We were very busy.

He called me the next day and begged me to lift the black cloud that *I* had brought over their vacation. Ye gods!

My heart was broken. Again. She wanted nothing to do with us, not really; and my dad went right along with it. Not only did he not resist her, but he made it seem like it was *my* job to rectify the situation. She left town and we never saw her. But as soon as I picked him up at the airport, I did as I had done in my teenage years: I gave him a strong piece of my mind. *How could you do this to me?* I made sure he knew it was a personal offense. He offered no explanation at all.

I was wounded and angry but welcomed him back into our home without hesitation. Our relationship had evolved into the for-better-or-worse kind. I had to suck it up, dig down deep and come up with the love, stability, and tranquility he needed if he was to live to see another week or even day.

It's hard to believe that such a thing is possible and I wouldn't believe it myself if I hadn't been put to the test. There was a Power Source in me that was as strong and effective as it was mysterious.

It gradually came out that during Nancy's visit she had planted an idea: I might just have other motivations besides his welfare.

Realistically speaking, grabbing his money might have been a real temptation if the man had been worth much; after all, no one's motivations are completely above reproach. But there wasn't much beyond the pension, which I couldn't get in any case. Many years earlier Louie had assisted Dad and Nancy in setting up their IRAs and each had assigned their children as beneficiaries. Targeting his money was therefore pointless.

But there is a world out there of pay-back and retaliation. If I were inclined this way—say I was angry or power-hungry—I could set out to "steal" the pension by fomenting their divorce. And then assign myself a sizable monthly check for "rent."

Such ideas were foreign to me and beyond ludicrous. I was new to the world of inheritances and naïve about people who did such things. All my forebears had been working class people who had left only meager estates, if any at all. Plus, I did not see my dad as owing me anything; I felt blessed to have been fed, sheltered and to have had my college paid for.

I had to shrug off the whole episode as irrational and get on with helping Dad live and enjoy life. We fell into a happy routine as spring approached.

We rented an electric cart for Dad to get around the
neighborhood and the neighbors all came to recognize him and wave.
Daily he would take himself to the nearby shopping center to browse
and waste money on stuff. Burlington Coat Factory was a favorite
because he could tool up and down the broad aisles with ease. He
also grew fond of the tiny French bakery, Arely, where he highly
recommended the spinach salad.

When I asked Dad if he had told Nancy about all the fun on his
scooter, he looked at me wistfully and with big eyes. *Oh no, never. That
would not go over well at all* he shook his head. He could not let her
know that our home was in any way preferable to hers. Again, the
lack of honesty and twisted communication was all beyond my
comprehension.

For Presidents' Day weekend I decided to book a short trip for
us. He had mentioned several times wanting to ride on a train again
so I bought Amtrak tickets to take us up to Orange County. Julie
would meet us at the station for a tour of her college in Azusa. Then
we'd spend the night near Disneyland, take in some live jazz at
Brennan's, and take the train back the next morning.

Everything went just fine on the outbound trip. The scenery was
enthralling and letting someone else do the driving was a real treat for
me. I started to unwind. My in-laws joined us at the exit station and
the relaxation continued as we strolled around the compact and lush
campus of Azusa Pacific. It was when we drove south to Disneyland
that the trip itself began to go south.

Dad was quite weak and after the long afternoon he would need
a wheelchair to go even a modest distance. But the good folks at our
Downtown Disney restaurant insisted that they could not secure the
chair for us from Disneyland. The chair could be available upon
leaving the restaurant, but there were just too many no-shows for
them to have the chair available on the arrival end. We had no choice
but to be patient and deal with that.

Michael had driven up from San Diego at the last minute as a
favor to his grandma, Louie's mother. She had forgotten our

suitcases which she had kindly offered to manage. Because there were now six of us in the party, Julie and I walked to the restaurant from our hotel while my in-laws, Michael, and Dad drove. It was complicated. Tensions were running high. People were hangry.

It took Dad 30 minutes to walk the two blocks from the drop-off point to the restaurant. By the time the driving group joined Julie and me at the table, one of them blew a fuse and delivered me a scathing scolding for ever putting my decrepit father through such an ordeal. *What on God's greeen earth were you thinking? You are truly unkind and irresponsible!* Attempts by others to shush the outburst went unheeded. *How could you conceive such a tortured outing for your father? You should be ashamed!*

By now the whole table sat in stunned silence and others were starting to stare. I gritted my teeth and managed a meager explanation. *He asked me to bring him on the train. He wants to hear the jazz* I muttered as I choked down my appetizer. Dad, being nearly deaf and having detoured into the restroom, missed the whole encounter.

He was none the wiser as the music lifted him to his happy place and his tummy was filled with fried catfish. Dad's obvious delight, along with our intimate back and forth comments and chuckles (talking lips to ears, so he could hear) demonstrated how unfair my accuser had been. An apology did come by the end of the meal, but my night was nearly ruined.

I was an emotional wreck after the loud public rebuke. Fortunately, Julie and I held annual passes to Disneyland and could enter for a couple hours. After taking a half dozen or so spins on the Matterhorn, Haunted Mansion, and Big Thunder Mountain, I was relaxed enough to get some sleep. The fun of being tossed this way and that released my tense muscles.

The relaxation didn't last long. The next morning more drama ensued. Julie, Dad, and I had all agreed to be ready to leave around 10 to make the train. As Julie and I were dressing we called Dad's room to make sure he was up. The phone rang and rang, no answer. Perhaps he couldn't/didn't hear the phone, so I went and pounded on the door. No response. I called his cell phone; no response. I began to fear the worst. After 30 minutes of this, I called Security to come to open his door.

A uniformed guard packing heat came off the elevator. We had no idea what to expect in his room. My imagination ran wild, to worst-case scenarios. What if he were twisted on the floor in the shape of a pretzel, unconscious? Or lying peacefully on the bed with hands folded on chest, eyes staring into space? Or maybe he was in the bathtub stark naked, having slipped and died from a blow to the head. What if…?

The guard opened the door to…nothing. The room was empty.

Our theory B involved his wandering away from the hotel. So Julie and I took our bags and scurried aboard the elevator, heading for the car.

As the door opened onto the crowded lobby, there was Dad standing in the middle facing the elevator doors, fingering the top of his earlobe. He rolled his eyes and shook his head. He impatiently demanded *Where the hell have you been?* and proceeded to publicly chew me out. For the second time in 24 hours.

He had defaulted to the procedure he always used with business colleagues; they all knew to meet in the lobby at an appointed time. He couldn't understand why I didn't know this. Evidently, it was all my fault.

As relief flooded over me, my knees went weak and I had a sudden urge to throw up. The effort to hold that in caused me to not hear much of what else he said. He was oblivious to the fact that he had just been brought back from the dead. He only backed off the blaming when I looked him straight in the eye and said *You don't understand. We thought you were dead. DEAD!* We all went to the car in silence.

Toward the end of March more trouble was brewing, completely unbeknownst to me; although I did regularly hear loud conversations coming from his bedroom. It was tax time and Nancy had not dealt single-handedly with the tax preparer in the 19 years of their marriage. She was a damsel-in-distress. From the confines of my garage, Dad arranged a return trip to Tennessee.

Despite the train trip fiasco, he was in denial about his frailty and lack of independence. When he announced his departure date to me I had a near meltdown at his lack of wisdom. *If you leave you will not be invited back* I told him. *It's just too complicated, Dad, to get all the legal documents adjusted and to lose the continuity with your doctors. Besides, your health just isn't strong enough. You probably wouldn't survive the return trip.*

He looked at me with shock and disbelief. This possibility had not occurred to him, even though Nancy had told him to expect my resistance. But he believed, again—and would up until he drew his last breath—that he could control the outcome of any situation through carefully chosen words and crafted explanations. Truth was just a secondary issue.

I stood my ground. If he left this time he would not see San Diego again.

He could not believe that anyone would be so unreasonable. The day of this confrontation he dragged the small desk chair out of his bedroom and planted himself in the middle of the hallway. I had been dressing to go teach the class and his scheme was to block my path. He said nothing as I wiggled my way past him but I got the message. *It's not going to work Dad. You will not be coming back if you leave.*

It was our ultimate showdown. Secretly I was praying with all my heart that he would stay.

On April 3rd, 2007 he left. I advised his wife of the severe back pain he had developed the day before leaving, and made sure the cardiologists here and there were in sync.

He wasn't long at home. He had to be hospitalized within 10 days of returning. From there it was determined by the professionals involved that he should not be left alone in the house, so he was moved to an Assisted Living facility. I felt certain that the arm wound incident had been conveyed to the Tennessee doctors back in December. Because of his poor memory, probably the result of reduced oxygen to the brain, he was placed with Alzheimer's patients. I knew for a fact that he did not have dementia.

As Dad reported these developments to me from Tennessee he always maintained a cheerful, upbeat attitude. He didn't want me to worry or feel sorry for him. He emphasized how hard Nancy had worked to make sure he was in a comfortable place. He talked about how nice everything was, how good the meals were, and how fun all the activities.

He proudly told me about an incident when he was with a busload of the residents and they stopped at a Cracker Barrel restaurant for lunch. It seems that he stood up suddenly and before the group could disembark, he made an announcement. *I'd like to say grace for everyone before we go inside!* And offer grace he did.

This was definitely not the man I grew up with.

Even though his contentment seemed quite sincere, I suspected he also didn't want to hear me say *I told you so*. I would not have done that, but there was plenty of cause for concern.

No one helped him hang the pictures in his room. No one helped him with the iPod Shuffle I sent for Father's Day loaded with all his favorite music, including *Time Out*, Ramsey Lewis and BB King. When Lucy heard about this she drove the 30 minutes to take it out of the package and turn it on for him. She said a huge smile broke out on his face. When he was left alone on his birthday in May, David's widow came through with a cake and gifts.

When he figured out how to exit the Alzheimer's ward just to sit on the porch rockers and watch the sunset, he was abruptly moved to a lockdown facility.

I went to visit him in August and again in October when the foliage was at its peak beauty. I picked him up and we took mini road trips to the Smokies and across I-140, which meandered past lakes and rolling hills. We shared a meal or dessert and coffee, often in silence. I took David's older daughter to see him and we sang hymns in the car to an Alan Jackson CD. I hung his pictures for him and we took selfies. He was always pleasant and affectionate.

But during these visits, he had traces of melancholy. There was something he wanted to say but couldn't. He kept a small paper pad and pen in his shirt pocket to assist his memory, like a good engineer. But this was not a memory issue. There seemed to be tears always just below the surface. Tears of regret, I thought. Months before, when I was so angry over his choice to leave San Diego, I had asked him if he realized what he had forfeited in his younger days, when he left my mom. *Mistakes were made* had been his only response.

One day in October we stopped near Townsend at a diner for lunch. It had dingy lace curtains, shabby carpet and other décor which could not have been touched in decades, but it was bustling and the patrons were jovial. He asked me if I had come just to see him since I had never before come to Knoxville during that month. *Yes, Daddy.* He stared at me blankly.

He ordered a fried fish sandwich and I did likewise. It was over-breaded and greasy but he made little groans of satisfaction as we ate. It was a mediocre meal in a dreary place but it brought unspeakable joy to us both. This irony pressed on my heart and my own tears could not be restrained. They came streaming but I made sure he didn't see.

He lingered long at the door when I said goodbye that day. He was softly smiling and didn't want to let go of my hand. I smiled back.

As the holidays approached my anger was again aroused when I discovered that he was left alone on Thanksgiving. He pretended it didn't matter, but how could it not? Virtually all of the other residents were picked up and taken away by their families. He never complained, even slightly; he simply told me the truth when we talked that day.

I left a voicemail for Nancy at home respectfully asking her to please let me know when she couldn't attend to him for holidays so that I could arrange for someone else to be there. I was seething but I did not let it show in my voice. I knew it would be counterproductive and possibly even backfire on him. But I did want her to know that it

211

did not go unnoticed and that there were more than a few other people who cared about him.

During the days at my house I had witnessed his great frustration when I handed him a stack of photos; it overwhelmed him and he would set it down when he thought I wasn't looking. So for Christmas, I sent him one of those electronic gadgets that displays photographs digitally. It could easily be hooked up to the TV so that viewing the photos was like watching a TV show.

The gadget worked like a charm. I had enclosed a note for the staff with simple instructions. The day after Christmas I got an elated phone call. I was in the coat department of Macy's with Mom, shopping for bargains. When I saw his number on caller ID I prepared my gentle excuses to keep it short. *Janet! Great. So great.* His speech was halting. He couldn't form sentences. *Enjoy! Wonderful.* Then the aide took the phone. *He is SO delighted!* she translated. *He wants you to know how much he's enjoying the photos.* I assured him that I would call back very soon when I was in a quieter place.

It never happened. On Saturday morning December 29, 2007, Nancy called me to report he had not awakened for breakfast. He was deeply in a coma. Sunday morning, while we were singing hymns and hearing God's Word from the pulpit in San Diego, in Tennessee he died. He had suffered a stroke in his sleep.

But his story wasn't quite finished.

Chapter 14

The day of Dad's death coincided with Louie's birthday. The usual celebratory dinner was planned with the extended family but Mom and I begged out. We couldn't be jolly or make small talk. Instead, we took ourselves to a lowly Mexican diner and loaded up on cheese and warm tortillas. We didn't have much to say. There were no tears; just silence and reflection.

We gathered up our most dignified clothing and prepared for single-digit weather in East Tennessee. Mom had been scheduled to stay much longer in San Diego, but we all five flew back to Knoxville together.

The funeral was on January 2, 2008. I don't recall speaking to Nancy at all after the news that Dad had died. She must have called to tell me about the funeral; her pastor contacted me to read scripture in the service. Of course, I was pleased to do so. Beyond that I was not consulted nor told about any part of it except where we were to sit.

When we arrived at the church we met with Nancy and her family in a parlor near the sanctuary. There were the usual friendly introductions. Nancy received my sympathy with polite aloofness.

I had no idea what had become of my dad's body. Would it be in an open casket in the church? Closed casket? Ashes in an urn? Turned out he had been cremated, but there was no evidence of that in the service. I felt just a little bit cheated, and I was too docile to ask about it. I suspected her opinion of me was full of spite and suspicion.

The Episcopal church was filled. In small towns in the South if you even remotely know the family you show up for weddings and funerals. The service was sedate and standardized. I got up to read scripture and sat down again. The pastor spoke of what others had told him about Dad: that he had sung in the choir during earlier years, and a couple of other forgettable verities. He made no bones about the fact that he didn't know my father and said *Because he was an active member of our congregation we will conclude that he is now with the Lord.* Wow. OK.

No testimonials were given nor were they invited.

The reception afterward at the church was fairly pleasant. We took some great family photos. Mom and I got reacquainted with my brother's first wife, the red-headed nurse, who would soon be diagnosed with a large brain tumor and die. I saw the physician who was Dad's General Practitioner and with whom I had had my first official date in the tenth grade. I made some simple conversation with Nancy's children and met her siblings and their wives, but no real emotional connection took place except with one group: the other realtors with whom Dad had worked.

They were compassionate and determined to know me. They all seemed very intent that I should know how much they admired and cared for him. To a person, they spoke of mourning his life. I read between the lines that they had seen him as a tortured soul without many options, who had now gone on to a much better place.

Before leaving the reception we made a date with Nancy and her family to get together the next morning for a late breakfast. Then Louie, Mom and I and all the grandchildren went out to dinner. We were reminiscent without being morose and passed photos around, telling jokes and anecdotes.

The next morning we received a call from Nancy's sister-in-law saying several of them were ill and the breakfast was canceled. No alternate plans were made or suggested. I later left Nancy a voicemail requesting the tiny iPod Shuffle and the photo player, and asking if she could meet me at the airport with these items. I later thought the better of laying any claim to anything of his and I canceled that meeting. Plus, I didn't want to feign any more friendship with her. All this was accomplished via voicemail.

During these events Louie had contacted the investment company which held Dad's IRA to request distribution, thinking that I was the beneficiary, as had been determined when the account was opened. He was told that I was no longer the designee. This meant that I had not inherited even a red nickel from him. I wasn't so much surprised by this as I was curious about how it had come to be so. It was just not like his personality to do such a thing.

But of course, there was only one answer. He had been instructed to do so.

The next night we gathered at the House for carry-out fried chicken. Before eating we stood in a huge circle in the awkwardly-shaped family room beneath the redwood beams and before a roaring fire to say grace. It was a sweet moment in which we briefly forgot that the circle wasn't unbroken. We had transcendence; the missing parties seemed very close.

The fire almost didn't happen, but not for lack of kindling or know-how. Mom had blocked the chimney long ago with an aluminum plate stacked with bricks on it to keep birds from nesting. Someone would need to walk over the barely-sloping roof to do the job. She came unglued. *NO!! No way!! The house will burn down and we'll all die! Please stop! Stop!* She was panic-stricken over the thought of a fire in that fireplace. Did she remember the struggle in that first winter? Was she spooked by her sister's raging chimney fire a few years before? While I was trying to calm her with logic, my niece skipped up a ladder and took care of business. The flue was opened, the fire lit and the ambiance in the room was complete.

We pulled out the pop-up screen and ancient slide projector to review my dad's life during the 25 years they were married. We howled with laughter over the Christmas cards taped to the wall of their first house and Mom's red-haired wig on Mr. Flaherty at the first cocktail party. We laughed and cried and unwittingly purged much of the pain residue from my dad's dishonesty.

It seemed that at that event the House was cleansed also. I never again felt uncomfortable there nor witnessed anything inexplicable. No more lights in the middle of the night or heavy atmosphere, icy fingers or female voices.

The House had finally matured into the domicile it was intended to be.

Several weeks after the funeral one of Mom's friends was playing bridge with the choir director from Dad's church. He let it be known that my father's ashes were unclaimed in a cabinet there. It must've been causing some buzz. By June, they hadn't been disturbed and no word had come from Nancy about any plan to have them interred, scattered, enshrined on the mantle or otherwise disposed of.

Enough was enough. By default, it became my job to plan my Dad's Scattering Event. I was utterly clueless, but how hard could it be? I thought of the type of ash that one cleans out of a fireplace or grill, and concluded that it should be easy to disperse them and make them disappear into the earth. As scripture confirms, *Ashes to ashes and dust to dust*. Right? I was not about to leave my Dad to languish in the church office underneath someone's work counter or in the chapel.

I picked a date in July and designed an amiable and innocuous event. I sent invitations to Nancy, each of her children, my nephew and niece, and David's widow. I mentioned something about the business at hand and also the provision of a picnic lunch. I asked for RSVP's of course for food planning.

As I expected, I did not get any response from Nancy or her family, except for her son's wife who was known to be a gracious and well-mannered woman. She left a voicemail with her regrets a couple days before the event.

When her call came through I chose not to answer, not wanting to force her into an awkward conversation. We both knew Nancy's temperament. I knew she would understand the position I was in because of her mother-in-law's abdication of responsibility. It would be difficult for me not to mention that, but in very poor taste if I did. So we understood one another without direct communication. I felt a twinge of compassion for her.

Everything about this situation was awkward, but even I didn't know how awkward it would become before it was over.

My nephew and niece, her husband, Mom, Lucy and I gathered on a gray, rainy, humid day to make our sentimental tour to a couple of Dad's favorite places to leave his ashes at each. We started with his walking park and then headed up to the Smokies toward Metcalf Bottoms, where we had had a dozen or more picnics with my children. We stopped in Townsend for lunch at the same diner where I had last eaten with him.

The only problem we encountered was the gravelly texture of the ashes. These ashes were not at all what I expected and were just not going to behave themselves and return to the earth unnoticed. I became stressed over their conspicuous nature, along with the thought of the possible trauma for unsuspecting passersby who might see our activity and be forever robbed of an unadulterated recreation spot.

I had growing angst about the whole affair. *I think I'm going to be sick* I announced as I was working my way to the bottom of the bag.

You do realize this just might not be entirely legal my niece's husband diplomatically observed.

I stopped dead in my tracks. The need for a permit for such things had never occurred to me. Why would it? I'd never been through this before, to know that's one of the details funeral homes cover for their clients.

Now I was also a criminal. On top of everything, this could just not be happening to me. I could feel an imaginary movie camera zooming in on the debilitating horror on my face. In my head, I let out a scream the likes of which has not been heard since Hitchcock's

Bates Motel. I set the bag down on a picnic table and slumped onto a bench in a state of shock and horror.

The younger generation came to my rescue and took care of business. They unceremoniously released Dad's ashes into the waters of the Little Pigeon River flowing about 20 feet away from me. I limped back to the car shaken but relieved. I had not wanted a burial at sea, but it seemed like the only decent option left. I was certain Dad would not have minded.

The whole episode was unnerving but satisfactory. It left me shaking my head at the idea of a wife not wanting to be involved in this informal semi-ceremony. But I will give her this: at least Nancy had saved us a trip to the church to pick up the ashes. The way we came into possession of them was...convenient, if not shockingly bizarre.

A few days before traveling to Knoxville I received a strange call from Mom. *Janet, there's a box on the dining room table for you. It came in the mail. I'm not certain what it is, but I think I know. It's really heavy. It's from Nancy. I'm not going near it.* Ye gods, can she really have done this unthinkable thing? Send my dearly departed father through the US mail?

Yes, she could and she did. Dignity be damned.

The crowning touch—a gloriously ironic, hilariously awful detail—was that she had used her real estate business card, complete with her lovely smiling photo, for the return address. This was what Mom saw first when she found the box by the front door.

So there was my dad, finally brought full circle back to his modest masterpiece, his architectural work of art, sitting atop the Heywood Wakefield Dogbone dining table with his second wife's portrait smiling up from the Priority Mail, free-with-shipping box in which he was interred.

Chapter 15

When I saw the box with his remains in it I silently vowed that I would never put my family through such an ordeal. Incidentally, Nancy also had deposited a well-worn red suitcase on the front porch sometime in the weeks before, which held various photo albums from Dad's interim singlehood, his high school yearbook, and the cremated remains of his mother. We scattered Grandma W along with her only son, which hopefully reassured her greatly. It would seem neither Nancy nor Dad knew quite what to do with a family member's remains.

Life went back to normal for a few years. Mike and Julie graduated from college and Julie took a teaching job in China. Mike stayed in San Diego, also teaching for a charter school. I continued teaching the Bible class and loved every minute.

Several times I met Mom in March in Savannah. We went there first in 1999 after reading *Midnight in the Garden of Good and Evil*; we wanted to see what all the fuss was about. The city fully lived up to its hype and entertained us in grand fashion. I continued going to Knoxville in the summer; we always made the side trip to Myrtle Beach. My travels with her are among my most beloved memories. She was my best friend.

In 2010 my next parental challenge developed. My mother started lying to me in shocking ways. At least that's what I thought it was. Once when I caught her doing this I let out a stream of ugly expletives. Within a few hours, I was overcome with shame and phoned her back to apologize. I braced myself for the well-deserved reprimands, but she didn't remember a word of it. I knew then it was a completely different problem. What I thought was intentional deception actually was her faking her way through.

During my summer visit I tried to suggest that she keep a journal for things she couldn't remember. She chuckled in mockery at such a silly idea, saying that keeping a diary was my thing, not hers. This was big-time denial. I was frantic and didn't want to leave her; after my return to San Diego, I called her every day. Fortunately, I had an autumn visit planned to attend my nephew's wedding reception. I persuaded her to come back with me for an extra-long Christmas visit to avoid the cold.

I received quite a shock when I arrived at the end of October. She had lost 30 pounds. She could only eat Chunky Soup and saltines. Her recliner was full of cracker crumbs.

I had to surreptitiously prepare the House for possibly being put on the market from California. I organized, purged, packed and donated stuff trying not to be noticed. I would put some kitchen item away; she would complain *why did you put that there? That doesn't go there.* It was imperative that she not realize that she might not return; this would certainly cause her to dig in her heels and refuse to leave. I was a nervous wreck. Duplicity is just not in my comfort zone. After all, God knows the truth and He doesn't let me lie easily.

On top of all that, to leave this house vacant was like leaving my firstborn child at daycare and not going back to pick him up. I tried to tell myself that many people in the world owned second homes in distant cities and it would be fine. But I guess I'm just too bourgeois. I called upon my closest friends in the neighborhood (for whom I had diligently babysat as a teenager), and they were more than willing to keep an eye on the place and water the plants. The wife said she might love to use it as a reading retreat. Mom was deeply loved and guarded in this neighborhood. That, along with the high visibility of the House, gave me the needed confidence to actually lock it up and walk away. For good measure, a group of us prayed over it before we left.

Mom was soon diagnosed with a treatable non-Hodgkin's lymphoma. During the IV-drug treatment ordeal it became clear that she also had dementia. She was 86. I went to the Alzheimer's Foundation website and reviewed the 10 warning signs; she was almost a textbook case.

This confirmed that she would need to live in San Diego permanently and the House would need to be sold. I was stricken with grief and nostalgia. But I had a husband willing to take her in and also a spare bedroom; Louie was fully compliant with the idea and I was beyond grateful.

When Julie returned from China nine months later we had a full house. In the summer of 2011, she and I made the arduous journey back to finish the purging. Mom had not been a packrat at all, but almost 50 years in a house does create a stockpile. I also needed to find a trustworthy realtor.

My first contact was Nancy, thinking she would want to represent her husband of nearly 20 years' earlier accomplishment. Also, I wanted to show her that I had no hard feelings; but she never responded to any of my communications.

There was a realtor in Mom's neighborhood and I set an appointment with him for early in our visit. As he approached the house, he saw an exercise bike on the porch to be picked up by the charity truck. *Oh! It looks like you're into working out! I have just the equipment you need* and he launched into his sales pitch.

I was speechless. He had not even mentioned my parents' distinctive and beautiful House.

I couldn't believe he wasn't fawning over the place. I politely walked him and his wife around and they pointed out some necessary fixes. Then he commenced his lecture on starting low with the sale price. *You've got to strike while people are excited! You mustn't lose that crucial opportunity!* I pretended to listen but only heard my instinct which was shouting *don't make a commitment...there's no need to rush into anything*. I thanked him and told him I would be in touch.

Julie and I worked ourselves into near exhaustion daily but reserved the late evening hours for watching the first season of Downton Abbey. The cable service had been disconnected, of course, so we were confined to DVDs. No one needs cable when Downton Abbey is available on DVD. The costumes! The sets! The manners! The human frailty on parade within the grandeur of a fabulous ancient mansion! It gave us the inspiration and mental break needed to keep going.

I started to ponder the ability of a house to inhabit human lives and help shape their destiny.

When the work was complete and we left for San Diego, Lucy took a realtor friend over to see the House. This realtor was as unimpressed as the first fellow and suggested I open with a price just under the appraisal value. When I gently resisted she replied *well maybe you should put it up For Sale by Owner* knowing full well how difficult this would be from San Diego. She didn't want to be bothered. But before she disconnected, she shared some useful staging tips which proved to be very handy.

We didn't have enough time to complete the cosmetic work, nor did we even know where to start with it. But the deep slump in the housing market made it advisable for any property to show like a movie set, so one more visit to Knoxville was warranted at least. The next available travel date when I could garner a helper was the following March. Louie would come with me and this time I *had* to find a realtor.

Throughout the winter months, I was dogged by my dilemma. How in the world would I find this perfect realtor, long-distance, who would appreciate the style and intelligent design of my father's House? Time was ticking by. Any day now a meteor could land on it and demolish it. Halloween vandals could permanently deface it. My mother could have a stroke and need long-term nursing care which the House must finance. Aunt Martha and her husband were growing louder in their criticism. *That house should have been sold months ago! Months!* My prayers grew desperate. I was empty-handed and frustrated when late one night the solution virtually dropped into my lap.

About midnight I was idly thumbing through a file of Mom's miscellaneous clippings. *How to remove hard water stains; 101 Uses for Vinegar; Complete Handbook for Lower Back Pain; A Rancher Revolution?*

Whaaat? Stop right there. Here was a clipping from a community newspaper, with the fresh-scrubbed face of a young man attached to an article about the same architectural style as the House. The author, who was a realtor, showed enthusiasm and good knowledge of his subject. He was identified as a historic home specialist. I had never heard of *midcentury modern* but his descriptions were exactly like the House. The date on the clipping was April 14, 2008, just before the dramatic real-estate bust. It would be a miracle if he were still employed in that field. It also happened to be my birth date. I saw it as no coincidence that I found this clipping.

The next day I left him a voicemail; after a few anxious days we connected. He had returned to graduate school for a new career but his real estate license was current, and he was delighted that I had responded to the three-year-old article. You just never know. We talked for over an hour and made a plan to meet in March.

Louie and I braced ourselves to get a few weeks' worth of work done in six days. When we arrived, we set about further purging and packing, painting and hoping for some much-needed direction from a realtor who would become our business partner. When he eventually came we had a great rapport, as expected, and I breathed a big sigh of relief, knowing that with his expertise the rest of the work would more or less fall into place.

When Scott first came in he was like a kid in a candy shop. He slowly went from room to room taking in every detail. He pulled out his phone and started snapping pictures. He pointed out details to me that I had never given a second thought, like little holes in the light fixtures and the period fabric of my mom's bedspread. He exclaimed over the cabinet handles on the built-ins of the kids' bedrooms, brushed nickel drawer pulls and even the atomic motifs on the plastic wastebaskets. The intercom and clothesline in the laundry room also amused him; I was sad that he couldn't see the built-in kitchen wall phone with a retractable cord (very modern but a real pain trying to talk in the other room with the cord constantly pulling you back). He went into near ecstasy when we went outside and he saw the underground trash system with flip-open lids operated by foot pedals. *There were no leash laws in those days and dogs would turn over the trashcans* I patiently explained. Incidentally, this system also worked against raccoons. In his own words:

> Many stored images flooded my mind the first time I came around to the driveway and saw the house to the left. I remembered the midcentury home of the Brady Bunch and period homes I had studied or been exposed to in general. If it had only been an empty shell, it was such a fine period example that I could easily mentally paint what the interior should be. It did not disappoint.
>
> I was excited from my first approach by the double entry doors, then the foyer flooring, then the lighting, both hanging and natural. I was in sensory overload and didn't know where to look next. With each new area, corner, and fixture I remember being thrilled that it was so well-preserved and true to the period. Unexpected goodies came flying at me: the hanging lamp in the workshop which could be manually raised or lowered for detail work; the underground trash can bins; the retractable clothesline in the laundry room; the intercom system between kitchen and kids' bedrooms; and the Hi-Fi in the living room with large wooden speakers which I imagine filled the house with great background music during parties.
>
> The modern flow of the floor plan was truly inviting. The simplicity of the house, the overall unobtrusiveness of the whole design allowed me to notice such small details as perforated spotlight covers. These minor details are now seen as very important to the correctness of a period home. Standing in a nearly unmolested, midcentury modern home allowed me to almost immediately feel at

home and welcome. I felt like I was on the set of *Mad Men* and wished I were in a polyester suit with slim tie!" *Scott Hendrix, REALTOR*

He was going to be a tremendous help, but I didn't know exactly how much help until one magical, epiphanic moment.

The garage needed painting, desperately. The main wall facing the outdoors was dingy white; the opposing side walls were still the original orange from the early 70s. We were preparing to paint it all white when Scott vehemently intervened. *Oh no! You need to leave it exactly as your dad designed it.* He was respectful but adamant.

My brain came to a screeching halt like a phonograph needle dragged suddenly off the record. Thoughts were suspended for several moments while I took this in. *The way my dad designed it. My dad…designed it.* My dad…with my mother's help, but *he* specifically, had created a House that a historic home specialist not only appreciated but wanted to preserve. My dad. Daddy.

What happened next was not cerebral. It was absolutely emotional and probably even spiritual. What had been mere head knowledge all my life flowered in my heart as respect and even awe. What had been completely obscured by my pain was unveiled and came into full view.

Suddenly I connected the distinctiveness and beauty of the House with my father's total person: his soul, his talents, and his taste…his love of the design process and architecture; his sense of style seeking its ultimate outlet; his determination to bring grace and beauty to middle-class life and to do it within his means. All with my mother as his muse. He had had a vision and he made it happen; he had put a pencil to drafting paper and turned a dream into a brick-and-mortar reality.

Whatever measure of pride and exhibitionism had been involved now faded to the background. God had been working in him with or without his acknowledgment.

At that moment my father became a man worthy of not just my love but my honor. A fully honorable man.

225

To behold and admire the creation is to love the creator.

My emotional attachment to the House started fermenting. I wrestled with the thought of selling it and could find no peace. But it was just not practical for me to try to keep it. It needed to be occupied and enjoyed. One thing I knew for sure: I would not sell it for the appraised value which was $180,000. We would list it at $225,000 and if it didn't sell for that, so be it. I would not undervalue this treasure. Scott was hesitant in spite of his enthusiasm but ultimately cooperated.

Louie and I left for San Diego. I reserved my goodbyes for the day when it was actually sold.

After returning to California I had in mind to find a gift for Scott to show my appreciation, which I would save for after the closing, should there be one. Browsing in the gift shop of the Museum of Art, I almost came undone when my eye fell upon a gorgeous coffee table book. *Atomic Ranch* by Jim and Michelle Gringeri-Brown nearly leaped off the shelf and into my hands.

I grabbed it, and randomly flipping it open, I took a big gasp. There was a photo of the green American Standard toilet from my mom's bathroom. *Ye gods* I thought to myself. Even the commode is period-appropriate. I flipped more pages and there was the Heywood Wakefield dining room set. My heart was pounding and I went to pay for the book immediately. I was so emotionally overwrought I almost forgot to ask for my member discount.

The photo of the toilet put me right over the edge. I had a serious problem. Day and night I wrestled with the question *How can I keep the House and also sell it? How?* Naturally, I prayed the question, and the answer came in words so distinct it was, again, almost like hearing a voice. *You write a book about it* I heard.

And then I remembered my long-ago premonition, received in December of 1995, about writing a book. *Can it really be possible? Are You sure about that?* I responded. As if.

Three days later I met a good friend for coffee. She was in the leadership group I supervised for the Bible class. I was bending her ear about the whole finishing process with the House in Knoxville and how it had made me come to fully love and appreciate my father. Her eyes got very big and she leaned in over the table. I had not mentioned any prayers or premonitions or inaudible voices. *You have to write a book about this* she insisted. *I can't tell you how important this is.* Later she would tell me that the compulsion to share that information seemed to come also from an inaudible voice compelling her to speak up. So then I unpacked the whole long story, never being one to keep my mouth shut when there's a story to be told.

Several days later she came to class and asked me for some exterior photographs of the House. A few more days later when I gave her the photos, her face was momentarily frozen. Then she could barely contain herself. *That's it! That's the one!* She was madly tapping the picture with her index finger. I chuckled under my breath and said *For heaven's sake Mari, what are you talking about?* Would there be no end to strange insights connected to this House?

That's the house I saw! I saw it! she exclaimed. But she definitely had not been outside of California. During a quiet prayer time, Mari had mentally visualized my father's House. I asked her if this sort of thing happened often for her. *NO* she emphatically replied.

With that, I knew I had my 17-years-awaited commission for the book I was to write.

I had no earthly idea how it would be accomplished but I believed that all creativity is a gift from above. The desire and ability to create is nothing less than the echo of God's Spirit. He sheds it abroad on the human race, rather indiscriminately it would seem; wherever it lands, it is to be received and unleashed with joy and abandon.

This would certainly be the very best way to honor my father: to show the whole man, with all his qualities both good and bad; and how the power of God's grace enabled my unconditional love.

Epilogue

As I've said, like my father I am visually oriented. The length and direction of shadows have great meaning to me. They evoke strong emotion. The very long shadows are Christmas: my grandparents' visits, crisp air, silent wind, hard ground. And another year goes by. This hasn't changed regardless of my age or location.

Giant trees contribute to this. We lived in a place with four distinct seasons marked by great and wondrous clusters of deciduous trees. They decide much. They were romantic and gigantic and made the passing of time like a fairy tale. They guarded us, protected us, and charmed us. As my mother grew older she gradually removed each one from the yard of the House. The maple that you could see from the kitchen through the skylight, choked by its own roots; a tulip poplar grown into the utility lines; the raintree, infested with bugs and with a split-through trunk; the white pine, too close to the House with its destructive root system. Dad took many tree photos; sadly, most of them got tossed.

I saved every one he took of Mama. His camera loved her. In his photos, she always looked natural and fresh; often happy; smart, stylish, and utterly un-self-conscious. These photos stand as a monument to their union, frozen in time. Along with the House. You could almost forget that the marriage didn't last.

There's one photo I recall from the day of my baptism. It was taken around my first birthday. My brother was three and he is wearing a striped tee tucked into shorts and brown orthopedic shoes. He has his hands in his pockets. Mama is wearing the same suit in which she was married, but with a new hat and gloves. She is beaming. I'm wearing a giant bonnet and matching dress with white orthopedic shoes. I'm trying to take a step. It's a bright sunny spring day in 1956. We all look so happy in front of the big church, the hoity-toity church.

The baptism took its effect—I am forever bound to Jesus, to have and to hold, to worship and adore, to obey and follow. Not perfectly but earnestly.

During one of my tri-annual trips to San Antonio for the Bible class, I discovered that their huge property lies adjacent to the war-games facility where David was when we had our final conversation. I found this to be oddly comforting, that the places we each considered to be heaven-on-earth were situated right next to each other. Thousands of miles away but almost exactly halfway between our respective homes.

The House was sold within six weeks of going on the market for 20% over market value (whatever that means) and Scott became a sort of hero for me and his fellow agents. It was sold to a retired couple. They ended up listing it again a year later because the husband did not fully adjust to the location. I put in a bid to buy it back, planning to rent it to Scott. I was outbid, however, by a cardiologist and his wife whose mother lived close by. So it goes. It was time to let it go.

The Stuart Davis print is now in my living room, badly discolored but more beloved than ever. Blue Fissure hangs in my stairwell where its moody darkness gets ample light. The Heywood Wakefield furniture is all safely in storage along with the accent pieces, a few light fixtures, the china, and even the everyday flatware. Julie dreams of using them in her home one day. Or, I may decide to move to the Southern California desert and find a small midcentury rancher of my very own, now that I'm single. In any case, the love embedded in these pieces will not be lost, forgotten or in any way diminished.

Mama passed very peacefully in December, 2016, with Julie holding her hand. They had earlier been discussing Mama's days as one of *The Girls of Atomic City* (see Suggested Reading). She was coherent right up to the end; even though her memory loss was severe, she had her wits completely. We calculated that she died close to, or even on, the exact moment I dismissed the class leaders from my final training meeting before retiring from the Bible class.

Some people may think it's not such a big deal to honor or love your father, even an unfaithful father. It is true that he was a good provider of the basic necessities: food, including steak-on-the-grill every Saturday night; clothing, including allowing Mama to let her own love of design flourish; and shelter, in a one-of-a-kind ranch style House which seems eternally young. He gave me David, my first friend and playmate, and he enabled us to be raised by an ever-present mother who loved us unconditionally. He gave me a 100%-financed college education. That should make it easy, right? It was all above and beyond the call of duty and way more than what many, if not most fathers provide.

But did it counterbalance the pain of rejection? Not even close.

The pain generated in me an abnormal hunger for love and permanence; an unrelenting drive to compensate for the feeling of male rejection. This was more than just an emotional or psychological dysfunction; it was a matter of life and death. Two people died because of it. My own unborn children.

There were other casualties too, of course. Unwittingly, Mama had taught me how to be an enabling wife. And that, coupled with my fear of male abandonment, led me to overlook and deny the dysfunction in my own marriage. But likewise unwittingly, Mama provided much of the solution to this. Her strong, steady love while living in our home in her final years gave me the strength and courage to say *No. More. Enabling.* And the marriage was ended.

While I do regret many, many of my choices, I also know that God can be glorified in my healing. As we trust Him to do so, He provides the means to accomplish that.

He made it clear at the cross: pain is part of the process. The root of pain is man's brokenness, the blame for which was laid on Jesus as He died.

God did not let go of Dad or me—He waited patiently and in love, and watched as we each realized the depth of our brokenness. As we each came to the end of ourselves. He stood by with arms forever outstretched so that we could grab hold and find our healing in Him.

The last thing I would have ever wanted to be is a religious fanatic (except for the Audrey-Hepburn-as-nun fantasy). As I grew up Daddy had used the term with scorn. But I am, with no apologies.

I had seriously underestimated the power of God. He can enable us to do amazing and marvelous things, like love someone you once hated. *The* single most amazing and wonderful thing: to love the unlovable. The more I experience this power the more committed to it I become. I am sold out to Him, hook, line and sinker. I am like a dog with a bone: obsessed, determined, and possessive. And He is the same with me. I am His and He is mine.

Even in the worst of circumstances, life is now one grand romance, waiting and watching to see what He will do next, like the clouds above the Myrtle Beach shore; and how He will prevail in the end. He always does. I finally found the grandest romance of them all. I think my father did too.

After the House was sold and he had been dead five years or so, I was working in a card shop. It was a happy place. We sold fancy greeting cards and gift wrap, and well-curated gift items. I was at the register one evening when a middle-aged gentleman came to pay for his items. He wore horn-rimmed glasses and was dressed in a short-sleeve button-down-collared shirt. A government security-clearance badge was clipped to his pocket.

I became overwhelmed. I was instantly back at home, six years old, watching Daddy arrive home from work. I could see him pouring a cocktail and sitting at the Formica table to chat with Mama while she finished preparing dinner. I could not hold back my tears.

My manager gave me leave to go to the back room and have a quiet respite. I thanked Jesus for momentarily allowing me to feel that pain which leads to healing. Blessed are they that mourn for they will be comforted.

I somehow sense that Dad would approve of my glorious obsession because he understood passion. His is left written all over a midcentury modern House in Knoxville, Tennessee.

Remember the red-haired foster child who had lived next door? The one with the limp? She was adopted by that couple, and gradually came to run and jump and play like all the other children, healed by covenantal love.

We love, because He first loved us. And the covenant of the Resurrection secures it.

Suggested Reading

Design

atomic RANCH: design ideas for stylish ranch homes; Gringery-Brown, Michelle and Brown, Jim; Gibbs Smith, 2006

Classic Modern: Midcentury Modern at Home; Dietsch, Deborah; Simon & Schuster, 2000

Cliff May and the Modern Ranch House; Gregory, Daniel Platt; Rizzoli, 2008

Mid-century Modern: Furniture of the 1950s; Greenberg, Cara; Harmony Books, 1995

Culture

The Girls of Atomic City; Kiernan, Denise; Simon & Schuster, 2013

The Ritz of the Bayou; Lemann, Nancy; Alfred A Knopf, 1987

Relationships

Boundaries: when to say yes, how to say no to take control of your life; Cloud, Dr Henry and Townsend, Dr John; Zondervan, 2017

The Emotionally Destructive Relationship; Vernick, Leslie; Harvest House Publishers, 2007

Acknowledgements

First and foremost, thanks be to God who plucked me out of the mire and gave me real life.

Thanks also to…

my faithful mother who, throughout my life, made her opinion known without judgment, always. Her steadfast love carried me through;

Bible Study Fellowship, International (bsfinternational.org) which gave me the tools and encouragement needed to know God and His Word, and trained me how to share it with others;

my wise and funny mentor, who listens and loves with style and wit;

Mark Richard, whose brilliant memoir *House of Prayer No. 2* inspired me and provided a working model;

my weekly support group, where I learned to share my story without fear; and for the loving input of that leader. They also were great listeners to my excerpts;

and my (usually) patient tech-native daughter, without whose skills the book would never have made it through publication.

Finally, a million thanks to all my early readers, pray-ers, and supporters, who believed in this project (at times, even more than I did); and when needed, spoke the truth in love. It has been a long time coming, as all of you know; and it wouldn't be here without the love of each one of you.

Made in the USA
Las Vegas, NV
30 March 2022

46584637R00142